essentials of public communication

essentials of public communication

James R. Andrews
Indiana University

John Wiley & Sons
New York
Chichester
Brisbane
Toronto

Credits: Cover photo: Terry Lennon
Part Opening Illustrations: Charles Waller
Calligraphy: Laura Ierardi

Library of Congress Cataloging in Publication Data:
Andrews, James Robertson, 1936-
   Essentials of public communication.

   Includes bibliographies and index.
   1. Public speaking.   I. Title.
PN4121.A674   808.5'1   78-18182
ISBN 0-471-02357-4
                                    1 Jul 81

Printed in the United States of America
10 9 8 7 6 5 4 3 2 1

To Ellen Kauffman and Iline Fife

PREFACE

An educated person is not only one who knows, but one who can *communicate* what he or she knows. There is no kind of education — education in the liberal arts, or technical or professional education — that can be complete or successful if the person being educated cannot talk clearly and convincingly in public situations. Nor is education successful if the person cannot respond intelligently to messages directed at him or her. A course in public communication, then, is one designed to help the student become more articulate and discriminating. The aim of this book is to further that design by describing for the student the *essential* components of the public communication process and directing the student toward ways of participating effectively in that process.

The underlying assumption of this book is that communication is a *process*. As such, it is not to be mastered simply by the application of standard formulas to stock situations. The dynamic of communication demands that the student be aware of the shifting qualities and emphases of the situation. It also demands that the student be aware that his or her own role in communication changes with the situation, thus creating new pressures and requirements. Recent research and theoretical probes in our field have clearly pointed out the dangers of a static approach to communication, of assuming that prescribed techniques, added together properly, equalled a given effect on an audience. And, certainly, the best of traditional rhetorical theory and criticism has always argued against a cookbook approach to effective communication.

Consistent with the idea of process, this book emphasizes the strategy and tactics of communicating as they affect both the speaker and the listener. The focus here is on the *choices* to be made in public communication. The effort in the book is to deal with the *why* of successful communication so that the student is equipped with generalizations useful in making choices. Furthermore, the book tries to help the student translate the *why* into *what he or she can do*. The book should provide the student with an essential body of theory; from those generalizations some predictions about public communication can be made. The book also offers practical and concrete directions and explanations that show how theory can be made useful and applicable in real situations. In short, traditional pedagogical and rhetorical thought, informed by current research in communication, and refined to extract what is most essential, has been used to give the student an informed rationale for practical action.

The book begins with a consideration of the participants in the public communication situation—the listener and the speaker—discusses their special functions and requirements, and examines how they interact. Then purpose and structure are examined as fundamental strategies, followed by a discussion of ways to make ideas understandable and believable through argument and audience involvement. A special chapter is devoted exclusively to outlining, a process that synthesizes the elements of speech preparation. This chapter includes real outlines, both good and bad, as they were actually done in a basic speaking class. Finally, style and delivery are considered, and a summary, including a detailed checklist for both the speaker and the listener, is presented. Hopefully, the intent, organization, and development of this book will help it to do what it is supposed to do: serve as a stimulating and useful teaching aid that helps both the student and the teacher succeed in the difficult task of improving understanding of public communication and sharpening skills in sending and receiving messages.

The ideas in this book are naturally a distillation of much of what I have been taught in classes, what I have read, and what I have learned from my colleagues and students. I sincerely appreciate the efforts of all those who have provided so much stimulation and information over the years. I specifically acknowledge the help of Kaylene Long, Clark McMillion, and Paul Prill in gathering material, Judy Hienmiller in typing and proofreading, and Marie Annala in preparation of the final manuscript, and Marcia Watts in typing and general secretarial assistance.

My wife and son deserve special thanks for the support they have cheerfully and unselfishly given me throughout this project.

There are two people to whom I am most particularly grateful:

Professor Ellen Kauffman and Dr. Iline Fife. Each has been to me a friend, an adviser, and an inspiring teacher of speech communication. I publicly acknowledge my gratitude to them.

I am also grateful for the constructive reviews this book received from Dr. Fay A. Yeager, Douglas College; Dean Malcolm O. Sillars, The University of Utah; Professor Patricia Hayes Bradley and Professor William E. Wiethoff, Indiana University; Professor Michael G. Leff, The University of California; and Professor Timothy Y. C. Choy, Moorhead State University.

All those who have aided in some way with this work have undoubtedly enhanced its value. Ultimately, of course, the responsibility for the final product, with whatever shortcomings it may have, is mine.

James R. Andrews

Bloomington, Indiana

CONTENTS

Contents xiv

PART ONE

communication and people

CHAPTER 1 *the listener*

All of us have been members of audiences: we've sat in classrooms and listened to teachers speak; perhaps we've heard ministers preach or politicians running for office address a campus rally; we might belong to clubs or organizations where we've listened to reports given by officers or committee chairpeople; and no doubt at some time or another we've been part of the mass audience that watches and listens to messages directed at us from the television set. We've been entertained, amused, interested, and excited. We've also been bored, frustrated, distressed, and depressed. Some speakers have helped us make intelligent decisions and some have hoodwinked us. Some messages have provided information that improved our lives and some have caused us to waste our money and our time. Sometimes we have responded to speakers and messages like mature, reasonable people; sometimes we have foolishly acted without any serious thought about our actions and motivations. Being human, we have won a few and lost a few, but, also, being human we have a unique ability to communicate and a real potential for communicating well.

Communication is a process. That is, it never stands still, it never stops moving, it is never frozen in place. You can experience a piece of this process, you can listen to a speech given in class, for example, but this is only a small part of the communication milieu that surrounds us. If you've ever looked at the ocean you know that the water is never still. Even on the calmest day there are waves, ripples, and currents that do not rest. You cannot identify a single section of water that is unrelated to the body of water in which it exists. You can, however, scoop out a bucket from the ocean, detach it from the rest, and carry it on to the beach.

The purposes for which you *use* the water, like the purpose of communication, are limited by the nature of the environment from which it comes: you can get your friend's attention by pouring the water on her, but you can't give her a drink of the salt water. Communication is part of the total environment that surrounds us. We can't attend to any message as if we knew nothing except what the speaker is telling us. When we listen to a speech we bring our world along with us; we filter what we hear through the screen of our own experience, our own prejudices, and our own knowledge. We ourselves are very much a part of the communication process and what we do and how we react will influence the process.

Yet "influence" is not a very specific description of the impact one can have on communication. To carry on our comparison with the sea, how extensively can one "influence" the ocean? There is an old legend about the eleventh-century Danish King of Britain, Canute, who was supposed to have attempted to demonstrate his power by seating himself on his throne at the water's edge and commanding the tide to retreat. He was no more successful than is the small child who hopes to stem the steadily advancing water with a wall of sand. Nevertheless, land can be reclaimed from the sea and jetties can stop erosion. We can travel over the top of the ocean or lay a transcontinental cable on its floor. No one can completely control the ocean nor is its complicated nature and operations fully understood, but neither is it totally unfathomable or unmanageable. Similarly, there are no sure-fire, ready-made formulas for success in communication, but it is possible to be effective if one recognizes his or her own, and the situation's, limitations, and if he or she knows how to use communication principles in the best way possible.

As you begin to learn how to be effective as a communicator you need to understand that you play different roles at different times in the communication process. So what is "effective" for *you* depends on *who* you are in any particular situation. Consider, for example, a speaker who hopes to persuade an audience to give money to a cause he espouses. Let us suppose that the speaker is successful and listeners each give $5. Now if you were the speaker in that case you could probably congratulate yourself for communicating effectively. If you were the listener, the exchange may or may not have been effective. If the speaker showed you how you could use your money in a way that helped people you wanted to help and that made you feel good, then you were part of an effective interaction; if, on the other hand, the speaker swindled you out of $5 and you later felt that you could kick yourself for being so stupid, then you were part of a situation that was ineffective for you. Communication is, after all, an effort on the part of someone who *initiates* a message to get someone else to *respond* to that message in a way that the communicator has predetermined. How effectiveness is judged, then, depends on how both parties to the exchange come out.

If you are the initiator of the message, the speaker in a public communication setting, you have a reason for acting: you talk to people because you want them to *do* something. You want them to learn or to buy or to believe or to feel; you want a *reaction* from them or you wouldn't engage in the communication process. Now it is true that there are speakers who don't seem to want to communicate, who don't care how angry or bored, or uncomfortable they make their audiences. These are the people who don't know or don't care that the end of communication is response, people who like to hear themselves talk, or like to get their aggressions or hostilities out regardless of how those to whom they are speaking react. But it might be better for such people to take up finger painting or handball or some other means of self-expression, because self-expression is what they seem to be bent on doing rather than *communicating*. If you were to go out to your car one morning and find a tire flat, you might aim a few vituperative remarks at the car; such self-expression won't bother the car and it might make you feel less tense and upset. But no matter how angry you feel you wouldn't go to a neighbor's door, pound on it loudly, and demand that he or she hurry down to help you fix the flat tire. If you have any brains at all, you will realize that asking a friend for help is a time to communicate and not a time to vent your frustration. Because you have a specific response in mind, you will try to ask for help in a communicative way, that is, in a way designed to get the desired response. You communicate *effectively* when you get the response you hope for (Figure 1).

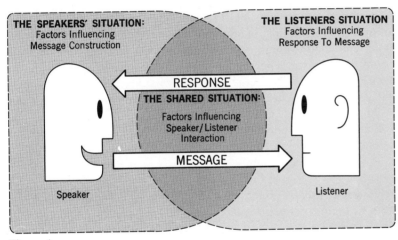

Figure 1

Communicating in public, of course, is a much more complex matter in many ways than is communicating with a friend you'd like to help you, although your common sense will tell you that some of the same principles apply. If, for example, your friend is a late sleeper, you might wait before going to ask for help with the tire; if your friend is inclined to think that more physical exercise would be good for you you may wish to remind him or her of your bad back; if your neighbor is a rather frail 80-year-old lady, you may consult her if you need comforting sympathy, but you will look elsewhere for practical help. When you talk to more than one person you must be as equally careful that you know something about those persons and their relationship to your message. You must know something of their predispositions, tastes, prejudices, and knowledge. And you must know what the audience you address can or may be prepared to do about your request, for the audience that you try to influence is made up of many listeners. If you hope to get a response from those listeners you need to consider what characteristics they share as a group and what qualities individuals bring with them to a communication situation.

We know by experience that different audiences — that is, the different factors that are important in the makeup of audiences — effect the nature of our messages. If you were majoring in physics and a friend, who was trying to decide on a major, asked you what it was like to study physics you know that you would tell him or her something quite different from what you would tell your little five-year-old brother who asked essentially the same question. In both cases you might need to define the goals of the study of physics, mention the topics of lectures, describe what you do in laboratory experiments, but obviously you would need to use a different vocabulary, make different comparisons, use different examples because your two listeners have such different experiences, different levels of maturation, different amounts of information, and so forth. Knowing this, you choose to talk about things in a way that the listener can follow. The same thing, of course, is true when you plan for an audience: you need to think carefully about what you know about that potential audience. The best way to go about considering the audience is systematically. Let us consider what kinds of things you find out about an audience that helps you to understand who you are talking to by asking the questions: Who are the listeners? What are the circumstances under which listening took place? Where do the listeners stand?

Who Are the Listeners?

A variety of factors go into making people what they are, and many of these factors come into play when planning a message for an audience. One who would understand and participate in the communication process must consider what it is that has an impact on our perception of events and our ordering of the importance of issues, and must understand that how we see things and what we think are important tends to mold our value structure. Let us examine some specific audience characteristics and, then, after discussing each, explore their implications for public communication.

1. The *age* of audience members will influence the reception of a message. Listeners see the world through the eyes of their own experience. Those, for example, who were college students in the 1960s, many of them subject to the draft during the war in Vietnam, were often in conflict with an older generation who had lived through World War II or the Korean War with very little significant protest being raised. Many older Americans believed they had responded to the patriotic call to fight for "the American way of life" and found it very hard to understand the reluctance of those who, 15

to 25 years later, would not do the same thing. For their part, the protesters saw those who supported the war as morally bankrupt and willing to sacrifice callously the lives of the young; they were able to taunt President Lyndon B. Johnson with the chant, "Hey, hey, L.B.J., how many kids did you kill today?" Students of today, caught up with a different set of problems, oftentimes regard the passionate divisions of the 1960s with mild curiosity or indifference. The famous "generation gap" could occur because people of different ages, seeing the world from different places, fail to understand how things might look from the other perspective. Imagine, for example, that you could receive in the mail tomorrow a notice that compelled you to leave school, your family, and friends and begin a process that would lead you to kill other people and take the real risk of being killed yourself; or that you wondered every time the phone rang whether or not a voice at the other end would tell you that someone you loved was dead or missing in action. Being in that situation yourself would influence the way you thought about and acted toward American foreign policy not only at the time but for the rest of your life.

People react in different ways, of course, to similar experiences, but living through certain events, and living in the context in which those events occurred, shapes the way a person sees subsequent events. Being young or old means, in part, having lived through times that were always changing. Experience, naturally, is not a question of age alone; two people of exactly the same age can have had widely divergent experiences. We will discuss experience in that sense later. The point is that passing through a time in which events occur makes us see and feel about those events in a unique way. And, since human beings are always searching for understanding by comparing the unknown with the known, we look for similarities between the present and those events that have touched our lives in the past. *How* they have touched us, of course, is another question that is not determined by age alone; in spite of the generalization that conservatism increases with age we all know that there are young conservatives and old liberals. The shared experience of a generation, however, unquestionably effects an audience's outlook. Of course, this is not the only factor to consider in approaching the question of how age influences an audience.

Matters of immediate concern are different for different age groups. Getting a job, keeping a job, and living comfortably when you've retired from a job, for example, might be the three uppermost concerns for three age groups. What behavioral scientists call "saliency" is often determined by age; that is, matters of personal relevance are affected by age: it is understandable that older persons will tend to be more concerned about the future of the Social Security program than will college students whose interest will be more engaged by the fate of legislation providing federally funded educational loans.

Shared experience and particular kinds of concerns have their impact on values. Different age groups may have different values that are reflected in several ways. What is important for anyone who hopes to facilitate public communication to remember is that the *worth* or *importance* of values depends very much on *whose* values they are; an inclination to dismiss a way of thinking or a model for living as stupid or irrelevant can sabotage efforts to communicate successfully. Young and old may well be unable to talk profitably to each other if the younger persists in thinking that the other's obsession with the form or appearance of things (what will the neighbors think?) is nothing more than hypocrisy, while the older consistently maintains that the other's efforts to establish independence and a logically consistent moral code signals disrespect or rejection.

2. The *sex* of the listener can influence how a message is received. As the myths of "natural" female roles and relationships with men are exploded and the realities of sex roles change, as men and women in modern society are liberated from the narrow confines of prescribed roles and attitudes, the expectations of how listeners will respond have been modified. It can no longer be assumed that women want to hear about fashion and men about sports. Jokes that portray women as vain, silly, and nagging are surely considered in bad taste everywhere except in the staunchest bastions of bigoted male chauvinism. But while the expectations about and interactions between sexes are changing, listeners can be unsettled and uneasy about certain matters. Both men and women may feel defensive about the roles they play or hope to play. As options are opened up some may feel unsure either of exercising them or of continuing to exercise old options. A woman who decides for herself that she wants to and enjoys doing the demanding work of bringing up children and managing a household, sometimes wonders if she is inadequate because she doesn't want what is traditionally thought of as a "career." A woman who has an aptitude and inclination for engineering can be so influenced by the traditional view of the exclusively male domination of certain professions, particularly those dealing with the technical or scientific, that she may worry that she will somehow be considered unfeminine. Some men may feel personally threatened by what they perceive as the erosion of their exclusive preserves and feel, in consequence, that their very maleness is undermined. And those who have suffered discrimination and humiliation may be understandably sensitive to actions that they perceive to be regressive.

A person's sexual identity is crucial to that person's very being. It is inevitable that listeners' understanding of and attitudes toward a speaker and his or her message can be profoundly colored by the listeners' sexual identification. It is probably true that, in forming this identification, there is now less influence exerted by artificial and arbitrary expectations about what men and women should do, should like, should work at, and so forth. Nevertheless, such influence still does exist, and while the speaker should never pander to such attitudes, he or she cannot ignore them with impunity. Furthermore, because men and women have different kinds of experiences in our society, they will have different outlooks on many matters. That is, for example, saliency, again, will be affected by sex roles so that, say, the problems single women and widows face in obtaining credit will be initially more arresting to women than to men. (Indeed, *some* women more than others will find this a salient problem because of their immediate circumstances. As with all the characteristics under discussion, sex alone will not likely be *the* determinate for most listeners.) Additionally, there are tastes and interests for which the culture programs men and women differently. If a speaker wishes to use the testimony of a Green Bay Packers' star lineman, chances are that more men in the audience will know who he is than will women. When such instances occur, the speaker's responsibility is to avoid condescending to the women who don't know the player or making men who don't know him feel like misfits. Although the point will be developed later, it may be well to remind ourselves here that NO category — sex, age, or whatever — *automatically* predetermines a listener's set of responses. There are women, for example, vehemently opposed to, adamantly in favor of, undecided on, and indifferent to ERA, the Equal Rights Amendment. The distinction between generalizing and overgeneralizing is often hard to make, but if there is one thing that the women's liberation movement should have taught everyone it is that, while women do have concerns and experiences that are unique to their sex, there are aspirations, attitudes, and aptitudes that are *human* and cannot be pigeonholed on the basis of sex.

3. Listeners are affected by the *subcultures* out of which they come and in which they function in responding to messages. There was a time when it was generally believed that Americans were an homogenized people. We arrived as immigrants, were melted in the pot for a generation or two, and emerged with a peculiarly American character. Now as many students of America have observed there are certain characteristics, certain traditions, certain ways of looking at things, certain values that seem to be especially "American." In recent years, however, we have come to realize that the melting pot conception is not entirely accurate. Our various subcultures continue to be different and to influence us in many ways. There can be racial subcultures, national subcultures, religious subcultures, or geographic subcultures. Although all these groups will share characteristics with the general American culture, there may be marked differences that could effect listeners' responses to messages.

Blacks and whites in America have a different history and different cultural experiences through which to filter messages. Hopefully, the old suspicions, hostilities, and tensions between the races are easing. Blacks and whites both are coming to accept each other as different but not, as a consequence, evil. Unfortunately, violent, disruptive signs of racial animosity can still be seen. The issue of school busing, for example, can bring glossed-over antagonisms to the surface. Communication between members of different races can be extremely complicated and, too often, fraught with distrust and doomed to failure. Nevertheless, successful communication between members of different races does occur in an overwhelming number of cases and situations every day. The problems arise in public communication partly because of the failure to understand that there can, logically and legitimately, be racial influences operating in listeners' approaches to issues. For example, the matter of the administration of justice might be viewed in a very special light by urban blacks who are accustomed to being brutalized and bullied by white police; the question of how to find more jobs may cause some white listeners to fear that they are to be sacrificed in order to find jobs for unemployed blacks. We have come to realize more and more that, as each race has its own integrity, each also has its own perceptions and problems and, furthermore, that recognizing racial influences is not racism. A racist denies the essential humanity of those who are different and thus limits severely his or her potential for communicating successfully: they can talk only to other racists. Those who appreciate the distinctions between people of different races are better equipped to talk fruitfully with a wide and varied audience.

The forebears of most Americans come *from* someplace else. With the exception of the American Indians, people from other countries began migrating to America in the seventeenth century, continued in the eighteenth, reached a flood in the nineteenth, and still arrive in the twentieth. Depending partly on when they arrived, partly on habits and taste, and partly on where they settled, their own national history, customs, and experiences colored their outlook. It is understandable that listeners who identify with their heritage will be concerned with both the speaker's perception of their origins as well as how the content of the message affects them as a group here or their erstwhile countrymen far away. That is to say that it should be obvious that Poles will find Polish jokes unfunny or that Italians will deeply resent the association of all Italian names with the Mafia. And, moreover, issues that seem to effect directly the country from which one's ancestors came will both be more important to and shape the reactions of one who identifies with the particular national group. For example, an Irish-American is likely to be significantly interested in the fate of Northern Ireland and likely also to have strong, well-formed opinions of who is right and what the outcome should be. A nation, with its particular network of viewpoints and values, can influence even its transplanted citizens and their descendants, particularly in matters that can be related in some direct way to that country.

Perhaps it is less accurate to talk of religious subcultures than of religious beliefs that are integral with or strongly associated with other subcultures. But, in any case, a listener's religion — or his or her lack of religious beliefs—can influence the reception and evaluation of public communication. It is obvious that there are issues on which certain religious groups *tend* to take uniform stands such as Catholics on abortion or Jews on support for Israel. There are more subtle and not always predictable influences, however. Religions with a strong hierarchical sense in which obedience and conformity are highly regarded may foster different views toward authority than those that stress individualistic participation in religious life. Some religions emphasize personal salvation and regard the intrusion of religion into the social or political sphere of human behavior to be inappropriate. Others insist that all matters relating to the human condition must be of concern to the church and its members so that religious precepts can be brought to bear on secular problems. A person's personal religious views, moreover, can be important when he or she judges the morality or sincerity or ethical position of other participants in the communication process. In 1976 when Governor Carter ran for the Presidency his well-known religious evangelism caused some to react positively to what they saw as "a good Christian man," and others to distrust the intelligence and openmindedness of one who held fundamentalist opinions. An old saw advised would-be communicators not to talk about religion—it is too personal and potentially explosive a topic. But whether or not one chooses to talk about religion, religion can well influence the listener as he or she integrates a message on other issues not on the surface "religious" in nature or tone.

Where listeners live can make a difference in how they process the message in public communication. People who have grown up in the country develop different habits and different life-styles from those brought up in the city. The horrors of muggings, commuting on unreliable trains, or moving always at a frantic pace loom large to the rural resident, while the city dweller imagines that the dullness and lack of stimulation in the country would bore him or her to death. Or perhaps the reverse is true: the untasted excitement of the city lures one, the longed-for peace and safety of the country the other. Each may have a different set of problems that are more important to them: how do we reduce crime, how do we improve mass transit, how do we keep food prices down may worry urbanites at the same time the questions of how we reduce property taxes, how we save the family farm, or how we keep meat prices up are troubling the residents of a small farming town. Moreover, different sections of the country have, through the course of our history, developed unique regional perspectives. The Californians, the Easterners, the Midwesterners, are people who do not all have the same ethnic mix in their population, the same industries do not dominate their economies, the same religious views do not find predominant expression. The South, long proud of its traditions while at the same defensive over its racial history and practice, is in a state of transition. Its geographic advantages—particularly the year-round warm weather—are creating a "Sun Belt" where many older Americans are living. The political and social impact of such a shift is not yet precisely clear, but it does suggest that there may develop in this region a particular way of looking at social and political problems. All this is to say that different parts of America exert somewhat different influences on those who grow up and live there: these differences can be the ones that are fostered by state or regional pride such as the kind that blossom so blatantly in the little speeches from the floor of a national political convention, or they may be engendered by the nature of the specific community since obviously Newark, New Jersey is not Franklin; Fort Wayne, Indiana not Spencer; Dallas, Texas not Plainview; and Los Angeles, California not Modesto.

4. The *educational level* of a listener will influence his or her reaction. Two audiences might want to hear a lecture on the latest developments in high-energy physics, but what they would expect from the speaker and what they might be prepared to deal with would be different if the listeners were a junior high school science class and a college class of physics majors. Other factors in this case—age and experience, for example—certainly make a difference, but the same principle applies even between a first- and second-year physics course. Education should provide us with specific knowledge, with attitudes toward and strategies for the rational solution of problems, with an awareness of the choices open to us, and with ways of evaluating the appropriate choices to make. How well a listener has been educated will determine in part whether he or she has particular information about the topic under consideration and whether he or she can intelligently evaluate the quality of the message. Much public communication, for example, takes the form of claims. It is claimed that using a product will make us happier or healthier, that voting for a candidate will improve our economic situation, that reading a popular book will enhance our sex life. The educated listener is one who should have facts at his or her disposal, one who would, for instance, possess information about history, economics, and political behavior and would be thus better equipped to evaluate those claims that a candidate for office might make. The listener who has had a good education should have had a variety of intellectual experiences with which he or she can relate specific aspects of the message being received. Take, for example, someone who is studying the subject you are now: public communication. You will learn in this course that you should be skeptical about generalizations that are made in public messages. So if you hear someone argue that force must be used in response to a foreign policy crisis because we are faced with the same kind of dangerous situation that faced American in the 1940s when we confronted the forces of nazism, you will ask for evidence that this is so and will not automatically agree because nazism is evil. And you will be able to determine whether the evidence that is offered is any good because you have

studied history. You will be able to make some judgment as to whether the situation before World War II is similar to circumstances now. You will take principles you have learned and knowledge you have acquired and apply them. If you find the evidence unconvincing, and cannot test it by your own knowledge or experience, you will suspend judgment. You will be acting as an educated person.

Of course it would be foolish to assume that listeners who are educated will always respond in such a rational way. There are many other factors operating that prevent any one characteristic from absolutely dominating a listener's behavior. Also, many people are *trained* in some skill by educational institutions but are not educated in the sense of having acquired information and being able to apply it in a variety of situations. One's training may range from relatively simple skills, like driving a bus, to much more sophisticated and complex ones, like being a doctor, but such mastery does not necessarily produce an educated person, as we have been describing such a person. Furthermore, education, which should not be confused with training, should neither be confused with intelligence. There are some very intelligent people who have not had formal education just as there are some who have had the advantage of attending good universities but are not terribly smart. But, with these warnings in mind, one can generally expect educated listeners to be more critical and to have more information about certain topics. "Certain topics," of course, is the key to the part education plays in shaping the listener's response; as with all the characteristics we have been talking about, the precise role education plays depends on the specifics of the public communication situation.

5. The *occupation* of the listener will influence the perspective from which he or she views the message. What one's job is will influence both one's attitudes and one's grasp of specific information. The cattlemen and the city homemaker will be interested in a news story about beef prices, but how they respond to the same information will be different: both have serious financial constraints operating on them as a result of their occupations and both want to do their jobs successfully. It may be, at times, that their goals are just incompatible, but it may also be that, while a reasonable compromise is possible, their occupations help to form attitudes that make compromising messages difficult to respond to. You can readily see that what we do will make us feel differently about the world around us; teachers, doctors, construction workers, dancers, postal clerks, and lawyers all spend time in ways that are unique and in dealing with problems that are important particularly to them. How is this going to affect my job, is a question often brought to bear on a public message. We should also realize that some people have jobs that they find boring or tendious or fruitless. Such an unhappy situation is bound to do things to a listener; it can make him or her want to reject messages that don't help to escape from a reality associated with

drudgery and even dispair; or it may attune the listener to messages that suggest ways to change one's condition.

An occupation provides people with skills of varying complexity; the consistent practice of these skills is what establishes one's expertness. A listener who is an engineer brings a whole set of competencies with him or her to a speaking situation and will respond to technological information as a specialist just as a teacher will respond to arguments about how to improve our schools or the lawyer will respond to proposals for no-fault automobile insurance. Yet it is also true that our occupations can act as a prism through which we see many questions in ways that are not always so obvious. On the question of how to improve our schools, for example, a motel owner may be appalled by the suggestion that schools be kept open all year around since that could mean that people would travel less in the summer and his occupation would be threatened. The listener may be asking him or herself what such a plan or proposal means to a steamfitter, a hairdresser, a dentist, or a sales clerk, all the time that the message is being sent. Perhaps the answer will be, "nothing in particular," but the chances are that the question will be raised in the mind of the listener.

6. The *income* of a listener may influence his or her response. Again, the extent to which this factor is important and the precise ways in which it functions depends on the nature of the public communication event. The topic of the message may be one that interests different income groups; how to devise tax shelters, for example, would probably have limited appeal to those of low income—or perhaps some of those hearing such a message would not perceive it as giving helpful practical hints, but, instead, as an example of how the rich exploit the law to evade paying their fair share. Indeed, the perceptions of groups as to how their income level compares and should compare with others may have deep-seated effects on the communication process. Middle-income families, for example, who see themselves as burdened with taxes and yet excluded from the benefits of social welfare extended to the poor, tend to look on a wide variety of political and social proposals with the jaundiced eye of those who feel they are going to foot the bill. It was from the middle classes who felt imposed on by the system that the epithet "limosine liberal" came, denoting the distrust felt for those seen as wealthy backers of social legislation to help the poor at the expense of the middle classes. And some messages, such as those designed to sell goods by creating the illusion that everyone must have or will have this product, that it is part of the American way of life to have this product, have the potential to create hostility and frustration among those whose income is far too low to begin to consume the items that an advertising message maintains they must. In any case, the extent of financial resources available to a listener will surely help determine his or her receptiveness to any proposals that involve getting or spending money.

7. The listener's *principal roles* will effect his or her reactions to a message. At different times and in different places we are different people. While you are in a classroom, for example, you will tend to think of yourself as a student, when you're at home you might think of yourself as a daughter or son, when you're playing basketball as a member of a team, when you're working on voter registration in your dormitory as a member of a political party. We can, of course, be many things at the same time. The perceived purpose of the message and the setting in which it occurs will influence the role that a listener assumes. For example, when you listen to a political candidate you might be very much aware of your role as a student and be concerned about his or her position on increases in tuition in state institutions; whereas the elderly retired couple that live in your neighborhood, in their roles as taxpayers, will be interested in the candidate's views on property tax relief.

As roles change, status may change as well so that how people react in a communication setting can shift as these factors are modified. Take, for example, a young man who is a basketball player. When he engages in communication with his coach he both processes the message he receives and forms those he sends with the realization that the coach is in charge, the coach's directions are important and they are not to be evaluated for their worth as much as they are to be understood to be acted on. If the same person is also captain of his basketball team and is discussing possible strategies with other team members, his status changes as his role is modified. His own messages now become more authoritative. As a listener he is less apt to accept automatically the suggestions or advice that come from his fellow players, although, if the team is a good one, he will listen carefully and weigh opinions thoughtfully since they come from others whose knowledge and experience he respects. The same player attending an alumni dinner may receive a host of messages that are purportedly designed to help him improve his game. He will undoubtedly listen differently to these messages; they will seem far less relevant or authoritative coming from those who are not actually involved in the activity themselves no matter how avidly they support the team or how closely they follow the game. But, since his role in this situation is partly to promote public relations he will listen politely, according status to those older, and probably in their fields successful, persons, but ignore practical suggestions as coming from an outside source. Consider, however, the same young man talking with one of the same businessmen about a job. The successful builder may be listened to only with toleration on the subject of how to improve the team's shooting average, but if the basketball player becomes someone looking for a job in the real estate business, his role, and his status vis-á-vis the builder, changes. Accordingly, his pattern of listening will change. Another good example is afforded by the graduate student who at 10 A.M. may lead a discussion in an introductory history class and expect that the listeners will accept her remarks on the causes of the American Revolution as coming from an authoritative source, while at 11 A.M. she may give a report on the same topic in a graduate class and expect an audience of much more critical listeners.

Note also that status can change without role change. This can be a result of actions over time or as a consequence of environmental factors. In your speech class, for example, you may achieve high status by giving consistently interesting and informative speeches; or perhaps your speeches on a particular subject, such as space exploration, will be good enough to establish your expertness in scientific areas and give you status when such questions are discussed in class. Yet you could, while still in your principal role as a student, be enrolled at the same time in a history class of 150 students where your status is no different from the other students in the course.

So listeners' roles will not always be the same, and thus the ways in which listeners process the message will vary and will affect the nature of listeners' responses.

8. *Memberships* held by the listener will have an impact on the listener's response to communication. Just as we play many different roles so, too, do we associate ourselves, formally and informally, with different organizations. And these associations contribute to the listener's identity, the listener's conception of what he or she is. Being a member of the Sierra Club, for example, marks for the person who is his or her commitment to preservation of the environment. One who is a staunch supporter of the club is likely to see the environmental aspects of questions as others in the club would, and, furthermore, to identify such aspects of questions when they are not immediately apparent.

Also, as with roles, there are times when certain memberships are more important than others. Quite obviously, when you attend a meeting of a particular group (a fraternity, a political club, the Future Farmers of America) the reasons for being in that organization will hold a prominent place in your life at that moment; messages that you hear will be heard by you as a member of that particular group. Indeed, most of what you hear at a meeting will be *designed* to be relevant to your group. At other times the goals of that group might be quite meaningless when the communication setting seems to you to have nothing to do with that particular membership. It is this phenomenon that religious speakers often work against when they remind listeners that the principles they hold as they attend a religious service are supposed to be applied in every facet of everyday life. But it is very hard to keep any one membership foremost in all decisions you are called upon to make: whether or not you are an active Democrat or Republican will most likely be of no consequence to you as you decide how to respond to a certain manufacturer's plea to buy his brand of toothpaste. And even in the political arena there are times when party membership is not a crucial matter in the listener's processing of communication. For example, when there was a serious threat to the New River in North Carolina, one of the oldest rivers in the world, liberals and conservatives, from Senators McGovern and Humphrey to Helm and Goldwater, supported legislation to save it. Most of the listeners in this case (senators and congressmen), did not see their party membership as an important factor in evaluating the message in this case. So the importance of memberships increases and decreases as listeners see the issue at hand as being related to membership.

There is another aspect of membership that should be mentioned. There are times when membership in a particular group or identification with the goals of a group is so important that either all messages are evaluated by its standards or irrelevant messages are virtually screened out. Consider two somewhat different examples. A young man might be a member of (or aspire to membership in) a fraternity. That membership may be so central to his life that he judges messages about where to eat by asking himself whether members of that group would eat that kind of food, or what to wear, or who to vote for on the basis of his perception of the political tastes of other members. Now, ostensibly, none of these things would seem to have a direct relationship to the goals and activities of the organization, nevertheless, many issues are transformed by the listener into ones that seem to him to relate to that particular membership. Another example is afforded by the National Rifle Association and its members and supporters. This group is dedicated to the defeat of all gun control legislation. So important are its goals to NRA members that they will often subordinate all other issues to this overriding one; they will end up voting for or against a political candidate because of his or her position on this single issue and may ignore the candidate's stand on the economy, or foreign affairs, or the environment — issues that might seem crucial to others, but, to the NRA member whose group identification is strong, issues that pale by comparison with the one with which he is obsessed.

Listeners' group memberships will influence their perceptions, then, but not always to the same degree and in the same way. There will be times when some memberships are seen as important to the matter at hand and other times when the same memberships don't even occur to the listener as relevant. In still other cases, memberships will conflict (you might, as a good Democrat and a loyal member of the Sierra Club, be in a dilemma when the Democratic representative from your congressional district votes against environmental protection legislation and asks for your support in his or her bid for reelection), and the listener will need to resolve such conflicts in order to respond. Who the listener is, therefore, depends partly on who the listener thinks he or she is affiliated with, and membership becomes an important factor in shaping the listener's reaction to public communication.

The question of who an audience is, is a very complex one. There are so many forces that act upon our lives to shape our identity and to direct the way we will function in a communication setting. A listener's age, sex, and subculture, along with educational level, occupation, income, and the listener's role and membership will act together to focus the listener's attention, to define the relevance of the message for the listener, and generally to guide the listener's reactions. Every listener, of course, lives in a total environment in which factors other than those discussed can come into play. But one could begin to compile a fairly accurate profile of an audience by asking what was known about the characteristics that have been outlined here. But before the picture of the listener as audience is complete, it is necessary to refine our knowledge about the listener's identity by understanding just what it is that has made the listener a part of the public communication process.

What Are the Circumstances Under Which Listening Takes Place?
Audiences come together for some reason or set of reasons. A protest meeting, for example, is very specific. The problem has been sufficiently defined for people to get together to do something or to learn what they might be able to do. They have grievances that they would like to have redressed or they have actions they want taken or prevented: they would like better telephone service, or they hope to forestall a rise in tuition, or they want safety conditions in the plant improved, or they want a streetlight at an unguarded corner. In such cases, what is important for the listener is clear, and the identifying factors must be seen in the light of the situation. At a public utilities hearing, for example, where the purpose of the meeting is to hear arguments on the need for a rate increase, many of the listeners will define themselves more in terms of their age and income than they will their sex or educational level.

Listeners will also gather when their goals are not as specific in relation to public messages, but under circumstances that still exercise some restraints on the communication. The Kiwanis Club or the Student Government Board or the American Legion have particular goals for which they associate, but these do not prescribe a particular topic although they should limit the possibilities. A speaker in such a situation will choose to talk about something that he or she deems pertinent to the group, and listeners will be particularly aware of the groups' perspective on the subject. When politicians, for example, talk to B'nai B'rith they tend to discuss their position on aid to Israel, a lively question for that organization; listeners will doubtless evaluate what they hear under those circumstances with a heightened awareness of the group's position since the situation will accentuate group membership and other associated characteristics.

The setting for a speech, then, can effect the relative importance of the various characteristics that depict listeners. On St. Patrick's Day or Columbus Day, audiences gathered in honor of the occasion will be more attuned to ethnic factors; a speech given at a church guild meeting will likely be perceived by listeners who are particularly aware of religious standards and practices. And, of course, situations exist in which communication can easily occur in such a way that several characteristics are brought into play at once. Listeners watching a television commercial, for example, may well respond to the message in their roles as parents, may decide if the person in the commercial is like them on the basis of race, may determine if they can afford the product with the income they have, and may judge whether the product is good or bad for their children by judging its worth against religious standards or the standards of an organization to which they belong.

There is also the so-called "captive" audience, made up of listeners who have or believe themselves to have no special or intrinsic interest in the communication to which they are exposed. Sometimes listeners may view the communication as a price they have to pay in order to receive some other reward, something to be endured in the pursuit of a different goal, like the thousands and thousands of parents who sit each year at graduations listening to tedious speeches in order to catch a glimpse of their son or daughter in the crowd of graduates, or see him or her walk across a stage to receive a diploma or degree. That event is usually a happy one and commencement addresses are endured with fortitude and even good humor. But some audiences are not as tolerant, and sometimes it would be better not to communicate at all rather than arouse the hostility of listeners. There are also certain situations in which the audience perceives itself as captive, and the communicator's very difficult job is to demonstrate to listeners that they have a good reason to *want* to listen and they do not need to be compelled to do so. An example of this situation can be the speech classroom, unfortunately. Hopefully, you will realize by the time you've read this book and talked the matter over with your instructor that you have a lot to gain by improving your listening skills and that listening carefully to other speakers is not only a favor done them to insure their attention to you, but a positive action that will help you be a better total communicator. Sometimes, however, listeners in a speech class will not be motivated by the situation alone and see themselves to be captive, thus putting a special strain on the speaker to convince them that what he or she has to say ought to be attended to. This sort of problem is faced every day by the creators of the television commercial. You don't turn on television to watch the commercial; you don't wait with eager anticipation for one to come on, and, in fact, you usually time forays to the kitchen or the bathroom to coincide with them. If you stay and watch the screen, the commercial must convince you that it is worthwhile to listen to it; it must transform you from the feeling of captive to the feeling of willing partner in the communication event.

There are, moreover, factors in the physical setting that will help an audience define itself but influence the characteristics that form its identity. The size of an audience, the intimacy of the listeners with each other, the proximity of the listeners to the speaker, the time of day, and the normal functions of the setting in which the communication occurs, can all have some effect on the listeners' view of themselves and hence their perceptions of and reactions to the message to which they are exposed. If you attended a speech in a classroom with an audience of 20 or so students and one or two professors, the chances are that your student role and the professors' teacher role would be enhanced; listening to the same speech in a large auditorium with hundreds of other people could blur such role distinctions. Attending a speech in a church of which you happen to be a member, even if the speech is not associated with that church at all, could reinforce those perceptions formed by your membership in that particular religious denomination. Someone who works at night might already be thinking of his or her job while listening to an excerpt from a political candidate's speech on the nightly news, heightening that listener's occupationally related perceptions. The listener who sits alone watching a message come to him or her via radio or television will be less likely to make the specific personal identifications and associations that would be made by the same listener hearing the same speech in a hall surrounded by fellow union members.

When, where, and why public communication takes place, then, will influence the listeners and how they interact with other elements of the communication situation. Before considering how the speaker and the listener both may shape this interaction, the third question about the audience needs to be addressed briefly.

Where Do Listeners Stand?
Given the characteristics of listeners and the circumstances of the communication, a listener's tendency toward positions on specific issues can be predicted. In trying to answer the question, "Who are they?" several examples were given of how listeners with certain characteristics would tend to react to issues. Listeners can range in their attitudes toward any particular controversial position from definitely favorable through undecided to definitely unfavorable. A listener can approach a noncontroversial, informative topic as an expert, as one who has general knowledge of the area, or as a complete novice. Not only will *who* the listeners are predispose them in a certain ways, it is also apparent that *why* they are listening will have a direct bearing on where they are in their thinking, beliefs, and knowledge in relation to the topic being discussed. Those attending a meeting to protest school busing, for example, can leave little doubt about how they feel on that subject. And those who have come to hear a lecture on the latest research in astrophysics are not likely to be students with little or no knowledge of physics. What the listeners feel or know and the intensity and depth with which they feel or know it will both be influenced by who they are and will, in turn, contribute to the listeners' makeup. That is, a staunch American Legionnaire is likely to be opposed to unconditional amnesty for

Vietnam draft evaders and his strong feelings about draft evaders will reinforce his perception of himself as a dedicated member of the American Legion.

It needs also to be recognized that there are networks of attitudes and beliefs that influence one another. It may not be easy to define precisely what a "liberal" or a "moderate" or a "conservative" is yet it does seem possible to do so operationally. And operationally is the way Americans tend to proceed, seeing things that seem to go together and to be going together in the same direction without worrying about any ideological orthodoxy. So, while there are contradictions and anomalies, quite often the listener's position on one issue will tend to define his or her stand on another so that "liberals" who favor an activist government might support extension of the social security program and government jobs to combat unemployment, while the conservative, distrustful of government, might wish to restrain the growth of the Social Security program and argue for private initiatives to improve the job situation. Yet, as if to underline the lack of doctrinnaire consistency, the liberal will tend to be suspicious of the defense bureaucracy while the conservative is eager to meet its every professed need. That there are "liberal" and "conservative" positions on many crucial questions is not due to a clear philosophy but rather, in part at least, to the way the whole network of factors—made up of peoples' conception of their own identities—develops and functions in public communication.

Where the listener stands in relation to the specific topic, along with the characteristics that identify that listener and the setting in which that listener functions, will provide a comprehensive picture of the make up of the audience. Figure 2 sums up the major listener considerations.

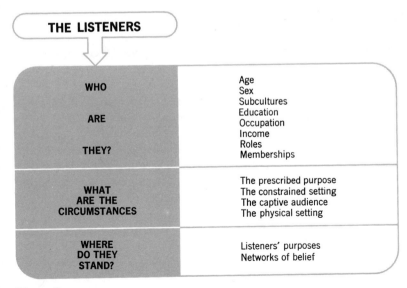

THE LISTENERS	
WHO ARE THEY?	Age Sex Subcultures Education Occupation Income Roles Memberships
WHAT ARE THE CIRCUMSTANCES	The prescribed purpose The constrained setting The captive audience The physical setting
WHERE DO THEY STAND?	Listeners' purposes Networks of belief

Figure 2

There is, however, one other perception of fundamental importance that listeners will have or will form in a communication situation. Before considering the ways in which the listener and speaker can put the knowledge of the audience to most effective use, it is best to consider the listener's perception of the source of communication.

Select Bibliography

The following citations, and those listed in all the bibliographies, offer further practical and theoretical information related to the chapter topics, and they provide a starting point for the student who wishes to undertake more intensive study and research into the topic.

W. Clifton Adams, "The Interrelationship among Need for Social Approval, Persuasibility and Activation," *Central States Speech Journal,* **23**(1972), 188-192.

Karl Anatol and Jerry Mandel, "Strategies of Resistance to Persuasion: New Subject Matter for the Teacher of Speech Communication," *Central States Speech Journal,* **23**(1972), 11-17.

John R. Anderson, "The Audience as a Concept in the Philosophic Rhetoric of Perelman, Johnstone, and Natanson," *Southern Speech Communication Journal,* **38**(1972), 39-50.

Dean C. Barnlund, "Toward a Meaning Centered Philosophy of Communication," *Journal of Communication,* **12**(1962), 198-202.

David K. Berlo, "Social Systems," *The Process of Communication.* New York: Holt, Rinehart and Winston, 1960.

John J. Carney, "The Unperceived Audience," *Today's Speech,* **13**(1965), 15-16.

Theodore Clevenger Jr., *Audience Analysis.* Indianapolis: Bobbs-Merrill, 1966.

Vernon L. Cronen and Richard L. Conville, "Belief Salience, Summation Theory, and the Attitude Construct," *Speech Monographs,* **40**(1973), 17-26.

Gary Cronkhite and Emily Goetz, "Dogmatism, Persuasibility, and Attitude Instability," *Journal of Communication,* **21**(1971), 342-354.

A. G. Greenwald, "Behavior Change Following a Persuasive Communication," *Journal of Personality,* **33**(1965), 370-391.

A. G. Greenwald, "Effects of Prior Commitment on Behavior Change After a Persuasive Communication," *Public Opinion Quarterly,* **29**(1966), 595-601.

Roderick P. Hart and Don M. Burks, "Rhetorical Sensitivity and Social Interaction," *Speech Monographs,* **39**(1972), 75-91.

Paul D. Holtzman, *The Psychology of Speakers' Audiences.* Glenview, Ill.: Scott, Foresman, 1970.

Carl I. Hoveland and Irving Janis, *Personality and Persuasibility.* New Haven: Yale University Press, 1959.

Cal Hylton and William B. Lashbrook, "Apathetic and Neutral Audiences: A Computer Simulation and Validation," *Speech Monographs,* **39**(1972), 105-113.

Dominic A. Infante, "Predicting Attitude from Desirability and Likelihood Ratings of Rhetorical Propositions," *Speech Monographs,* **38**(1971), 321-326.

Dominic A. Infante, "The Perceived Importance of Cognitive Structure Components: An Adaptation of Fishbein's Theory," *Speech Monographs,* **40**(1973), 8-16.

Dominic A. Infante and Jeanne Y. Fisher, "The Influence of Receivers' Attitudes, Audience Size, and Speakers' Sex on Speakers' Pre-Message Perceptions," *Central States Speech Journal,* **25**(1974), 43-49.

Richard L. Johannesen, "Attitude of Speaker Toward Audience: A Significant Concept for Contemporary Rhetorical Theory and Criticism," *Central States Speech Journal,* **25**(1974), 95-104.

William B. Lashbrook and Jean Sullivan, "Apathetic and Neutral Audiences: More on Simulation and Validation," *Speech Monographs,* **40**(1973), 317-321.

Howard Martin, "Communication Settings," *Speech Communication: Analysis and Readings,* Howard Martin and Kenneth Anderson, eds. Boston: Allyn and Bacon, 1968, 58-84.

Paul R. Mattox, "The Effect of Audience Set on Message Perception," *Western Speech,* **29**(1965), 79-86.

Henry E. McGuckin, "The Persuasive Force of Similarity in Cognitive Style between Advocate and Audience," *Speech Monographs,* **34**(1967), 145-151.

Carolyn W. Sherif, and Roger E. Nebergall, *Attitude and Attitude Change.* Philadelphia: W. B. Saunders, 1965.

Victor D. Wall, Jr., and John A. Boyd, "Channel Variation and Attitude Change," *Journal of Communication,* **21**(1971), 363-367.

Lawrence R. Wheeless, "The Effects of Attitude, Credibility and Homophyly on Selective Exposure to Information," *Speech Monographs,* **41**(1974), 329-338.

CHAPTER 2 *the speaker's image*

We have all had the experience of listening to a speaker and reacting negatively to him or her without being certain that it was the content of the speech alone that we were responding to. Sometimes a person's voice may irritate us; sometimes we may identify a speaker as a member of the opposite political party from our own (or, perhaps, a "politician" of whom we are distrustful simply because we distrust all politicians); sometimes we may associate the way a person dresses with a life style that we reject. We might be hearing a speaker for the second time and remember that our first impression was that the speaker was boring or confusing. We might question the ability of a speaker to discuss the topic at hand. On the other hand, we have also had the experience of following someone's advice not so much because we are convinced by the array of facts, or because we see clearly what will happen if we take certain actions, but just because we trust the person who is giving the advice. In other words, it is possible for listeners to react to a message on the basis of what they *think about* the speaker him or herself and not on what the speaker *says*. This is something that we all do routinely. For example, if a friend you've been in several classes with, someone you like and whom you think knows and shares your interests, recommends that you take a course, you might be likely to take it without finding out too much about the specifics of that course—the friend's recommendation is enough. We often do this kind of thing when we are deciding on what movie to go see or what restaurant to eat in, what car to buy or from what store to get clothes. And it is quite probable that we will often make very important decisions that affect the course of our lives on the basis of our reaction to a *person* sending a particular message. Many people have gone into careers because someone they admire pursued such a career; you might have decided on which college to attend on the basis of the advice of a counselor, or friend, or brother or sister whom you trust. We often find ourselves voting for a political figure for the basic reason that we tend to trust or believe him or her more than the other candidate: we might not understand either candidate's specific proposals for improving the economy, for example, but we'll accept one position because the person advocating it just seems a more likely person to get the job done. Sometimes such a method of making decisions may lead us to take actions that are not in our best interest or not to our taste; sometimes we simply *must* rely on others to give us advice in areas where we can never hope to assimilate enough information or gain enough experience to make a sensible decision. But whatever the result, there is little doubt that the source of the communication him or herself will have some impact on listeners.

Ethos in Persuasion

Students of the communication process have pondered this question for a long time. Aristotle, whose seminal study of rhetoric, or the art of persuasion, had the single most significant impact on our thinking about and teaching of public speaking, was led by his observations of public communication in ancient Greece to postulate that the speaker's *ethos* was a potent persuasive factor. By *ethos* Aristotle meant the communicator's character, intelligence, and interest in the audience's well being. The *kind of person* that was speaking, then, would, in the most successful communication, come through the speech to the listeners and effect their reactions to the total communication event. Later theorists refined and modified this concept until today we think of ethos as almost synonymous with the term "image." That is to say, the communicator as *reflected* for an audience is the source of persuasive potential.

Who, after all, is the *real* person that addresses an audience? We make judgments about people—who is honest, who is smart, who cares about us, who is reliable—on the basis of what we know or hear. You have probably had the experience of disagreeing with a friend over a mutual acquaintance; you might think the person is very kind and intelligent while your friend thinks him thoughtless and not very smart. Although people can behave differently at different times and in different places, both of you cannot be right in describing the essential character of the person in question. You are both reacting to what you have seen *reflected,* and on that basis the person has an ethos which depends on your perception. So we are not talking only about a communicator of good character, but a communicator that the audience *believes* to be of good character; not only one who is intelligent, but one whom the audience *thinks* is intelligent; not only one who has the good of his or her audience at heart but one who is so *perceived* by his or her listeners. This means, of course, that ethos is both relative and fluid; it will not be the same for every listener and it can change not only over time but in the course of a single speech.

Political figures often afford good examples of the nature of ethos. In the 1972 election campaign Senator George McGovern was seen by some voters as a rather wild, unstable radical. His comments on corruption in government some perceived to be exaggerated ravings born of desperation. Other voters saw the same man as a dedicated and honest leader who would restore American values. Whoever was nearer to assessing the "real" man, the important point is that people *saw* him in different ways: for some his ethos was strong and positive, for others weak and negative. President Nixon, who was seen by many as the wise, experienced, moderate leader was still viewed with distaste and suspicion by those for whom his ethos had always been negative. And Mr. Nixon's subsequent fate in the wake of the Watergate revelations shows how much ethos can change: the man who was renominated by acclamation to lead his party in 1972 was not even mentioned at the Republican Convention in Kansas City in 1976. So negative had Mr. Nixon's ethos become that no politician was eager to have his or her name associated with the former president.

Ethos, then, is not the same thing as ethics. Ethics might be described as a set of behavioral standards, standards that some might argue are universal and unchanging while others argue that such standards are related to the culture and situation out of which they grow. In either case, they represent a code, and an ethical person would be one who lives by that code. *If* the audience knows (to the extent an audience can ever know) that a person does, indeed, live by the code that they would approve then *they would consider him* an ethical person, that is, he would have a positive ethos. Perhaps the same person, living by the same code, said or did or was *reported* to have said or done, something that listeners *thought* violated the code in a way that was unacceptable to them, then the communicator would have negative—or less positive—ethos. "His "ethics" might not change, but his ethos would because of the audience's *interpretation* of his ethics.

    All of this means, then, that what an audience thinks of a speaker will make a difference in how well he or she can communicate with that audience. Let us examine the nature of the set of perceptions that listeners have that we have been calling ethos.

Ethos and Ethics

Students of the communication process generally agree that there are two aspects of the ethos a speaker brings to a situation that seem to influence an audience most significantly. That is, how we assess a speaker will depend in large measure on how much we *trust* him or her and on the extent to which we consider the speaker an *authority*. The extent to which these two factors are viewed positively will be reflected in the speaker's ethos, and listeners will tend to be persuaded more easily by a believable source. If, for example, a teacher urged you to attend a particular college, factors such as cost, distance from home, kinds of academic programs, size of the institution, and so forth would probably enter in to the discussion. Even as you evaluated the evidence, however, much of this evaluation could

The Influence of Source

27   The Speaker's Image

depend on how you viewed the source. If you admired the person and trusted his or her judgment you would tend to believe the assertion that X Community College is a friendly place without asking for specific proof. Or, if the teacher is a chemist and tells you that the home economics program in which you are interested is a very good one your reaction to that assertion can well be determined on how you view the authority of the source; if you reasoned, "What would a chemistry teacher know about home economics?" then you would either discount that claim or you would ask for further proof; if you thought, "teachers know about the educational system regardless of the specific field," then you might accept the argument as proven without asking for more evidence. The speaker's past associations, public positions, and reputation in general comes with him or her to a communication situation, but how it effects that situation will depend on how the audience perceives all these factors.

Listeners, then, will be prepared for a communication even partly by their prior knowledge of the source and how that knowledge affects their interpretation of the trustworthiness and authority of the source. The ways in which audiences gain knowledge of public figures — through new media or through others who relay what they have gleaned from the news media — can be somewhat complicated. Basically, listeners will be influenced in their views of a speaker's ethos by the nature of the experience they have had with the speaker, how important that experience was, and how recent it was.

In many communication situations, however, the source is almost neutral; the speaker may be totally unknown and therefore not bring a positive or negative ethos with him or her. This lack of strong ethos, however, may not be as total as it seems at first. Although a listener may not know the speaker's name, or may know very little of the speaker, what *is* known can form some impression. The extent to which the speaker matches the listener in psychological, social, and cultural senses can promote the speaker's ethos. For example, listeners tend to identify with someone their own age and their own sex, with someone who goes to the same church or belongs to the same organizations. One of the purposes of introducing a speaker is to help the audience establish ties with the source as well as to establish the authority of the source to speak on a given topic. But even with little introduction and in a situation in which the source has no established image in the minds of his or her audience, ethos will still be a factor. Take, for example, the speech classroom. In a small school where students know each other, its quite possible that ethos can be what is often called extrinsic or external to the immediate situation — that is, some students will be known by their colleagues and will have a positive or negative ethos. But in large institutions where students might never see each other the two or three times a week they meet in a given class, or even in smaller institutions where it is possible to encounter a class of strangers, even in these cases, the ethos factor is still important in public communication. Here listeners will be evaluating the speaker *as* he or she communicates, the ethos of the source will actually be formed in the minds of the listeners as they participate in the communication process. That means that what a speaker *does* in the immediate situation will shape listener perceptions of him or her. The nature of the message content itself, how the speech is delivered, the speaker's awareness of the audience, the kinds of authority that the speaker relies on, the structure and clarity of the message, and how interesting the presentation is, will all contribute to the developing ethos of the source. If, for example, a listener perceives the message to be an attack on social welfare legislation, the speaker's ethos will be enhanced or diminished depending on the liberal or conservative convictions of the listener. Or consider the situation when a listener can't hear a speaker; sitting in the back, straining to catch what is said can be a very irritating experience and can lower the listener's opinion of the source. A speaker talking to a student audience about grading would tend to have a more positive ethos if that speaker demonstrated his or her realization of the pressures to succeed that are put on students by parental expectations, by the desire to get into a professional or graduate school, and by the uncertainties of the job market. A speaker urging that American foreign policy in Africa take a certain direction can enhance his or her own authority by bringing before the audience the testimony of persons who are generally regarded as experts, such as the secretary of state, the chairman of the Senate Foreign Relations Committee, the president of Kenya, and so forth. A speaker who is hard to follow, who keeps jumping back and forth from point to point, who is dull and uninteresting, will not be thought to be competent or prepared by the listeners and thus his or her image will be negative. All of these examples come to the conclusion that ethos is dynamic: it can virtually be created and it can change during the course of a speech.

Ethos and Situation

While ethos is important, it is not always important in the same way and to the same degree. There are times when the ethos of the source is almost irrelevant, although it can never be totally so. You might, for example, be studying for an exam and go to a review session held by a graduate student or an instructor about whom you know very little. In this case you are likely to be highly motivated to understand the message and you won't care, or perhaps even think, about the person who is sending the message. At other times, you might know something of the communicator's political view and as a result distrust or dislike the speaker; the topic on which the person is speaking, however, might be "How to buy real estate," and you are convinced enough of the source's competence in that area to listen for information that you think will help you. In other words, the ethos for you changes as the topic makes certain aspects of ethos more important. Of course, it is possible that ethos from one area

29 The Speaker's Image

will spill over into another with good or bad effects for the speaker. Advertising often attempts to capitalize on the ethos of a popular person, encouraging spill over as it solicits endorsements for products from a popular entertainment or sports figure. It is also possible that a listener can form such a bad image of a particular source that the resultant ethos will intrude on every message, regardless of the relevance of the speaker's personal qualities to the subject matter. And in some public communication situations and settings, ethos can be all important. In advertising, for example, which attempts to create an ethos for the product; the product in effect becomes the source. This view of product as source is encouraged by the idea that what you will hear and see is "a word from our sponsor"; it is the sponsor—Johnson's War, Texaco, Xerox—that is "talking" to you. And that sponsor hopes you will like and buy the product. It is what the consumer thinks about the product that is essential. Perhaps one reason that professional advertising has become such a significant part of political campaigns is that the purpose there is often to sell the candidate as the "product" and not to worry about concrete or specific issues. In any event, the importance of ethos or the factors that make up ethos will vary as the setting, the speaker, and the audience varies, but the persuasive potential of image alone is never absent from public communication (Figure 3).

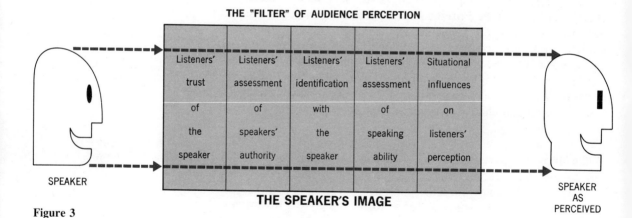

THE "FILTER" OF AUDIENCE PERCEPTION

| Listeners' trust of the speaker | Listeners' assessment of speakers' authority | Listeners' identification with the speaker | Listeners' assessment of speaking ability | Situational influences on listeners' perception |

THE SPEAKER'S IMAGE

SPEAKER

SPEAKER AS PERCEIVED

Figure 3

Select Bibliography

The following citations, and those listed in all the bibliographies, offer further practical and theoretical information related to the chapter topics, and they provide a starting point for the student who wishes to undertake more intensive study and research into the topic.

Kenneth E. Anderson and Theodore Clevenger, Jr., "A Summary of Experimental Research in Ethos," *Speech Monographs,* **30**(1963), 66-70.

David K. Berlo, James B. Lemert, and Robert J. Mertz, "Dimensions for Evaluating the Acceptability of Message Sources," *Public Opinion Quarterly,* **33**(1969), 563-576.

E. Berscheid, "Opinion Change and Communicator-Communicatee Similarity and Dissimilarity," *Journal of Personality and Social Psychology,* **4**(1966), 670-680.

Gary Cronkhite, "Identification and Persuasion," *Central States Speech Journal,* **15**(1964), 57-59.

Gary Cronkhite and Jo Liska, "A Critique of Factor Analytic Approaches to the Study of Credibility," *Communication Monographs,* **43**(1976), 91-107.

F. S. Haiman, "An Experimental Study of the Effects of Ethos in Public Speaking," *Speech Monographs,* **16**(1949), 190-202.

Carl I. Hovland and W. Weiss, "The Influence of Source Credibility on Communication Effectiveness," *Public Opinion Quarterly,* **15**(1951), 635-650.

Elihu Katz and Paul Lazarsfeld, *Personal Influence.* Glencoe, Ill.: The Free Press, 1955.

M. Karlins and H. Abelson, *Persuasion: How Opinions and Attitudes are Changed.* 2nd ed. New York: Springer Publishing Co., 1970.

Stephen W. King and Kenneth K. Sereno, "Attitude Change as a Function of Degree and Type of Interpersonal Similarity and Message Type," *Western Speech,* **37**(1973), 218-232.

James C. McCroskey, "Scales for the Measurement of Ethos," *Speech Monographs,* **33**(1966), 65-72.

Herbert W. Simons, Nancy N. Berkowitz, and R. John Moyer, "Similarity, Credibility, and Attitude Change: A Review and a Theory," *Psychological Bulletin,* **73**(1970), 1-16.

Christopher J. S. Tuppen, "Dimensions of Communicator Credibility: An Oblique Solution," *Speech Monographs,* **41**(1974), 253-260.

Karl R. Wallace, "An Ethical Basis of Communication," *Speech Teacher,* **4**(1955), 1-9.

Jack L. Whitehead, Jr., "Factors of Source Credibility," *Quarterly Journal of Speech,* **54**(1968), 59-63.

Henry Nelson Wieman and Otis Walter, "Toward an Analysis of Ethics for Rhetoric," *Quarterly Journal of Speech,* **43**(1957).

CHAPTER 3 *speaker/listener interaction*

The qualities of effective listening

Listening as an active process
A strategy for listening

The listener's identity
The listener's purpose
The influence of setting
The speaker's target
The listener's knowledge of the speaker
The speaker's purpose
Defensive listening

The qualities of audience adaptation

Identifying values
Identifying relevant dimensions
Stereotypes
The listener's perspective
The realistic purpose
The arrangement of ideas
The sense of ideas
Feelings and motivations
Talking with an audience

A final word about communication and people

Select Bibliography

The best and most comprehensive advice that can be given a listener is to be sure to know what's going on. That, of course, sounds very simple, but it is not simple at all. Very few of us know what's going on in a public communication setting all the time, and most of us would probably not like to admit how often we are persuaded to do things without us being aware of just how such persuasion occurred. And then there are a few of us who hardly ever know what's going on.

In essence, a major portion of this book is devoted to helping you know what's going on, that is, to helping you become a better, more effective listener. You will most likely find yourself consuming a lot more communication than you will find yourself producing it. But with what we've said so far about the listener and the speaker as a background, we can begin to talk about some basic ideas that will be elaborated later on. As an overview, we discuss a fundamental principle of listening and then suggest the outlines of a strategy for listening that should contribute to making that process more effective.

The principle that should determine your approach to listening is simple: *listening is an active process.* We often tend to forget that when we are not talking we are still very much a part of the communication process. Especially we can forget this in a public communication setting where constant recognizable feedback is not called for and where overt interaction is minimal. Many students in a public speaking class, for example, think that it's not very important to be in class when someone else is speaking except, perhaps, as a courtesy — so that there will be an audience for others. But listening to speeches ought to be as important as giving them if one works at it. The widespread dismissal of the listening process as unimportant is reflected by the kind of comment that some students make (students who have not studied the effect of such comments on ethos) when they ask instructors, "Did we do anything important when I was absent on Tuesday?" The implication is that if no assignments were given or tests administered or materials handed out, then the instructor only talked, so nothing important happened. But how they responded to that lecture was, or could be, of vital importance to each listener. The point, of course, is not so much that one is there as that one *does* something; not that one just listens, but that one listens actively and critically. Being active means that you've got to move—you have to keep your mind going, and going on the same track as the speaker, and not let it stop and float about, aimlessly drifting from topic to topic until the sound that you don't really hear finally stops. And listening critically means that you *assess* what you hear, trying to make it relevant to what you need to know or weighing it carefully before you decide to act or not act. There is a kind of restless, relentless, skepticism about the good listener who worries an idea the way a dog does a bone, devoting full attention to it, not letting it get away until all the juice is long sucked out of it, and rejecting a brittle, and even dangerous chicken bone for a good substantial T-Bone. Since a piece of communication is designed to get a response from you, you ought to ask yourself what it is doing to and for you as you listen. The search for the answer to such questions can never be a passive one; it can be a most productive one only to the extent that you pursue a careful and complete strategy aimed at getting the most for yourself out of public communication. Let us now lay out the basic tactics that should form your strategy with the understanding that much of what will come later in this book will add more to your understanding and ability to apply such a strategy.

1. *Think about your own identity.* Perhaps that sounds foolish. Yet it must not be forgotten that we all have many facets to our lives, represented in part by the characteristics discussed earlier in this chapter. The topic, the setting, and the general situation in which public communication takes place will influence the roles we play as listeners. If you can approach a communication situation aware of its relationship to you in your personal and social attributes and in the roles you play and the memberships you hold, you will begin to uncover your own initial positions on topics and your own predispositions and biases. No one can totally eliminate bias, nor can one be purely objective. But one can, through a self-analysis, at least indicate to oneself what some of the forces are that are at work. The aim is to face the situation realistically and honestly so that we know what we bring to the communication situation and who we are in relation to it.

2. *Listen with a purpose.* The speaker has a purpose in getting up to talk and the audience members ought to have one as each sits and listens. Do you hope to learn something? Is it something general or is it very specific? Can you relate the topic to your life and decide what aspect of it will be useful to you? If so, you can aim to identify the practical aspects of the message as it pertains to you. You can't, of course, be certain of your own purpose before you begin to listen to a speech, although the topic will give you an indication of what's

happening as will the resolution of other issues (issues that will be raised as this discussion goes on). The point is that you can provide your own focus in the situation; you can take from and respond to a message on your terms. This is not to say that you should ignore the speaker and his or her function; the speaker might want to tell you something that you will be very happy to have heard about, but which you initially find meaningless. All that is being urged here is that you try before and during the course of the communication to relate yourself personally to what is happening and try to understand the relationship of the message to you.

3. *Understand the setting.* As pointed out earlier, the setting in which communication takes place imposes restrictions and expectations on the communicator. A political candidate who has bought 30 seconds of radio time is very limited in what he or she can say. A speaker in an outdoor rally and one in a classroom will be working under different restraints. The listener will need to be aware of the handicaps and the advantages afforded to a speaker just by the immediate surroundings if that listener is going to evaluate accurately what the speaker is doing and can do.

4. *Try to understand who the speaker is talking to.* If the listener is going to appreciate and understand the choices made by a speaker, then the speaker's target audience must be identified. Given the topic and the context out of which the communication event arose, the listener can determine who the audience immediately addressed is—that is, who is sitting in front of the speaker listening to him—and, also, who the larger audience might be. The President of the United States might give a speech to the American Legion or a national labor convention; in both cases the subject matter and specific material will be strongly influenced by those groups. Nevertheless, the President will be aware of television and newspaper coverage and of the mass audience beyond the immediate one. The kind of appeals a speaker makes, the kinds of arguments he uses, even the topic he selects, may be puzzling to the listener who does not understand that public communication may have wide ramifications and may be directed at audiences unseen or unimagined by the naive listener.

5. *Examine your assessment of and knowledge about the speaker.* The listener ought to get his or her perception of the ethos of the speaker out in the open. The ways in which ethos will influence you ought to be made explicit so you can determine whether they are sensible to you. If, for example, you know the speaker is someone you detest and you will not do as he urges no matter what the message is simply because it might give him some pleasure and satisfaction, then you should not fool yourself into believing that you won't take the desired action because it is too expensive, or it doesn't seem logical, or because you are too busy. If the matter is not of vital importance, then it may not make any difference whether

or not you follow the course of action recommended. But suppose it's a very serious matter that will effect your health and well-being. Can you afford to base your decision on purely personal grounds? If you fool yourself, you will never even question whether you should act solely on the basis of the ethos of the source, and thus, you may lose the opportunity to listen effectively and consequently act effectively. Furthermore, you should be realistic in your assessment of the speaker. Gossip, half-remembered impressions, and secondhand accounts of the actions of others that one hears can influence a person's ethos significantly. The listener who hopes to be as effective as possible will be skeptical in assessing the speaker's reputation as in other things. In most cases, it is unwise to assume that any communicator's life is an open book to the listener. To be too confident of who and what a speaker is can lead the listener to over and underestimate the ability or integrity of a communicator. This is not to say that all a person has said and done in the past can or is to be ignored. In a sense we all stand on our records. The listener should satisfy him or herself that the speaker's record is as straight as it can be.

6. *Consider the speaker's purpose.* The listener who knows what the speaker is trying to do is better prepared to respond effectively. Speakers may not always be clear, or they may intend to mislead an audience. It will not always be easy to identify the speaker's purpose. However, what the listener knows about the setting, the speaker, and the general nature of the topic should be clues to pinpointing the goal of the speaker. Sometimes the speaker's purpose is one that is completely compatible with the listener, as in the kind of classroom situation where the lecturer hopes to gain understanding and the listeners really do want to learn something; in such a case the listener will want to know the speaker's purpose in order to co-operate actively with the speaker in its achievement.

7. *Listen defensively.* If the speaker is truly trying to communicate, he or she hopes to get the listener to do something; it could be a direct action such as voting in a certain way, or something less overt such as agreeing that more money should be spent on higher education. It could be in your interest to respond as the speaker wishes or it could not be. As a listener your major responsibility to yourself is to respond as intelligently as possible. This means that you cannot jump to conclusions, but instead must suspend judgment until you are convinced that you are making the best choice for you. To do that you must defend yourself against the appeals and pressures put on you by the communication event. Now defending does not necessarily mean rejecting; you might ultimately accept the speaker's arguments and respond as he or she would wish. You might be skeptical of a television message and end up finally buying the product or voting for the candidate. *Being defensive does mean that the listener works to uncover and evaluate the basis of his or her own responses.* As the ways ideas are explained and advocated in public communi-

cation are discussed in the subsequent chapters of this book, the attempt will be made to provide listeners with specific tests to help them evaluate messages. All these suggestions will be directed toward the general stipulation that a listener should understand *why* he or she is reacting in a certain way to a message and then ask him or herself if that is a sensible thing to do. For example, if you as a listener have decided to buy pantyhose because they look good on Joe Namath you should know that his ethos has convinced you and ask yourself if such a gimmick really is proof of the superiority of that product over others. If you tend to feel silly because you are acting as you do, then you should reevaluate your decision.

In examining your own motives you should try to uncover the extent to which you are acting on the basis of the image or reputation of the source. Furthermore, you have to determine how you are responding to the ideas in the speech, asking yourself how clear they are and how well assertions are supported by hard evidence. And certainly you should consider the extent to which you are responding on the basis of your feelings, that is, because you feel sympathetic or frightened or hostile or loving. In this connection the listener must ask him or herself how appropriate those feelings are considering the case at hand—are they the right ones that you believe you ought to have in that situation? Has the source of the communication identified his message with strong (but in this case irrelevant) feelings you have as, for example, associating your feelings of independence and self-esteem with a kind of cigarette (Figure 4)?

The tools of defensive listening are discussed along with the techniques of successful speaking. It is thus hoped that all those involved in the communication process will be better equipped to

---

DIRECTIONS FOR EFFECTIVE LISTENING

AN OVERVIEW OF ACTIVE RESPONSE TO PUBLIC COMMUNICATION

1. Think about your own identity.
2. Listen with a purpose.
3. Understand the setting.
4. Understand who the speaker is talking to.
5. Examine your speaker assessment.
6. Consider the speaker's purpose.
7. Listen defensively.

Figure 4

make that process more effective. But now let us examine, again as an overview, the fundamental considerations a communicator must deal with in his or her interaction with listeners.

Qualities of Audience Adaptation

That communication must be specifically designed for an audience ought by now to be recognized as a guiding principle in this book. The audience must be central to a speaker's thinking; all that he or she does should be calculated to elicit a response from listeners. That being the case, all that a speaker does is underpinned by the need for audience adaptation. It is important, therefore, to have a clear understanding of audience adaptation before proceeding to sketch the outlines of an effective speaking strategy.

Perhaps it would be best to say first what adaptation is *not:* adaptation is NOT saying what an audience wants to hear. Sometimes beginning speakers feel anything from a slight uneasiness to moral outrage over the notion that they must tailor their remarks for a particular audience. But if one hopes to accomplish something with that audience then adaptation is essential. This is not to say that the communicator only reinforces and never tries to change an audience's beliefs or attitudes. This is also not to say that the communicator never disagrees with an audience. It *is* to say that the communicator recognizes the essential humanity of all listeners, and tries to focus his or her message on their very real concerns and necessarily limited knowledge.

Audience adaptation, then, is the search for relationships between the speaker, the message, and the audience, and the use of the results of such a search to promote identification between the speaker, the message, and the audience. *How* one is to do this is a principal concern of this book; but the outlines of a strategy for accomplishing this goal may now be sketched.

1. *Search for and identify audience values.* The speaker devotes considerable energy to discerning values that are shared with his or her audience. The cataloguing of characteristics is partly done in order to see audience values and to try to understand and perhaps sympathize with those that are contrary to the speaker's. What are the things that are of real worth to the listeners? For certain audiences patriotic values may be extremely important, for others the need to get ahead, for others the value of education will be paramount. Of course, all of us possess a network of interlocking values, some of which conflict with others. Americans tend to admire individualism as a trait while at the same time place great stress on the need for teamwork; they profess the Golden Rule of doing unto others as we would have them do unto us, and, at the same time, value material success that often can be realized only at the cost of outwitting or tricking or outmaneuvering someone else. We hear of

the "work ethic," the "business ethic," the "Puritan ethic," all denoting various sets of values at work in our society. The best communicator is one who sees what values are relevant to the communication situation and will help an audience resolve value conflicts. Values, of course, are not the only listener features that a speaker must study.

2. *Identify and communicate relevant audience dimensions for the audience itself.* From the list of characteristics that were reviewed earlier in this chapter, those that directly pertain to the speech should be known to the speaker. The setting and the topic will suggest the obvious ones to him or her, but successful communication may exploit what is beyond the obvious. Since all of us have many roles, many memberships, and are shaped by a variety of factors in our backgrounds, we are not always aware of all our own interests at once. When we are thinking of buying a new car, for example, our roles as consumer may conflict with our role as parent; we might want to buy a car that is inexpensive and good on milage, but that same car may be too cramped to get the children into comfortably for a long trip. Different speakers with different purposes may choose to emphasize our different roles and to downplay others —ultimately the listener will have to decide for him or herself—but the communicator who hopes to influence the course of action has every right to make as strong a case as possible for the supremacy of one aspect of a listener's life over another. It might even be that the listener, preoccupied with the immediate considerations suggested by the setting and the topic, can overlook aspects of his or her own life that are, indeed, relevant, and these the speaker can point out.

3. *Do not stereotype.* It is important here to observe that, as much as we know or seem to know, about listeners, we cannot overgeneralize about people or assume that they all fit into neat little pigeonholes. One should not assume that all older people have the same view of sexual morality, for example. Older people may live together without being married because of the threat of severe loss of income due to Social Security regulations. Many young people are surprised to think of grandmothers and grandfathers doing such a thing, just as many older people might be surprised to learn that all young people do not believe in premarital sexual realtions. Labels often deceive us into stereotypical behavior, as well. All women and men who believe in "liberation," for example, do not mean the same thing by it. Liberation to one woman might mean the freedom to pursue a career and be married at the same time; to another it might mean the right to choose *not* to get a job and to remain happily at home without being made to feel guilty about her contribution to society; to another it might mean rejection of all traditional male/female relationships. So as we try to construct a profile of listeners we should remember that we are talking about trends in behavior

among certain groups and never can we predict absolutely that certain characteristics predetermine responses.

4. *Do not lose your own perspective.* While it is necessary to see the listeners' perspective, you do need to be warned that your own point of view should not be overwhelmed by your considerations of the audience. Being openminded does not mean being empty minded; you don't want to submerge your own convictions merely to please an audience. You must try to understand the people you hope to influence. Understanding is not the same thing as agreeing: to sell oneself or one's ideas for any price, including audience acceptance, is prostitution, and that is something quite apart from communicating effectively.

5. *Speak with a realistic purpose.* Your investigation of audiences will indicate to you the wide and conflicting variety of interests and needs of listeners. As has been pointed out, the network of values and characteristics is complex and not easily rearranged. You cannot assume that one message will cause very drastic effects. The web of relationships that make up our lives is tough and not easily reconstructed: a person who has strong religious beliefs is not likely to shed them because of a five-minute speech urging agnosticism. A lifelong Democrat will probably not be moved to vote Republican on the basis of a two-minute television spot. Yet we all know that it is possible for people to change their religious convictions or to switch political parties. These actions are usually the result of a multitude of experiences, however, that will undoubtedly include a *series* of messages. The teachers, the advertiser, the preacher, the political candidate all plan a series of messages in the hopes of getting audiences to understand, believe, and act. A speaker, then, must recognize that there are limitations imposed on what can be accomplished, and those limitations grow primarily out of the nature of the audience, along with those imposed by the setting and the topic. Yet with limitations are opportunities, too. The speaker needs to keep foremost in his mind the challenge to get a response from listeners. A realistic purpose, then, is one that accurately assesses how far listeners are prepared to go and is structured in terms of a *desired response.*

6. *Arrange ideas clearly and intelligently.* What the speaker knows about the audience should help him or her in stating and choosing those ideas best designed to get the response desired. If the speaker, for example, hopes to get an audience to understand how electricity is produced, that speaker will need to know how much the audience is likely to know about certain physical laws and principles of electricity before he or she can decide how best to frame ideas that will promote understanding. The speaker will also decide, based on his or her reading of the audience, whether it is necessary to arrange ideas in a step-by-step way, describing each facet of the process from the dam to the light bulb, or whether to talk about engi-

neering principles and how they affect the process. The way the purpose has been stated will help direct the speaker in being clear and direct for his or her listeners.

7. *Demonstrate the sense of ideas.* One of the things that a study of audiences should do for you is to convince you of the diversity of possible responses to messages. Ideas that are perfectly obvious or readily accepted by us we discover, sometimes to our great amazement, are unclear or controversial to others. Understanding audiences is the clue to understanding the kinds of material that are needed to make ideas more understandable or believable. The communicator needs to know in constructing a message whether a contention calls for elaborate proof or not; whether, for example, the audience will accept his or her contention that it is important to get a good education and thus enable the speaker to go on to develop an argument for his or her particular plan to improve it, or whether he or she will have to devote considerable attention to adducing evidence to show that education is a good thing in and of itself. And, of course, the nature of the proof offered should be tailored to the listeners' needs and experiences. The same speaker would be advised to consider examples of how education improved farming or small business practices if he or she were trying to demonstrate value to an audience in a small town in Indiana or Iowa and forget about its effects on literacy in certain areas of New York City. So the communicator, then, seeks to substantiate ideas adequately for the audience by identifying those that a listener will need to have supported and by choosing the kind of support with which listeners can relate.

8. *Recognize the relevance of listeners' feelings and motivations.* All of us have feelings about things that we care about. We are only upset or angry or happy or excited or apprehensive when we care about something. If we hear a message that excites no emotion at all or arouses no interest on our part then that message will be judged by us as totally irrelevant. There are many needs that we all share and emotional states that we experience, and these will be discussed in detail later, but it is essential that the speaker realize that emotion is not an evil force. Quite often we tend to think of a split between logic and emotion, the former being "good," the product of education and intelligence, while the latter is "bad," the result of some primal passions that should be kept under control. But without feelings both learning and persuasion are impeded. If you were asked to take a specified action and you felt that that action would make you feel good you would, of course, be more likely to take it than if you thought the action would be a waste of time since it had no relation to you. Sometimes our feelings might lead us to do socially undesirable things: greed might cause us to support a clearly unsafe and unhealthy way of manufacturing a product, for example, because we as stockholders in the company will make more money if costly changes in the process are not called for. We might act out of a very

positive feeling—love, for example, and still injure the loved one by overprotecting him or her. Or out of fear we might decide to equip our home with fire safety devices and thus protect ourselves and others from harm. Both good and evil can arise from actions motivated by needs and feelings; what the speaker should be mindful of is that for actions to occur at all the listener must be emotionally engaged at some level and with some intensity.

9. *Talk* with *not* at *an audience*. Every speaker should aim to be articulate. Listeners form impressions of a speaker and his or her ideas partly on the basis of what they see and hear during the delivery of the message. To be articulate is to be direct and clear, to let the language chosen and the delivery of the speech support the ideas and never to intrude on them. Often students of public speaking are advised to be "conversational," and insofar as this means to avoid the stilted, unnatural qualities of a read or memorized address, this is good advice. Being conversational, however, should not mean being sloppy, or disjointed, or fragmented as our conversation sometimes can be. The ability to speak directly and unaffectedly with an audience is not one that always comes naturally and may take some work and practice. It is important to remember that in most communication situations the potential for either engaging or turning off an audience is there, and what happens will be partly a result of what the listeners actually experience during the course of the communication.

At the heart of whatever strategy a speaker develops in his or her efforts to communicate is the concept of the responding audience, the listener who is the object of the communicator's attention and

DIRECTIONS FOR AUDIENCE ANALYSIS AND ADAPTATION

AN OVERVIEW OF PREPARATION FOR SUCCESSFUL PUBLIC COMMUNICATION

1. Search for and identify audience values.

2. Identify relevant audience dimensions.

3. Do not stereotype.

4. Do not lose your own perspective.

5. Speak with a realistic purpose.

6. Arrange ideas clearly.

7. Demonstrate the sense of ideas.

8. Recognize the relevance of listeners' feelings and motivations.

9. Talk with not at an audience.

Figure 5

the means to his or her success. The more the speaker knows of that audience, the more he or she can reasonably adapt to it (Figure 5).

A Final Word About Communication and People

In many respects, attitudes are as important as procedures in public communication. Public communication revolves around the relationship between the source of communication and the receiver. All of us who enter into the process play both roles and should expect that successful communication will be effective for both parties. To be successful we must understand what we and others bring to a given communication situation and how to use what we know to make the communication event more satisfactory.

What you should be able to do now is to begin to construct a profile of any potential audience you might face as a speaker, using the characteristics of the audience discussed in this chapter as a guide to the kinds of information that may be relevant. If you are going to give a speech in class, you should begin now to think about what your listeners are like and how you might devise a speech that is expressly for them. As you prepare to listen to the speeches of others you should review those aspects of active listening that will enable you to respond intelligently and in a way that will be satisfactory to you.

A communication class, naturally, can't teach you all you need to know about either the subject on which to speak or the people to whom you will speak. A course in public communication is not the place to learn extensively or systematically about the sociology of religion or the psychology of aging or the history of immigration. Your entire education is an ongoing process of acquiring and assimilating knowledge about human institutions and behavior. A sound approach to communicating and evaluating ideas in which you use most effectively what you know will help to make you a truly educated person.

Select Bibliography

The following citations, and those listed in all the bibliographies, offer further practical and theoretical information related to the chapter topics, and they provide a starting point for the student who wishes to undertake more intensive study and research into the topic.

Dominick A. Barabar, "Listening with the Inner Ear," *Central States Speech Journal*, 11(1959), 95-98.
Ernest S. Brandenburg, "Factors in Listening to Informative and

Persuasive Speeches," *Central States Speech Journal,* 5(1953), 12-15.

Virginia Buchli and W. Barnet Pearce, "Listening Behavior in Coorientational States," *Journal of Communication,* 24(1974), 62-70.

Michael Burgoon, "The Effects of Response Set and Race on Message Interpretation," *Speech Monographs,* 37(1970), 264-268.

Francis A. Cartier, "Listenability and Readability," *Speech Monographs,* 22(1955), 53-56.

Theodore Clevenger, Jr., *Audience Analysis.* Indianapolis: Bobbs-Merrill, 1966.

Milton Dickens and David H. Krueger, "Speakers' Accuracy in Identifying Immediate Audience Responses During a Speech," *Speech Teacher,* 18(1969), 303-307.

Carole H. Ernest, "Listening Comprehension as a Function of Type of Material and Rate of Presentation," *Speech Monographs,* 35(1968), 154-158.

James C. Gardiner, "The Effects of Expected and Perceived Receiver Response on Source Attitudes," *Journal of Communication,* 22(1972), 289-299.

Thomas B. Harte, "Audience Ability to Apply Tests of Evidence," *Journal of the American Forensic Association,* 8(1971), 109-115.

Kenneth A. Harwood, "Listenability and 'Human Interest,'" *Speech Monographs,* 22(1955), 49-52.

Paul D. Holtzman, *The Psychology of Speakers' Audiences.* Glenview, Ill.: Scott, Foresman, 1970.

Arlee Johnson, "A Preliminary Investigation of the Relationship between Message Organization and Listener Comprehension," *Central States Speech Journal,* 21(1970), 104-107.

Charles M. Kelly, "Mental Ability and Personality Factors in Listening," *Quarterly Journal of Speech,* 49(1963), 152-156.

Barbara Lieb, "How to be Influenced Discriminatingly," *Today's Speech,* 8(1960), 24-26.

James D. Moe, "Listener Judgments of Status Cues in Speech: A Replication and Extension," *Speech Monographs,* 39(1972), 144-147.

Ralph G. Nichols and Thomas R. Lewis, *Listening and Speaking.* Dubuque: William C. Brown Co., 1954.

Ralph Nichols and L. Stevens, *Are You Listening?* New York: McGraw-Hill, 1957.

Charles R. Petrie, Jr., "Listening and Organization," *Central States Speech Journal,* 15(1964), 6-12.

Charles M. Rossiter, Jr., "Sex of the Speaker, Sex of the Listener, and Listening Comprehension," *Journal of Communication,* 22(1972), 64-69.

Thomas G. Sticht and Douglas R. Glasnapp, "Effects of Speech Rate, Selection Difficulty, Association Strength and Mental Aptitude on Learning by Listening," *Journal of Communication,* **22**(1972), 174-188.

Robin Widergy and Gerald R. Miller, "Audience Commitment and Source Knowledge of Audience as Determinants of Attitude Change Following Counterattitudinal Advocacy," *Speech Monographs,* **39**(1972), 213-215.

PART TWO
communication strategies

CHAPTER 4 *communicating with a purpose*

Whenever we involve ourselves in a communication situation we are compelled to make choices. In public communication, most basically and obviously, we have to decide whether or not to talk or to listen. Once committed to participation, we start selecting what to talk about out of a universe of possible sources of material, or we start selecting what to listen to depending on the factors operating on us during the communication event. The fact is that communication involves a whole series of choices and the option that is open to us is whether or not we want those choices to be random or reasoned.

Suppose, for example, you were going to talk about how a President is elected in the United States in a speech communication class where you have been assigned a 10-minute speech. You may have just heard a political science lecture that relates to that subject, so you elect to work up a summary of your notes from the political science class. The network of choices involved in this case are largely random because they are inspired chiefly by ready convenience and not by the demands of the communication setting. The topic, for one thing, is probably much too broad to be dealt with adequately in the time. Then, the source of the material is too limited if the speaker hopes to communicate with particular listeners who can not be expected to have the same background as the members of the political science class who heard the original lecture — that original audience would have heard several other lectures, read the same textbook, prepared the same written assignments, and so forth, thus sharing many common experiences that prepare them in a unique way to receive the communication. The audience in the speech communication class would not have those shared experiences; they might not even particularly care about the subject or see how it relates to them, and they certainly would not have the impetus to listen that comes from the possibility that mastery of the information will be essential to passing an examination some time. All the choices that have to be made regarding how the material is organized — the nature of specific ideas to be laid out and how they will be developed, the precise sort of reaction that is expected from the listeners—all these choices are exceedingly restricted by the original arbitrary choice of reproducing a boiled-down version of a lecture. The same sort of objections would apply, of course, to a decision to give a speech that is, essentially, a rehash of an article from *Reader's Digest* or some other magazine that is not written for the 20 or so people who will listen to the speech, but for a much broader national audience that can be far different from the one the speaker is addressing. The initial choice, then, has really prevented the communicator from exploring and exercising the options dictated by the need for successful communication. He or she is thereby unable to plan intelligently a coherent set of choices in dealing with the audience for which, and the setting in which, public communication takes place—a set of choices that form a pattern that we will call strategy, and will discuss more fully below. And, of course, there is another fundamental objection that should be raised to any action that prevents the communicator from devising appropriate strategy: not only does it diminish the chances of creating a successful interaction, it also does a serious disservice to the communicator who would improve his or her ability to participate in the communication process. If one makes no choices based on the realities of the communication situation as he or she can best understand such realities, then very little learning will take place, for it is through the development of communication strategy that theoretical principles can be applied to practical experiences.

So the need of the communicator, then, is to determine a set of choices that is based on the communication needs of the audience and occasion and is consistent as well with his or her own goals and interests. In short, if public communication is to be successful, it must be the result of a careful strategy that grows out of the situation.

Situation and Strategy

A strategy, as we have said, is an overall plan that governs the choices to be made. Let us first examine the concept of strategy and then see how it applies specifically to public communication. Let us consider as examples of what strategy is and how it works some different constructs: military strategy, educational strategy, and finally, rhetorical strategy, or the strategy of public communication.

Strategy is a term most usually associated with the military and it is really from the military model that we derive the idea of strategy. Let us assume, for example, that two nations have gone to war. One of the first considerations of military planners will be war *aims,* that is, the determination of what the results must be in order for country A to say it has "won." The aims will grow out of the immediate and long-range situational factors. To simplify matters, let us consider the matter from the perspective of country A only. It may be that country B has infringed on A's border, that country B is a serious economic rival of country A, that country B has encouraged dissident groups to subvert A's political system, and that there is a long history of mutual antagonism between A and B. These are all situational factors that will shape A's aims, as will the state of both A's and B's armed forces, the alliance structure of each country, public opinion in each county, and so forth. Depending on the assessment A makes of the situation, different war aims could emerge. A might hope only to regain the land seized by B at the border, or A may hope to extend its territory at the expense of B, or it may hope to overthrow B's present government, or it may wish to destroy B's economic capability, or it may aim to overwhelm B totally and dictate the terms of a peace settlement. The aims will determine the strategy that is implemented. There are, however, strong forces at work that may prevent a rational consideration of aims and subsequent strategy. That is, certain situational factors may be distorted so as to impair a reasonable judgment as to the most attainable ends. The long historic legacy of bitterness between two countries may, for example, cause A, in patriotic fervor growing out of inflamed public opinion, to set as its aim the complete destruction of B—an aim that is unrealistic in the light of other situational factors. If the aim is not attainable, then no strategy will likely be effective.

Country A's aim may finally emerge as an effort to cripple country B's economic functions. Then a strategy or series of strategies might develop along these lines. The first might be called a "force" strategy that seeks physical destruction, the second might be a "diplomatic" strategy that attempts to isolate B from others who might buy her goods or supply her economic needs, and the third might be a "subversive" strategy that works toward undermining the confidence of B's citizens in their country's ability to succeed economically. Now each of these strategies will call for a set of *tactics* to make them work. That is, the force strategy might call for bombing of industrial targets, commando raids on factories, and a sustained military invasion that drives toward industrial centers; all these tactics are designed to further the strategy. And so with other strategies: an attack on B at the United Nations, the offer to provide country C with needed raw materials if it will remain uncommitted, and so forth, could serve as tactics to accomplish the diplomatic strategy; the subversive strategy may be advanced by such tactics as propagandistic radio messages beamed to the people of B or the use of agents to sabotage B's factories, or to stir up labor unrest. The situation and the emerging strategy and tactics, then, are intimately related.

The relationship works in *two* ways. Not only do the strategy and tactics grow out of the aims shaped by the situation, but, also, the execution of the strategy can cause reassessment of the aims. If, for example, A's bombers never reach their targets, commandos can inflict very little damage before being captured, and the invading army is driven back into its own territory, the force strategy will have to be abandoned. Depending on the degree of success of the other strategies, A might well have to reconsider whether its aims are possible to achieve, and may have to modify them considerably; they may, in the end, hope only to keep the situation the same as it was before the war began. So aims shape strategy and the success of strategy can reshape aims.

Strategy and its function might be better understood if put in another context; a teaching-learning situation. Educational strategy also grows out of a network of situational factors that lead to goals. The ages of the children, their known intellectual capacity, the expectations of parents, the normal requirements imposed on certain grade levels or by particular schools, can all form some part of the situation out of which the teacher creates reasonable aims. The educational strategist, like the military strategist, can miscalculate. Through lack of experience he or she might demand much more of students than can be reasonably expected, as when the beginning college teacher tries to reteach to freshmen what he or she has just learned in a graduate class; or, on the other hand, the inexperienced teacher of handicapped children may sentimentally assume that love conquers all and fail to demand that these children reach their full potential through work and discipline. The situational factors can be misread or they can be correctly interpreted; in any event they will lead to designated aims. Educators now talk widely about "behavioral objectives," or specific statements of what they wish students actually to *do* as a result of being taught; but, whether or not one talks about behavioral objectives or simply educational goals, the teacher will devise a series of strategies and attendant tactics to achieve his or her aims. Assume, for example, that the teacher is designing a unit on colonial life in America. That such a unit must or will be taught already constrains the situation. After careful consideration of situational factors the aim might be described as having the children understand the quality of life in seventeenth-century New England. (And, of course, this aim could be stated in a series of objectives that could be tested by the children's observable behavior.) To bring about such understanding a teacher could employ an "involvement" strategy consisting of tactics calling for the students to make clothes like those worn at the time, to cook foods eaten at the time, to construct models of houses, to reenact town meetings or religious meetings, and the like. The success of such a strategy in helping children to understand aspects of the colonial environment would depend on the aptitudes and interests of the children, and, as with other kinds of strategies, the failure of tactics to promote the strategy might call for different tactics (as the same involvement strategy certainly would if the students were high school rather than elementary students). Or, failure might call for the abandonment of the chosen strategy for others, or for the modification of aims.

These two brief examples of strategy in operation suggests aspects of a strategic model that we can now construct and apply to the strategy of public communication: rhetorical strategy.

Rhetorical strategies are the set of choices to be made in the design and execution of a message, based on comprehensive communication principles. In this book two fundamental strategies will be offered based on the principles that communication is purposive and that communication has structure and form. *Rhetorical tactics* are those specific methods and procedures designed to further strategic choices. In this book, two basic sets of tactics will be discussed: those dealing with arguing reasonably and with involving audiences.

The first element in shaping rhetorical strategy is the rhetorical situation. That is to say, from the total situation there are certain aspects that are particularly relevant to public communication. These situational factors may influence the choice of topic or they may influence the way the topic is developed by the speaker and responded to by the listener, or both. In the presidential campaign of 1976, for example, Governor Carter of Georgia and President Ford met in a debate in San Francisco. During that debate the President stated that Eastern European countries were not dominated by the Soviet Union, a comment generally regarded as a political blunder. That statement became a part of the rhetorical situation in the week that followed and led Governor Carter to choose to talk about the conditions of Eastern Europeans in his speeches throughout the week. So that comment by President Ford was a situational factor that influenced Carter's public communication. In the same week, however, a student in a public speaking class gave a speech on tax loopholes and how they should be plugged. For him, Ford's remark was irrelevant; while it was part of some overall situation, while most of his audience was likely to be aware of the Ford remark, it was not a part of the student's *rhetorical situation*. For him, student concerns about how to finance an education while parents were paying higher taxes *was* a part of the situation with which he had to deal. Or one could imagine a state legislator being invited to speak to the PTA at a time when a bill was pending that would reduce state aid to local schools: that situational factor would be so importnat that it would probably dictate the legislator's choice of topic.

For the speaker who must choose a topic the situation will play an important role. First, of course, the choice must come from the speaker himself. It is foolish to enter into public communication without some interest in and knowledge of the matter being discussed. The principal resource that a speaker has *initially* is him or her self. All of us have a wide variety of interests if we stop and think about it. We may have some future career goal that we're working for, or a part-time job now that's satisfying or interesting to us. We may have particular academic subjects that we enjoy or intellectual interests aside from our formal class work. Anyone who wants to be an engineer, or a teacher or a draftsman or a lawyer or a lab technician, has things to talk about in connection with these fields. If chemistry or history are favorite subjects, then there are topics from these areas of study that are interesting. Someone who likes to read poetry or play chess or solve word puzzles has things to talk to others about. The solitary and demanding hobby of building ships in bottles or the more active involvement in politics can lead to speeches of interest or concern to audiences. But it is essential that any communicator realize that what is to be discussed publicly must be of some interest to that speaker no matter what the situation, or the chances of successful communication taking place are practically zero. There is, however, a caution that must be injected here: the speaker must not confuse interest with complete preparedness. In order to enter into public communication, a speaker must engage in a demanding intellectual process first. So the speaker must not assume that a speech must be complete in his or her head before a topic is chosen.

The situational factors, then, working with the interests and tastes of the speaker will produce a topic. The factors could include the many aspects of audience that were discussed in detail in the last chapter, the needs of a particular occasion—such as a sales presentation or a classroom oral report—or the motivations for public communication that can arise out of the immediate context in which the speaker and listeners live, such as problems that affect the lives of the listeners directly. A speaker, for example, may assess his or her own interests, which include history and politics, analyze the student audience and identify their concern over job prospects when they finish college, and take into account the presidential election campaign going on at the time. From these situational factors the speaker may decide to speak on the topic, "Voter Apathy." Now what the speaker must do next illustrates the next phase in our model of rhetorical strategy.

From situational factors, interacting with the speaker and the listener, aims must be developed. Just as country A had to assess the factors that led to conflict and determine what it had to accomplish to win, so the speaker has to look at the entire speaking situation and determine what he or she hopes to accomplish; that is, the speaker must create a purpose. You will remember that in the first chapter we discussed purpose and suggested that the purpose of communication was to get a desired response from an audience. So as the speaker refines his or her topic, he or she will try to translate it into a specific statement of response. Since all that can be done to insure successful public communication rests ultimately on a clear conception of purpose, we consider it in detail here.

The speaker who has chosen "Voter Apathy" as a topic, now has several decisions to make. The restraints of the situation, such as how many people will be there, how long the speech must be, what time of the day it is, and so forth, combined with what he or she can determine about the audience should lead the speaker to decide first on the general nature of the speech; the speaker will decide on what kind of response he or she is aiming for generally before deciding on the specific response. In our example, the speaker could decide that the audience simply was unaware of voter apathy and needed more information about the problem, or the speaker might have a plan to overcome voter apathy that he or she would like to have the audience agree to and/or act on, or the speaker might believe that the audience already looks with disfavor on voter apathy but doesn't feel strongly enough to do anything about it. In such cases the speaker would posit then a kind of *general purpose*—to gain understanding, for example—and then move to a very specific statement of the response sought for, such as, "I want my audience to understand the precise ways in which voter apathy has affected the outcome of past elections." From this example, let us go back and look systematically at the kinds of general and specific purposes that govern public communication. In order to understand purpose best let us consider each general purpose and the specific purposes derived from it.

Informative Purposes

One type of communication is called informative and this aims *primarily at gaining understanding*. Often public service announcements on television and radio, lectures given in class, reports delivered at meetings of organizations, are all aimed at gaining understanding. In this type of communication the initiator or source hopes that the listeners will end the encounter having learned something they did not know before. The concern of the source or speaker is not that the listeners necessarily do something, or think something that they have not thought, or believe something, but, rather, that they *know something that they did not know before*. All communication is directed at getting something, and what the speaker hopes to get here is understanding. From this general purpose the speaker then moves to create the specific purpose or the statement of the desired audience response.

The specific purpose grows out of the topic and the general purpose, shaped by the particular demands of the situation. If, for example, you were going to give a speech in class on the problem of crime you would, after considering such matters as the factors influencing the audience, the relationship of crime to the audience, the amount of time available for the speech, and so forth, decide that the audience should know more about how crime affects them directly. This suggests a speech to gain understanding, and the speaker could devise several possibilities for purposes that could be accomplished in a limited amount of time. The following are all examples of specific purposes that could be set by the speaker:

I want my audience to understand the economic impact of crime.
I want my audience to understand the kinds of crime committed in the suburbs.
I want my audience to understand the crime pattern at this institution.
I want my audience to understand some of the major causes of crime.

Each of the examples is a statement of how the speaker wants the audience to respond, that is, what he or she hopes to accomplish in the speech. An appropriate strategy can be devised and implemented once the speaker is sure of what he or she hopes to do; and when we discuss how communication can be structured and developed in the chapters that follow we will really be talking about designing and carrying out rhetorical strategies. But what is important to remember at this point is that the fundamental step is deciding on how listeners are expected to respond before doing anything else.

This step is so fundamental it deserves some additional collaboration. Too often public communication is less successful than it could be because the speaker is not sure what that communication ought to be doing. A speaker once addressed a large crowd gathered to protest proposed fee hikes for state colleges. Now the listeners had come primarily because they wanted to know what to do to stop the increases and to show support for those who were fighting to keep fee costs as they were. The speaker delivered a long, angry attack on student apathy and implied that such stupid, unresponsive creatures deserved whatever they got at the hands of an unsympathetic legislature. The speaker could have talked about the need to become active, he could have attempted to get his audience (already motivated to act) to understand how they could take direct actions that would put pressure on the lawmakers. There were a wide range of appropriate purposes that he could have devised. Instead, he probably decided just to "get up and talk about apathy" with the result that he irritated and alienated an initially friendly audience and injected a depressing note into what should have been an enthusaistic show of unity and determination. If that speaker had thought carefully and systematically about the topic and the situation it is likely that he would have come up with a more sensible specific purpose.

Often beginning students of public communication will tend to hurry over the specific purpose without realizing how it determines so much that will happen. A speaker might be tempted, for example, to say that her purpose is "to talk about modern technology." Such a statement, of course, is not a purpose at all. It says something very vague about what a *speaker* will do, and purpose in communication refers to what the speaker wants to *get from the listener*. Furthermore, "modern technology" is a very broad and nonspecific idea unless it is related directly to what the speaker hopes the audience will understand about modern technology. Stated as is, the speaker would have a very hard time making choices about what material to include and what to exclude in such a speech. The result would probably be somewhat random, and the chances of a coherent strategy slim. To go back to our military analogy, it would be like country A deciding that the aim of the war was "to fight B" with the result that no coherent plans could be laid out, since conflict seemed to be an end in itself. It is just as foolish to assume that "talking about" something is an end in itself. The speaker in this case, after considering her own interests, the listeners, and the situation in which they all find themselves, might come up with a purpose like, "I want my audience to understand the ways modern technology makes learning easier." Such a purpose will call for a different strategy and will certainly lead the speaker to different material from that called for by a purpose such as, "I want my audience to understand how modern technology creates psychological problems for some factory workers." Both these purposes relate to the topic of "modern technology," but both will obviously need to be developed differently. The communicator who hopes to be successful, then, will plan the response carefully and never allow him or herself to be vague or unclear about precisely what his or her purpose in speaking is.

Persuasive Purposes

Persuasive communication aims at influencing the feelings, thoughts, and behavior of listeners by *eliciting stronger feelings, gaining agreement,* or *inducing action.* Traditionally, such persuasive purposes have been grouped under three persuasive categories, and we consider each of these now: communication designed to stimulate, communication designed to convince, and communication designed to actuate.

In *communication designed to stimulate* the communicator hopes to get his or her audience to feel more strongly about something with which they might already be in agreement. This is sometimes described as a speech that reinforces ideas or beliefs that listeners already have. There are times when public communication hopes to overcome apathy or to promote involvement or awareness on the part of listeners. All of us could think of ideas or principles that we would not object to but that don't seem to make much difference in our thought or action. There are political convictions, religious beliefs, or moral values that we might say we subscribed to, but that we do not have uppermost in our minds. There are many people, for example, who are nominal Democrats or Republicans. Yet they will be unable to tell you who their party's candidates for state or local offices are; they don't seem to care very much which party wins; and they might not even vote themselves. They might agree with Republican principles or agree with what the Republican candidate says in his speeches, but they just don't feel very strongly about it. One might engage such persons in a much more animated discussion of the merits of the local high school football team, or ways to improve production at the plant, or the quality of the latest college theatre production, or the pros and cons of staying in school versus taking a year off to get a job. The political communicator who would like all the Democrats or all the Republicans to support the party (by working door to door, by giving money, certainly by voting) knows that people must feel some personal motivation before they will be prepared to give such support. Part of the total communication in a political campaign, therefore, is aimed at getting those who already agree with the party's positions and candidates to feel strongly about their political allegiance. There are many other examples: religious speakers often try to get audiences to feel more strongly that the principles to which they may pay lip service are important in their lives; teachers may attempt to get students initially committed to furthering their education to feel more strongly that completing their degree or diploma is a good, positive thing to do; the president of a campus organization may try to create more enthusiasm among the members for the group's goals; a student may try to get a roommate to feel more strongly that his or her concentration would improve if a study break was taken. Communication with the aim of reinforcing existing feelings or beliefs, then, is based on the assumption that the listener and the speaker are already in substantial agreement: the coals are glowing, but they need to be fanned if they are to burst into flame.

If one were giving a speech in class to reinforce existing beliefs, and the topic was ways to improve higher education, a reasonable specific purpose might be, "I want my audience to feel more strongly that the costs of higher education must be kept as low as possible." Such a purpose states what the speaker hopes the audience will feel when he or she has finished speaking. It is limited in scope, too, and can be handled within the confines of the situation. Furthermore, speeches that are sometimes called "ceremonial" usually aim to stimulate existing feelings. In 1976, for example, when the United States was celebrating its bicentennial there were hosts of messages about America and the American heritage that were based on the assumption that the listeners agreed on the essential goodness of the country and its citizens. A student in such circumstances could give a speech with the purpose, "I want my audience to feel more strongly that the American past has favorably influenced the present." Now if that same student was travelling in Europe and was asked to speak to some German students about the American bicentennial the same assumption could not be made. He or she would certainly wish to develop a different specific purpose, one more responsive to the situation and audience.

In *communication designed to convince* the communicator hopes to secure the *agreement* of his or her listeners. We have all found ourselves in situations where we want someone to agree with our point of view. The issue might be a political one, such as who should be elected president, or it might be a question of taste, such as whether or not a recent film was as innovative and original as the critics said it was, or a matter of conjecture such as whether Michigan or Ohio State play the toughest football schedule, and so forth. Whatever the particular case, we have all had experience with this kind of persuasion. This does not mean, of course, that we all know to operate successfully in such a situation. We know that sometimes we seem to be able to get people to see things as we do and sometimes we don't. While the study of persuasion does not *assure* anyone of success, it does help those who would persuade to increase their chances of effectiveness, and surely one way to give oneself a better chance is to identify the precise persuasive goal that one has in mind. The goal, as are all goals in communication, is shaped by the situation. The speaker needs to understand what is reaonable and possible to accomplish. In seeking to gain agreement, the communicator has to realize that dramatic shifts of opinion and ideas are very rare. Sometimes, it is better to try a very small step that can be taken than to attempt a large one that is doomed to falter.

Consider, for example, an exchange student from an Eastern European country who devised as his purpose, "I want my audience to agree that the United States should overthrow its present form of government and adopt a Communist-style one." Given an average college student audience, such a speaking purpose would be virtually impossible to accomplish. It would be much more reasonable for the student to limit his persuasive goals to such specific purposes as , "I want my audience to agree that the people of Eastern Europe want to be friendly with the American people," or "I want my audience to agree that our system of government is not a bad system for our people." Now neither of these purposes can be accomplished without effort, and perhaps the speaker might not be able to realize fully even the more limited goal. It does seem, however, that such purposes are *possible* and that is a critically important consideration.

As in all communicative purposes, speeches designed to get agreement should be stated precisely in terms of response. The speaker who sets out "to persuade my audience about nuclear power," is in serious trouble before he or she begins. It is the "talking about" problem all over again. The speaker has a whole range of options open: he or she has to be absolutely certain of whether the aim is to get the audience to agree that nuclear power should be attempted on a limited basis, or to agree that nuclear power should be rejected as a possibility in the near future, or to agree that the development of nuclear power should be given first priority in our national energy-conservation program, or one of the many other possibilities that exist. It is only when such a clear purpose is established that strategy can be formed.

In considering the limitations that of necessity are imposed on the specific purpose, the communicator should not be so cautious that he or she becomes timid, afraid to take risks with an audience, to challenge listeners, to face difficult issues. Getting other people to agree with you is not easy. And limiting a purpose to one that *can* be achieved does not mean that you will always achieve it. And it certainly does not mean that a speaker should only tackle the sure thing. If you were to design purposes that you were convinced would *always* produce agreement, you would probably end up talking about trivial matters much of the time or, what is even worse, end up saying not what *you* think is right but what you believe *listeners* want to hear. Persuasion is not a knack that one can pick up by learning a few of the tricks of the trade. It is a difficult communication process that takes careful thought and practice; it takes the kind of intelligent planning that grows out of respect for one's own integrity and need to be an articulate human being, coupled with a respect for the listener's needs and feelings. That being so, planning a persuasive specific purpose becomes a thoughtful prerequisite to a well-developed piece of communication and not just a mechanical effort.

In *communication designed to actuate* the communicator hopes to have his or her audience take some *direct, overt action.* Every day we encounter appeals, pleas, suggestions, and demands that we act in certain ways. Politicians ask us to get out and vote, health experts ask us to get out and exercise; advertisers ask us to buy their products, Girl Scouts ask us to buy their cookies; a friend asks us to take care of her cats while she's in Florida, our parents ask us to spend more time at home. Our friends, our television sets, and even total strangers try to influence us in specific ways to do specific things. One who plans this type of communication has a very definite and concrete goal in mind: a direct action that needs to be taken. Anything short of the action is not sufficient to accomplish the speaker's goal. Suppose, for example, that you were particularly eager to see a certain candidate elected to the state legislature. Your friend, whom you knew to be not particularly partisan, was persuadable. After spending some considerable time in trying to get your friend to commit himself to your candidate and finally sensing that you had gained the agreement of your friend, you would be disappointed to hear him say, "Well, I guess you're right. Of course, I can't vote anyway because I never did get registered." Agreement, while somewhat satisfying, isn't all that you had in mind—you wanted a vote that would count in the election.

In planning a speech to actuate, the communicator needs to determine the precise action that he or she wishes to see the listeners take. If the topic of the speech is volunteerism, the speaker who hopes to get action will not be happy if the audience only learns something about the role of volunteers in charitable organizations, or if the listeners leave after the speech is over agreeing that volunteers are important—although both these reactions may be favorable. What should satisfy the speaker is the accomplishment of such purposes as: *I want my audience to pledge to spend two hours a week as a volunteer; I want my audience to refuse to do volunteer work; I want my audience to join the National Association of Volunteer Workers; I want my audience to visit the nearest neighborhood recreation center within the next week.* These are all different purposes and the precise one, of course, would be determined by the interaction of the speaker, the audience, and the situation, but all reflect the speaker's intention to aim for direct action. In many ways, this kind of speech yields the most tangible results; at least if you ask for 20 people to make sizable donations and end up with $1.15, you know that you have not done well. One cannot always tell, naturally, whether listeners will actually do what is hoped for, but this speech is not one that aims only for mental or emotional response. (The speech to actuate calls for listeners to demonstrate some overt, observable behavior.)

Entertaining Purposes

Communication that is entertaining is that which stimulates enjoyment on the part of the listeners. This is the type of communication that usually occurs in an after-dinner situation, or at a time when the audience does not expect to be asked to think very hard or take very serious action. In many ways this is a very difficult speech to give. Humor is hard to plan; professional humorists are likely to employ teams of writers and even they can and often do flop. Also, what might seem funny to you or a few of your friends one night might not seem so funny the next morning. A student, for example, was preparing to give a report in class on a famous debate of the eighteenth century given in the British House of Commons. He amused himself and his roommates with the idea that the debate could be reported the way Howard Cosell would have reported it.

The next morning at 8:30, however, what had seemed so funny sounded strained and overdone in the classroom presentation. Instead of being enjoyable, the experience was embarrassing for everyone. The student in this case made several mistakes. Foremost, of course, was to misread the situation and audience and assume that an entertaining purpose was suitable. It was not, of course; this should have been a speech to gain understanding. But, even if it is granted that the student wanted to inform and hoped that by increasing interest he could accomplish this, he had obviously not framed his purpose so carefully that the vehicle for presenting material didn't obscure the information itself. It was also fatal to try such a maneuver on the basis of the reaction of a few friends who might share one's sense of humor, and to try such a device without lots of time to refine it and to think about it. Being an intelligent person, the speaker would probably have thought better of his plan if he had given himself time to consider it.

Creating enjoyment, it should be pointed out, does not always mean being funny. In fact, most successful speeches to entertain will probably include a lot of informative material. Enjoyment comes from being interested and relaxed and not necessarily from being amused. Furthermore, different people enjoy different things: some people like to solve puzzles and play word games, some people like historical adventure, some people like to watch television, some people invariably find a cream pie squashed in a comic's face to be uproariously funny. What people enjoy is not always easy to predict, and often the clues one can get from audience analysis are not helpful. But if you think about it, you can probably guess with some accuracy what kind of music college students find enjoyable, what sorts of television programs most people watch, what movies are popular, what the serious interests are of those in particular majors, and so forth. A speaker could give a speech with the specific purpose: "I want my audience to enjoy my account of how the pyramids were first discovered," or, "I want my audience to enjoy my explanation of how horror movies are made," or "I want my audience to enjoy a description of my motorcycle trip through the Middle East." Now in all these cases, the listeners may learn something, they may even be actuated in some way — such as going to see a horror movie or taking a trip to Egypt or the Middle East, but that is not what the speaker hopes to accomplish. What he or she really wants is for each listener to have a good time listening to the speech. That means, of course, that the speech will be developed differently from a speech with another kind of purpose; to repeat what has been said many times in this chapter, the strategy depends on the purpose. It would be nice if every speech was enjoyable, and that is a worthy goal. But the point here is that only those communications that aim at enjoyment *alone* can be successful when enjoyment is the *sole result* (Figure 6).

PURPOSEFUL COMMUNICATION

Type	General response	Specific response
INFORMATIVE	Understanding	I want my audience to understand...
PERSUASIVE: STIMULATE	Eliciting stronger feelings	I want my audience to feel more strongly that...
PERSUASIVE: CONVINCE	Gaining agreement	I want my audience to agree with me that...
PERSUASIVE: ACTUATE	Inducing overt action	I want my audience to [take action]...
ENTERTAINING	Stimulating enjoyment	I want my audience to enjoy [my account of...]

Figure 6

Purposes and Multiresponses

As you read this chapter you may begin to think that some speeches could have more than one purpose. That is not exactly right—each speech will have *one* specific purpose—however, you would be right in discerning that some speeches will be designed to elicit more than one of the kinds of responses that have been discussed so far. There are communications that promote understanding, that reinforce ideas and feelings, that seek agreement, and finally call for action—such responses can be sought in one speech. What determines the purpose of such a speech is what the speaker hopes to accomplish. This will all be clearer if we consider some examples.

Were a speaker to talk about the Egyptian pyramids, several purposes are possible. Let us suppose that the purpose is this: "I want my audience to sign up for the special Christmas charter tour to Egypt." In such a speech the audience might well be given information that will help them understand how the pyramids were built, their feelings that it would be good to get a complete break from the routine of school might be reinforced, they might be led to agree that the charter tour is the most economical chance they will ever get to make the trip, and finally, some of them might sign up to go on the tour. In other words, a whole range of responses would *have to* precede the desired one in order to be successful. How, for example, could listeners be asked to agree that genetic research is safe and desirable if they do not understand the kinds of problems that are being investigated? How could listeners be expected to agree that nuclear energy is more efficient than electrical energy if they don't understand at least a few fundamental principles that explain how each works? And, to turn the examples around, how can a speaker get an audience to understand how energy for our daily lives is produced if the listeners are not convinced that such information is important to them? Getting an audience to understand how to conserve energy is very hard if that audience doesn't agree that energy *should* be conserved. Nevertheless, in spite of the fact that a range of responses may be called for, what determines the purpose is the communicator's hoped-for end result. To return to the speaker who wanted his audience to sign up for the tour: if the listeners had stopped, as it were, at any point along the way, the speaker would not have accomplished his purpose. If the listeners understood something about the construction of the pyramids but did not sign up for the tour, or agreed that it would be fun to go or cheap to go but did not sign up, or if they enjoyed the talk very much but did not sign up — the speaker would not be satisfied. Even though he had promoted understanding or gained agreement or stimulated enjoyment, if he had not signed up tour members he had not accomplished his specific purpose. Communication has the best chance of success if, as has been pointed out before, the communicator realizes what is possible and aims for the possible goal: that goal is the specific purpose.

It should also be realized that it is sometimes more effective to try to accomplish a long-range aim through a whole series of communications. To get changes in environmental protection laws, for example, took many years of public education — merely trying to get people to understand the nature and gravity of the problem — before any direct action could be urged. In the classroom situation, a speaker may decide to use his or her speaking assignments as a sustained campaign aimed toward some ultimate goal. Perhaps the speaker might want to urge some revision in the school curriculum. Perhaps the revisions may not be the ones that can be assumed to be automatically popular ones. The speaker may give a first speech with the specific purpose, "I want my audience to understand how curriculum changes are brought about and curriculum decisions are made"; the second speech purpose might be, "I want my audience to feel more strongly that the curriculum should meet their particular needs"; the third purpose might be, "I want my audience to agree that requirements should include more courses that help them to write and speak more effectively"; and the fourth speech purpose might be, "I want my audience to volunteer to work for the Student Committee for an Improved Curriculum." Such a sequence of speeches might have a better chance of bringing student listeners around to the speaker's position than would one that tried to do everything in a single communication.

Testing Specific Purposes

Since specific purposes are the foundations on which all strategy is built, a great deal of space has been devoted in this chapter to describing them carefully. It might be particularly helpful now to consider some quick ways to test the specific purposes you will develop and to be certain that you can evaluate purposes. Basically, there are three questions you can ask yourself to determine whether or not you have a sound, communicative purpose.

1. *Does the purpose call for a response?* "I want to talk about the need for tax reform," or "Tax Reform," or "Ten Reasons Why Taxes Should Be Reformed," or "My Views of Tax Reform," or "What you should know about your taxes," are *not* specific purposes. They might be topics or they might be titles, but they *do not* designate the response that the speaker wants from the audience. "I want my audience to understand what a tax loophole is and how it works," *does* indicate that the speaker has planned for a response from his or her listeners and accordingly *does* qualify as a specific purpose.

2. *Does the purpose reflect the realities of the situation?* The audience, the setting, and the occasion, as has been pointed out, should influence the purpose of communication. "I want my audience to understand the history of Russia," is absurdly broad to be given in a short space of time and *is not* a good specific purpose. "I want my audience to take up skiing as a hobby," *is not* appropriate to a Senior Citizens Club just as "I want my audience to plan for retirement" would *not* be appropriate for your college speech class. A purpose that *is* manageable might be, "I want my audience to understand the major immediate causes of the Russian Revolution," and the skiing speech might be appropriate given to the college speech class. (Of course, if the class is one in Normandale Community College in Minnesota the chances are that the purpose is appropriate, whereas if the class is at the University of Florida then the purpose surely would be less appropriate.) It would probably be too late to call the attention of senior citizens to the need for retirement planning, but one could give an appropriate speech with the purpose: "I want my audience to understand the services and opportunities that are available to retired persons."

3. *Is the purpose clear?* An audience can often be confused by a strategy that grows out of a vague purpose. And, unfortunely, communication is almost invariably unsuccessful when the communicator him or herself is not clear about what he or she hopes to accomplish. "I want my audience to understand about the Japanese Tea Ceremony," is *not* a good purpose because, although it is couched in the appropriate language of a purpose, it shows that the speaker does not know *precisely* what he or she wants the audience to do. The phrase "understand about," is a clue that the real clarity is lacking, that the *words* of response are being used, but the *idea* is probably the same as "talk about." The speaker may wish an audience to know how it is

performed, or how persons are trained to do it, or why it is such an important ritual in Japanese life, or even to go see a ceremony performed next Monday in a room on campus. All these are purposes that reflect a clear conception on the part of the communicator regarding the desired audience response.

What we have been concerned with in our discussion of specific purpose has been the way a communicator lays the groundwork for a successful rhetorical strategy. Audiences are also concerned with the purpose of messages aimed at them and a word needs to be said about listeners' purpose.

Agreement and Conflict in Speakers' and Listeners' Purposes

The purposes of both communicator and listener are often compatible. Advertisers who are trying to persuade people to buy their automobiles are listened to by people who, indeed, want to buy automobiles. A lecturer who wants the audience to understand the anatomy of the inner ear rightly expects to find that the medical students or audiology students who are listening *want* to understand.

Specifically, there are learning situations where the listeners want to understand what is said. There are persuasive situations where listeners will feel better about their allegiances or values if they are reinforced in them; where listeners will be introduced to and brought to agree with ideas that are consistent with the listeners' beliefs and attitudes; where listeners will be urged to take actions that will enhance and fulfill their lives. The listener needs to recognize that it is often in his or her interest as well as the speaker's to be informed, persuaded, and entertained. It has already been suggested that listening is an active process. Sometimes that process involves the listener in working hard to help the speaker do what he or she has set out to do. The listener cannot be — and cannot expect to be — *acted upon;* he or she might sometimes have to overcome boredom, fatigue, initial uninterest, or any other distracting factors, and interact with the speaker and the message as constructively as possible so that all parties in the public communication situation can be satisfied.

On the other hand, the listener does need to be aware that his or her purpose can be in conflict with a speaker's. It may be true, for example, that the listener wants to buy a car and the communicator wants to sell one. But the salesman wants to make the best financial sale possible and the listener may wish to spend as little as possible. The listener, for his or her own defense, needs to define precisely what it is that he or she hopes to accomplish in the communication exchange and judge the message that is directed toward him or her by that goal.

In public communication, of course, premeditation is not always possible. When you come into a speech class you are not sure of what topics will be discussed that day, and, faced with a speech on the role of women in intercollegiate athletics, for example, different listeners will have widely different initial responses on which to begin to form any purpose at all. The speaker will, if he or she hopes to be successful, try to relate the speech to the audience. As listeners perceive and evaluate such efforts, they can begin to decide what they ought to be getting out of the speech. If, for instance, a speech on pollution control legislation is given the listener, such factors as the listener's awareness of national problems or the listener's geographic location will shape his or her initial interest in the question. If the speaker is successful in engaging the listener's attention so that the listener begins to be aware of ways that pollution is directly harming him or her, at that point the listener may begin to form a purpose, such as, "I am listening to this message in order to find out how I can stop pollution in this town." Now the listener's purpose, unlike the speaker's, will be somewhat open ended and subject to some modification as the speech goes on. Nevertheless, to try to get the most out of the communication event as possible, the listener will attempt to achieve the focus and concentration that a purpose will help to provide.

Whatever purpose the listener finally evolves, he or she should be cautious in deciding whether or not it has been accomplished. One reason for legislation that protects people who sign contracts with salesmen by giving them a certain period of time to revoke the agreement, is that we often need time to think over our decisions. The speaker may well press for an immediate response to his or her message. The careful listener, however, will try to stave off any irrevocable action on the basis of a message he or she has just received until there is adequate time to reflect on whether or not the *listener's* purpose has, indeed, been achieved.

Summary

The design and development of communicative messages is governed by a series of choices—what we have called a strategy—based on a communicative purpose that grows out of and reflects the situation. Rhetorical purposes can generally be described as informative, persuasive, or entertaining and they are further refined into specific purposes for each communication event. These purposes state the desired audience response and are the foundation upon which a message is built. The listener actively and cautiously creates his or her purposes in a public communication situation and assesses messages in the light of this purpose.

At this point you should be able, with the help of the analysis of the audience and the total situation, to devise a specific purpose or a series of specific purposes for speeches you will deliver in class.

You should also be able to understand more fully the problem that a communicator faces in making public communication purposeful and be able to evaluate more adequately his or her purposes. The next issue that must be addressed is this: given the specific purpose, how does one go about making intelligent decisions on how to develop and evaluate strategy and supporting tactics?

Select Bibliography

The following citations, and those listed in all the bibliographies, offer further practical and theoretical information related to the chapter topics, and they provide a starting point for the student who wishes to undertake more intensive study and research into the topic.

Kenneth E. Anderson, *Persuasion: Theory and Practice.* Boston: Allyn and Bacon, 1971.

John E. Baird, Jr., "The Effects of Speech Summaries upon Audience Comprehension of Expository Speeches of Varying Quality and Complexity," *Central States Speech Journal,* **25**(1974), 119-127.

Lloyd F. Bitzer, "The Rhetorical Situation," *Philosophy and Rhetoric,* **1**(1968), 1-14.

Robert D. Brooks and Thomas M. Scheidel, "Speech as Process: A Case Study," *Speech Monographs,* **35**(1968), 1-7.

Donald C. Bryant, "Rhetoric: Its Function and Its Scope," *Quarterly Journal of Speech,* **39**(1953), 15-37.

Gary Cronkhite, *Persuasion: Speech and Behavioral Change.* Indianapolis: Bobbs-Merrill, 1969.

Charles R. Gruner, "Effect of Humor on Speaker Ethos and Audience Information Gain," *Journal of Communication,* **17**(1967) 228-233.

Charles R. Gruner, "The Effect of Humor in Dull and Interesting Informative Speeches," *Central States Speech Journal,* **21**(1970), 160-166.

Robert G. King, *Forms of Public Address.* Indianapolis: Bobbs-Merrill, 1969.

Charles U. Larson, *Persuasion: Reception and Responsibility.* Belmont, Cal.: Wadsworth Publishing Company, 1973.

Charles Petrie, "Informative Speaking: A Summary and Bibliography of Related Research," *Speech Monographs,* **30**(1963), 79-91.

Paul E. Ried, "A Spectrum of Persuasive Design," *Speech Teacher,* **13**(1964), 87-95.

Thomas M. Scheidel, *Persuasive Speaking.* Glenview, Ill.: Scott, Foresman, 1967.

Herbert W. Simons, *Persuasion: Understanding, Practice, and Analysis.* Reading, Mass.: Addison-Wesley, 1976.

Charles O. Tucker, "An Application of Programmed Learning to Informative Speech," *Speech Monographs,* **31**(1964), 142-152.

69 Communicating
with a Purpose

CHAPTER 5

the structure and form of communicative messages

The relationship of ideas to purpose

Determining a good idea

    Clarity of ideas
    Simplicity of ideas
    Situational considerations
    Ideas that make sense

How ideas relate to each other

    Sequencing ideas
    Ideas and patterns
        Chronological
        Spatial
        Topical
        Directional
        Climactic
        Problem-solving
        Contrastive
        Casual

Transitions and internal summaries

Outlining as a process of preparation

The whole speech and its parts

    Structure and the clarity of ideas
    Form and persuasiveness of ideas

Listener responses to patterns of ideas

Summary

Select Bibliography

When the communicator knows what it is precisely that he or she wishes to do and has determined that there is a reasonable expectation that it can be done, it is then time to develop and put together the main ideas in the message. The ideas are the backbone of the rhetorical strategy, because it is the ideas that hold the entire speech together and must carry the weight of achieving the specific purpose. That is to say, if the audience accepts the ideas, if the ideas are understandable and believable to the listeners, then the purpose should be accomplished. Consider, as a simple example, someone who wants to sell a washing machine. The specific purpose would be very clear, it would call for the direct action involved in buying the machine. As the salesperson has learned about the machine himself, he or she has gathered specific information that he or she uses in order to develop a set of ideas that he or she hopes will move the buyer to action. The salesperson might likely come up with the following set of ideas: (1) This machine costs less than comparable models. (2) This machine uses less water than others. (3) This machine has a variety of settings to meet every washing need. (4) This machine gets clothes exceptionally clean. (5) This machine comes in a wide range of colors. Such a set of ideas, given that the situational factors are right and the potential buyer really does want a washing machine, seem likely ones to accomplish the speaker's purpose.

But consider a more complicated example, one that might very well illustrate the kind of speech that you would give. You may wish to have your audience agree that the University should abolish the current grading system. Now if this was a speech that you were going to give in class you would have a different kind of audience from that that might face you if you were going to give the speech to the faculty senate. The different audiences then would mean that you might develop different ideas designed to further your purpose. Or it might be that you would give emphasis to some ideas for one audience, and deemphasize those ideas for another. In other words, certain ideas might need more proving for some people than for others. If the speech were a class speech you might devise a set of ideas such as these:

1. Abolition of the grading system would encourage students to be more adventurous in what they choose to take.
2. Abolition would reduce competition among students and promote cooperation in its stead.
3. Abolition would improve faculty-student relations.

Furthermore, in a speech of this type, the speaker would need to be aware of counterarguments and build into the speech those ideas that would rebut competing ideas in the minds of the audience. Anyone thinking about the question of grading would know that there are many who argue that the abolition of grading makes it difficult to distinguish in any way among students. This, critics of abolition would argue, makes it impossible to reward excellence. Furthermore, in a more practical vein, it would clearly be impossible for graduate schools, professional schools, and employers to make any judgment about the quality of the work the student has performed while in college. Now the speaker, given this obvious negative to his or her idea, might develop a fourth idea: the current system of standardized examinations (such as those required for admission to law school or the Graduate Record Exam, coupled with a system of on-the-job training and probationary hiring periods) would make it possible to distinguish among students for advanced education or jobs. Now, unlike the more simple washing machine example, the results in this case are much more problematic. But, in both cases the results will be influenced by the way the particular ideas are stated and are developed. Simply enumerating the main ideas, of course, does not guarantee that the purpose will be accomplished, but, delineating clearly those ideas is an essential first step in the development of the message. Let's examine one more example on still another level that demonstrates how complex and difficult the choice of ideas can be.

In the 1976 presidential primary, Ronald Reagan of California challenged President Ford for the Republican nomination. He had a very difficult task since a sitting president is unlikely to be denied his own party's nomination. Reagan, however, came very close to accomplishing this near-impossible task. His purpose in the speeches he gave across the country was to gain agreement with the proposition that he would do a better job as president than Gerald Ford was doing. In order to gain agreement he argued these ideas: I. Reagan better represented the true conservative principles of the Republican party; II. Reagan could act to solve domestic economic problems more effectively than they had been solved in the past; III. Reagan would carry on a more aggressive foreign policy that would better safeguard American interests abroad. At certain times Reagan did need to deal with the question of whether or not it was possible for him, as Republican nominee, to win the election, and he accordingly built in an idea to deal with this aspect of the situation: he argued that he was a proven vote getter who had won in the past and could do so in the future. It is very hard to determine how successful Reagan's ideas were. We do know, however, that he mounted one of the stiffest challenges against an incumbent President that has ever been carried out. And we do know that he won some primary elections, and that he was exceptionally popular with a large minority of the Republican party. Whether or not he might have developed different strategies that would have been more successful or whether or not there was anything more he could have done to win, the point here is that in a very complex kind of situation he developed certain ideas designed to promote his purpose. It is obvious that he was not entirely successful in proving those ideas for large numbers of people. But his effort was to come up with those that would best advance his purpose.

What the communicator does, then, is to *invent* the ideas out of what he or she knows about the audience and situation, out of the needs dictated by the specific purpose, and out of the nature of the subject itself. This invention *process* is one that the speaker must go through early in his or her preparation to speak. Assume, for example, that a student is giving a speech on the constitutional amendment process. She has decided that her audience needs to know precisely how the U.S. Constitution can be amended before she can try to persuade them, in subsequent speeches, that it should be made easier or harder to try to get them to take direct action in support of specific amendments now being debated nationally. So, her specific purpose would be, "I want my audience to understand how an amendment to the U.S. Constitution is adopted." She might begin by reading Article V of the Constitution, which describes the amendment process, the amendments themselves, and the commentaries on the way amendments are adopted. Further specific information about how amendments have been dealt with in the past can be gained from historical accounts and newspaper stories written at the time. As this information is sifted through, the ideas—and the material that will serve to enlarge and support those ideas—should begin to emerge and be brought into focus. With the purpose of gaining understanding, the speaker will shape those ideas that seem best designed to promote that understanding. Such questions as how the process begins, who has responsibility for proposing amendments, how they are ratified, how long the whole process can take will need to be answered if the audience is to understand exactly how amendments do become part of the constitution. Accordingly, the ideas generated will address themselves to such concerns. In this case they might be something like this:

1. Constitutional amendments often arise out of public controversy or controversial situations.
2. The Constitution provides that Congress propose amendments

or call a convention for proposing amendments if enough states request it.

3. Amendments passed by Congress or in convention must be ratified by three-fourths of the states.
4. There is no set time limit on how long it may take for an amendment to be ratified.

As the speaker develops the speech these ideas may, of course, be modified, discarded, or replaced by others. But the likelihood is that they will form the skeleton on which the body of the speech will be built. Given the fact, then, that ideas are at the heart of the speech, the remainder of this chapter is devoted to an investigation of the worth of ideas, how ideas effect each other in a speech, and what ideas can mean to those who listen to them.

Determining a Good Idea

Ideas are designed, then, when taken together, to accomplish the speaker's purpose. So, basic to deciding whether or not an idea is a good one, is the consideration of how well it is designed to get the desired response. There are, however, other factors that help determine how good the idea is: a good idea is one that is clear, one that is simple without being over simplified, one that is appropriate to the demands of the situation, and, above all, one that makes sense. Let us consider each of these characteristics.

Clarity of Ideas

There is a strong relation between language and thought; the way we talk and the way we say things can tell us a lot about the way we think. All of us have probably been guilty at one time or another of saying something like, "Well I know the answer to that but I just can't put it into words," or "I understand myself, but I just can't explain it," or, "I know what I want to say, but it just doesn't seem to come out right." All of these comments are, when you get behind them, just ways of fooling ourselves about what we really *do* know. If you can't say it, you don't know it; if you can't explain it, you don't understand it. If one is to be successful at communication one has to admit the facts to oneself: putting an idea into accurate, correct, and clear language is the only way to be sure that the idea is truly understood. Now even if this were disputed on some theoretical level, it is certainly true in the practical sense: an unexpressed idea cannot be a full-blown idea.

So clarity, then, depends on the way in which language is used. One of the first implications of this proposition is that an idea, in order to be clear, must be *complete*. That is to say, language fragments do not convey complete ideas; a full sentence is the best way to insure that an idea is stated in its most fully developed form. Such things as "the economy," or "taxes," or "ways to improve," or "the future," are not clearly expressed ideas. Such words written on a card might be reminders to a speaker, but what we are discussing at this stage is how ideas are developed. It is crucial, when inventing the ideas to support the purpose, that we leave no room for doubt as to the *precise* meaning of those ideas. Ambiguity at this stage is deadly. What the speaker must do is to be sure that the idea is fully stated so that she or he can test that idea against the purpose. If one hopes to get an audience to agree that the best way to stimulate and improve the economic situation is by the reduction of taxes, for example, then one must be sure that he or she has clear ideas that promote that purpose. "Jobs," is not an idea designed to do this whereas, "By providing consumers with more money to spend the government will thereby stimulate the economy and provide more jobs," is an idea.

Take, for example, a student who was giving a speech on the benefits of space exploration. The specific purpose was to get the audience to agree that substantial funds should once more be channeled into space research. On the initial outline the main ideas read like this:

1. Accomplishments
2. Medical
3. They will advance
4. Space relation to Earth
5. Altering environment

It is quite obvious, in the light of the foregoing discussion, that these are not clearly stated *ideas*. Points I and II are simply one-word notations that don't convey any meaning in and of themselves. In order to be a complete idea, point I might read, "In the past, space research has resulted in some very practical benefits." If this were the idea it would immediately become apparent that the speaker's job here would be to enumerate and prove how beneficial the program had been in the past. In this case the speaker reconsidered his initial thoughts and realized that this one idea could be the entire speech; he decided he could reasonably go back and change his purpose. On the other hand, he did not wish to neglect the fact that he was arguing for future policy and therefore had to demonstrate in some way that positive good would come out of the program in the future just as it had in the past. This caused him to think that he would develop ideas that followed just such a line of thought. He would rewrite his specific purpose in this way: "I want my audience to agree that the space program has benefited all of us and would continue to benefit us if funds were provided." He then looked at the remaining four notations on his outline and began to develop those in the light of his restated purpose, so his first idea became: I. *In the past space research contributed considerable knowledge of how the human body functions.* Under that point he could develop all his information about the medical advances made as a result of space research. He or she decided that points IV and V as listed could be consolidated into an idea like the following: II. *Our increased knowledge of space has contributed to our understanding of earth itself and its environment.* The point that he had listed before under III, "They will advance," is a complete sentence, but it is obvious that it is not a clear idea. What the speaker had in mind here was that, in the areas in which some knowledge had been gained in the past there would be even greater advances in the future. He finally developed a third main idea: III. *The kinds of knowledge that can be gained by continuing research could be of direct practical advantage to us as inhabitants of earth.* After having gone through this process the speaker was still faced with the problem of developing each of these ideas, still faced with other kinds of factors that in the future might cause him to limit those ideas or to expand them. But at least he now had the set of ideas that were clear in themselves and related to the purpose in mind. A comparison and restatement of the two sets of statements should clarify the evaluation from notation to idea:

1. Accomplishments

2. Medical

3. They will advance

4. Space relation to Earth

5. Altering environment

1. In the past space research contributed considerable knowledge of how the human body functions.

2. Our increased knowledge of space has contributed to our understanding of earth itself and its environment.

3. The kinds of knowledge that can be gained by continuing research could be of direct practical advantage to us as inhabitants of earth.

Simplicity of Ideas
Audiences, of course, must understand ideas if they are to respond to them. On the one hand it is important that an idea be directly and simply stated while on the other hand it is important that ideas not be distorted. The speaker's problem is to establish this balance, that is, not to communicate inaccurate ideas and yet not to complicate ideas so that an audience is baffled rather then enlightened.

With the purpose in mind the speaker must ask him or herself whether the idea is as basic as it can be and whether it is as unencumbered as it can be. If a speaker feels that the idea just cannot be made simple, that it is a very complex idea, then he or she needs to determine whether or not such an idea is understandable to the audience. If the idea cannot be simplified in order to be understood then the speaker may very well wish to reexamine the specific purpose to see if it is appropriate to the audience. It may well be that the speaker is trying to do too much in the time alloted and needs to focus more sharply. Furthermore, speakers often try to include too much information or even a whole series of ideas within one idea. The idea is, after all, the essence; it is what the audience must grasp, must respond to, in order for the purpose to be achieved. Each idea will be developed fully in order to make it understandable or believable, but the idea itself is the basic thought unit. Let us take two examples.

The speaker has as his or her purpose the following: "I want my audience to become involved actively in political campaigning." The first idea reads like this:

1. College students who take an interest in politics can restore idealism to the process as well as learning valuable skills themselves and making a practical impact on politics.

This idea obviously tries to fit too much in. It is not, in reality, a single idea. It is a complex and interrelated set of ideas. What the speaker needs to do is to sort out the idea from the material necessary to develop that idea. A revised form of this might be something like the following:

1. There are direct benefits to society when college students participate in politics.
2. There are direct benefits to each person who participates in the political process.

The speaker is saying, then, that if he can induce his audience to agree that there are both social and personal benefits to participating in the political process he hopes he will achieve his purpose. His next task, of course, will be to develop the ideas, that is, to enumerate the benefits that come from participation, to demonstrate that they are indeed beneficial, and to make them real and motivating for an audience. Thus the speaker will develop specific, convincing tactics to further the overall strategy promoted by the main ideas as a part of the total structure of the speech.

To take one other example of a main idea that could be improved through simplification, consider the speaker who is giving a speech in which she wanted her audience to understand the roots of our American legal system. In this speech she was discussing certain aspects of English history that bore on our own legal development. She began her speech with this idea:

1. Since Charles I was defeated by the Parliamentary forces, English monarchs have been deemed to be accountable to the law.

This idea as it is stated is accurate and perhaps clear enough. It does, however, present certain problems that could be solved by simplification. First, it obscures the major point that the idea hopes to make by burying that point within the historical context. Second, in doing this, the speaker has emphasized certain specific historical elements with which the audience might not be familiar and which might tend to distract them from the point that she is making. One way to recast this idea would be the following:

1. The principle that no one is above the law was established in England in the seventeenth century.

This statement emphasizes the point — no one is above the law — and does not obscure it with historical detail. What the speaker hopes is that the audience understands what basic principles were formed in history that shaped our own legal system. This idea complies with that purpose. Now certainly as the speaker develops the idea she will explain in detail the historical situation that brought it about, but the historical situation is subordinate to the idea she wishes to promote.

Simplicity, then, goes hand in hand with clarity as basic characteristics of a well-stated idea. Of course, clarity and simplicity are sometimes relative concepts, and it is necessary to remind ourselves that the ideas in the speech, just as other elements, grow out of the rhetorical situation.

Situational Considerations

We have already considered at some lengths the proposition that a speech is designed for an audience and that the speech is also influenced by the occasion that prompts it and the setting in which it occurs. It is sufficient here to reemphasize the fact that the ideas of the speech are ideas that the *listener* must respond to and therefore must be appropriate to that listener and to the context in which he or she listens. The level of complexity, for example, of any idea will be significantly influenced by the audience's relationship to the topic. If, for example, one has as his purpose to have the audience understand the kinds of scientific data that are gathered by the exploration of Mars by an unmanned satellite, it is easy to see that that purpose can be furthered through ideas that are highly technical, sophisticated, and complex. A speech to a colloquium in the astronomy department might call for exactly those kinds of ideas; a speech in a beginning public speaking class would call for a different set of ideas.

Ideas That Make Sense

In the next chapter we discuss in detail the question of what makes an idea a reasonable one. Much of this consideration rests on the relationship between the basic conclusions embodied in the idea and the evidence used to support that conclusion. At this point, however, a speaker must consider the initial impact of the idea on the audience along with the intrinsic sense of the idea. He or she must first ask whether the idea is a sensible one to him or herself and then consider how an audience might view it. Speakers have sometimes proposed as main ideas those that are on the face of it just not sensible. For example:

Most people would probably like to learn to throw the javelin.
Whether or not you subscribe to the student newspaper will be one of the most important decisions you will ever be called upon to make.
People who participate in college athletic programs need special tutoring since they do not have the intellectual abilities of other students.

These ideas just don't make sense. Perhaps if the speakers had thought more carefully about the ideas, had considered their implications — had tried to imagine how an audience might react — they would have avoided them. These ideas as stated are not sensible because they do such things as confusing the speaker's own interests with those of the audience (1), they overgeneralize on the basis of popular stereotypes (3).

Sometimes ideas will also seem not to be sensible to listeners if they appear to be romanticized, sentimentalized, or idealized or too cynical or pessimistic. For example, the idea that students come to college primarily to develop and sharpen their intellectual and artistic powers may not seem sensible to the average college audience. Many in the audience might either know from their own experience or from that of others that some people come to college in order to get better jobs, in order to kill time until they decide what they want to do with their lives, or because of parent or peer pressure. Now this kind of an idea is a little more difficult to deal with because it does not state some obvious misconceptions. Perhaps what the speaker is talking about is what he or she believes college students *ought* to do, or what he or she believes the true goals of a university ought to be. The speaker could keep the concept behind the idea intact, but would need to rephrase it considering how sensible the audience would think it to be.

A good idea, then, is clear, simple, grounded in the situation, and sensible. Let us now consider how an idea once developed relates in very specific ways to other ideas in the speech.

Sequencing Ideas

When one has developed a good idea or a series of ideas one must face the problem of how to put them together. We all know that there are times when we would like to say everything at once. We

How Ideas Relate to Each Other

would like to present the whole picture so that our listeners could see some kind of totality that would make all the parts more understandable. Unfortunately, we talk in a *linear* fashion. That is to say, one word comes after another, and one idea must come after another.

If, for example, you were taking a course in literature, it would be nice to understand the basis on which you could best judge and interpret a book that you read. On the other hand, rules or standards for judging the quality of a book would be rather meaningless and difficult to understand unless one had read several books. So what should one do first? Probably the best thing would be to do two things simultaneously, but that is impossible. The same thing is true for the speaker. As much as he or she might like to say everything at once, ideas do have to be taken one at a time. This means, of course, they have to be put in some kind of order or sequence. The process can be totally random — whatever pops into the speaker's head — or the process can be carried out in such a way that it will help the audience respond as the speaker hopes they will respond. The speaker, then, must decide which idea should come before which other idea, and in order to develop a sensible sequence he or she must develop a *pattern* of ideas based on the subject matter itself and/or the demands of the situation.

Ideas and Patterns

When the speaker is faced with the problem of taking a set of ideas and making them reasonable and coherent for an audience he or she will want to put them together in a way that is best designed to accomplish the specific purposes of the speech. Let us consider some of the patterns that typically would emerge as the speaker sequences his or her ideas.

Although the topic and the audience are both of importance in deciding on a sensible pattern, there are some patterns that are influenced more by the subject matter itself, such as *chronological, spatial,* and *topical* patterns.

1. *Ideas can be arranged in a logical time sequence.* This is often called a *chronological* pattern. If the subject matter of a particular speech deals with some historical development or if it involves a step-by-step, one-after-another approach, then a time sequence is sensible. If, for example, a speaker wanted his or her audience to understand the events that led up to the American Revolution, the speaker could very easily use a chronological approach that traced the occurrence of events through time. If one were explaining how a skilled craftsman wove a rug, he or she would probably begin with the first step that the worker undertook and follow the process in time step by step to actual completion of the rug. Following is an example of ideas arranged in a chronological pattern:

Specific Purpose

I want my audience to understand the rise of Nazism in Germany.

1. The Treaty of Versailles that ended World War I created several serious problems for Germany.
2. Financial crises encouraged the National Socialists, led by Hitler, to attempt an unsuccessful coup in Bavaria in 1923.
3. By 1930 the National Socialist Party, campaigning on a platform of opposition to the Versailles Treaty provisions, emerged as a major political party.
4. The violent election campaign of 1933 and the burning of the *Reichstag* resulted in the necessary political power for the National Socialists to establish the Nazi dictatorship.

2. *Ideas can be arranged in a sequence governed by space relationships.* This is often called a *spatial* pattern. When a topic is largely geographical, for example, or when a topic demands progression that moves from one physical area to another then this kind of pattern is a very sensible one. If, for example, one were describing the facilities that are available to students at the University library, one could quite profitably do this by telling the student where he or she should go from place to place from the main entrance to the very top floor. Following is an example of ideas sequenced in a spatial pattern.

Specific Purpose

I want my audience to agree that democratic institutions are threatened in Europe.

1. In Great Britain the power of the unions over economic life could lead to a proletarian dictatorship.
2. In Italy, the political success of communism threatens the existence of other political parties.
3. In Spain, the new spirit of moderate liberalism could lead to violent reactions from both the right and the left.
4. In France, dependence on Middle Eastern oil could stifle criticism of government foreign policy.

3. *Ideas can be arranged in a sequence that emphasizes distinct topics.* This is called the *topical* pattern. If, for example, one were advocating a particular position that offered several benefits to the listeners, those benefits could well form individual topics: if one were giving a speech on the benefits of higher education one could develop ideas related to the intellectual, social, or economic advantages of education. In other words these topics, which are interrelated, suggest independent ideas. Following is an example of the main ideas of a speech arranged topically.

The Structure and Form of
Communicative Messages

Specific Purpose

I want my audience to register and vote at the next election.

1. The results of the election could influence the amount of taxes that you and your parents pay.
2. Aid to higher education could be affected by the outcome of the election.
3. A whole range of other issues related to your everyday life could be settled by this election.
4. The process of registering and voting is a simple one.
5. Your vote can make a difference.

Sometimes ideas are sequenced in patterns that reflect the speaker's awareness of special audience considerations. Of course, the subject matter must also lend itself to such development. Such patterns are *directional,* and *climactic.*

4. *Ideas can be arranged in either a direct or an indirect sequence.* This *directional* patterning of ideas is based on the speaker's assessment of what the audience knows, believes, and expects. In discussing a controversial issue, for example, a speaker may wish to lead gradually to a conclusion by an indirect development rather than arouse the audience's hostility or antagonism before the opportunity to present the evidence is given. On the other hand, a speaker's position may be well known and/or the audience may be in strong agreement with the speaker, and, consequently, the speaker may wish to lay out the rationale for the position very clearly so that the audience's own feelings and beliefs will be reinforced by what is said. Consider the following examples of speech on the same topic developed both directly and indirectly.

Specific Purpose

I want my audience to feel more strongly that collective bargaining by faculty would improve faculty performance and benefits.

1. The regulation of professional matters related to such factors as class size, teaching load, adequate and comfortable office space would help instructors to do a better job.
2. Regulation of qualifications for teaching would result in the upgrading of instruction.
3. Financial security and job security would relieve unnecessary psychological stress and create a better climate in which teaching could be carried on.

Specific Purpose

I want my audience to agree that collective bargaining by the faculty will result in an improved educational system.

1. A good educational system depends on getting the best performance possible from the best faculty.

2. Faculty can do the best job when the conditions under which they work are designed to promote learning.
3. Faculty can do the best job when they can direct their energies to solving educational problems.
4. Securing a good faculty and providing conditions under which they can work well can best be done through collective bargaining.

5. *Ideas can be arranged in a sequence that goes from simple to difficult, from least important to most important, from emotionally neutral to emotionally intense.* This *climactic* pattern of development very much reflects audience needs and pressures. If, for example, one is addressing him or herself to a topic with which the audience is not at all familiar one might want to start with a very simple idea first so that the audience is not puzzled or confused. The speaker might also, as he or she assess the battery of arguments to be used, decide that it would be best to leave the audience with the strongest argument. In this case the speaker would arrange ideas so as to build up to that argument. There is, however, considerable difference of opinion and conflicting research results on whether or not this weak-to-strong indirect method is a good one. A good argument could be made for the proposition that it is generally better to start with the best argument, follow through with other arguments, and then return briefly to review the best one once again. At any rate, the ideas should all be sound ones, and therefore should not suffer too much by indirection. Furthermore, a speaker, like a playwright, may wish to build on his listeners' interests and attention until he or she reaches a climactic moment. That is to say, a speaker may wish to arrange ideas so that the audience becomes increasingly absorbed and interested in those particular ideas until the moment is reached when the audience can most strongly identify with what the speaker is saying. Following are some examples of ideas that can be patterned climactically.

Specific Purpose

I want my audience to agree that action to stop environmental pollution must begin now.

1. Pollution of air and water in this community has direct consequences for your health and your pocketbook.
2. Pollution effects can drastically alter the standard of living in this country.
3. Pollution can ultimately lead to the destruction of human life on this planet.

Specific Purpose

I want my audience to understand the basic operation of an automobile engine.

83 The Structure and Form of Communicative Messages

1. The gasoline-fueled automobile engine functions through the combined process of compression and combustion of the fuel in the piston cylinder.
2. The power that the engine produces is the result of many small but quickly timed explosions.
3. The essential parts of the engine for this process are the carburetor, piston and piston cylinder, spark plug, crankshaft and fuel mixture.
4. The sequence of the piston strokes is "intake-compression-ignition/combustion-exhaust/power."

Assuredly, as any ideas are patterned the precise pattern they do take is influenced both by the subject matter and the audience. There are, however, some patterns that clearly arise from an intricate interplay of the topic and the situation. Such patterns are *problem-solving*, *contrastive*, and *causal*.

6. *Ideas can be arranged in a problem-solution sequence.* The *problem-solving* pattern is one that lends itself to particular topics and also appeals to an audience who wants a careful, logical, well-rounded approach to a perceived difficulty. This kind of a pattern of ideas suggests itself when there are a variety of ways to deal with the problem and when one way might not necessarily be purely advantageous but may have certain drawbacks. Through a problem-solution pattern the speaker may well be able to demonstrate that the solution with drawbacks is still the *best possible* solution to a difficult problem. In this pattern the speaker's first idea would deal with the nature of the problem itself, what it is and who it affects; his or her second idea would establish the criteria for solving the problem; his or her third idea would encompass the possible solutions to the problem and his or her fourth idea would offer the best possible solution. It should be emphasized that the speaker using this kind of a pattern needs to make explicit the relationship between the criteria for solution and the best possible solution. After all, that solution which most nearly meets the criteria will be the best one. Following is an example of ideas that fall into a problem-solution pattern.

Specific Purpose

I want my audience to agree that prostitution should be legalized and regulated by law.

1. Illegal prostitution raises serious legal, moral, and health problems.
2. Any solution to these problems must take into account the sensibilities of the community, the difficulties of law enforcement, the protection of the public, and the individual rights of those involved.
3. Prostitution could be kept as a totally illegal act, as it is in most places now; it could be kept illegal and enforcement made stricter and punishment more severe; it could be legalized

without any restraints; it could be legalized only under careful government supervision.

4. Legalization under supervision is the solution that best meets the needs of society and speaks most directly to the more serious aspects of the problem.

7. *Ideas can be arranged in a sequence that contrasts those in favor of a particular proposition with those opposed to it.* This *contrastive* pattern is suited to a speech that deals with the acceptance or the rejection of a particular program, policy, or idea. If, for example, a speaker was discussing the Equal Rights Amendment he or she could well use this contrastive patterning of ideas to lay out the arguments for the amendment as opposed to the arguments against the amendment. Through a process of weighing both sides the speaker would then come to a decision for or against based on the pros and cons as he or she has laid them out. This method is one that should be used, as well as reacted to, with some caution, since it often gives the *appearance* of impartiality without the reality of that quality. On the other hand, there are instances in which failure to recognize arguments on both sides of the issue might suggest to an audience, particularly an audience familiar with those arguments, that the speaker is overlooking or ignoring or deliberately trying to hide arguments that would be disadvantageous to his or her case. Following is an example of the way in which ideas could be arranged contrastedly.

Specific Purpose

I want my audience to agree that the best kind of state sponsored student loan program is that which provides for a 100 percent state guarantee.

1. The state Senate and the House of Representatives have passed two different student loan bills, one that provides a 100 percent guarantee behind loans and ones that provide a 95 percent guarantee.

2. The 100 percent plan would make more loans available to more students and would qualify the state for 100 percent federal reimbursement for any defaulted loans.

3. The 95 percent bill would make financial institutions more cautious in lending and could result in savings of tax dollars.

4. But the drastic reduction in loans that would result from the 95 percent plan would defeat the purpose of the program in the first place and many worthy students would be unable to raise the money to attend college.

8. *Ideas can be arranged in a sequence that leads from cause to effect or effect to cause.* This *causal* pattern is a useful one when a speaker wants an audience to understand the development of a particular idea, event, phenomenon, or when the speaker hopes to

suggest modifications in a chain of relationships that will bring more desirable outcomes for an audience. If, for example, a speaker wanted his or her audience to understand why urban violence occurs he or she may attempt to do this by arranging ideas so that they will show the relationship of an event or circumstance to another event or circumstance, thus forming a chain of events that has as its final link the violent behavior the speaker hopes to explain. Following is an example of ideas arranged in a causal pattern.

Specific Purpose

I want my audience to agree that a better system of traffic lights and signs is needed in this community.

1. Three children have been killed or seriously injured in the last year on First Street while attempting to cross an unguarded crossing. (*Effect*)
2. At the crossing on the bypass several accidents have resulted when oncoming traffic has failed to stop for the red light. (*Effect*)
3. Traffic jams causing long delays and increasing psychological stress on drivers occur every weekday during the rush hours. (*Effect*)
4. Directions for lanes in which to turn, speed limits, and so forth, that are painted on the street, are completely worn away by the end of the winter. (*Effect*)
5. Something must be done about the poor traffic control procedures in this town. (*Cause*)

The above list of possible patterns is not exhaustive, but it does include the principal ways in which a speaker could sequence his or her ideas in such a way as to construct coherent patterns suitable to his topic and appealing to an audience.

Transitions and Internal Summaries

It is the speaker's task to do the best he or she can to help the audience apprehend the relationship of ideas to each other. The way the ideas are put together is, of course, crucial. But it also is very important that the speaker plan carefully the ways in which he or she will progress from one idea to the next.

A transition is a kind of bridge whereby the speaker moves from one idea to the next. The audience, after all, cannot be expected to be paying 100 percent of their attention to the speaker, nor can they be expected to understand the sequence of ideas as clearly as does the speaker. This is all new to them, and so the speaker must alert his listeners so that they will be mentally prepared for a new idea to be introduced and developed. This bridge can be a very simple one as when the speaker says, "Now that I have laid out the principal advantage, let me turn to the disadvantage." Or it can even be as simple a matter as enumeration: "And now consider the second way in which money can be raised." Sometimes getting from one idea to another might be accomplished in a more elaborate fashion because the complexity of the material warrants it. In this case, for example, the speaker might employ an internal summary. That is, he or she would very briefly go over the points made so far before moving to the next one. The speaker in such a case might say, "We've seen how the Stamp Act in 1766 aroused the first successful organized resistance on the part of the colonists to the British government and how British attempts to deal with the problems of taxation and defense, coupled with a growing spirit of independence in the colonies, caused an ever-widening breach between North America and Great Britain. Now let us see how the events in the months preceding the Declaration of Independence led the young colonies to a final break with the mother country." That kind of statement is, in essence, a short summary of what has been said. It helps keep the audience mentally on the track.

A good transition, then, helps the audience look back on what has been said and forward to what will be said and thus follow more closely the speaker's pattern and see more clearly the connection between ideas.

What a speaker is doing as he or she tries to understand the nature of the audience and the situation, tries to devise a sensible, reasonable purpose that will generate sound ideas, and tries to put those ideas together in a meaningful way, is to participate in a process that will ultimately prepare him or her to speak. This process of preparation can be visually represented through an outline. Sometimes speakers think of an outline as something to be done after the speech is prepared—a sort of formal partitioning of the speech. Still others think of the outline as a set of notes to be used in delivering the speech. Actually, the outline is neither of these things. It is the tangible representation of the process of speech preparation. It is built as the speaker goes through the intellectual operations necessary to get ready to speak to an audience. What has been discussed so far should be seen as generating a kind of skeletal outline of the major portion of the speech. The speaker who has defined a clear purpose, who has designed ideas to further that purpose and who has arranged ideas in an effective sequence has actually begun to outline. His or her next consideration is to find ways in which those well-ordered ideas can be developed in order to make them understandable or believable for an audience. That is to say, that the ideas must be *supported*. An outline then shows clearly the supporting relationships that exist within the speech itself. It should demonstrate for the speaker how his or her purpose can best be carried out using the material that is available to the speaker. Subsequent chapters will deal specifically with those tactics designed to support ideas, and with the integrative nature of the speech outline, but it needs to be

Outlining as a Process of Preparation

pointed out now that an outline should be forming during the preparation process.

The Whole Speech and its Parts

Structure and the Clarity of Ideas

As the speaker begins to impose structure on his or her ideas he or she should be able to determine the strengths and weaknesses of the speech as a whole in promoting the purpose. The structure, in other words, gives a kind of clarity to the whole speech that only becomes evident when all the ideas are carefully articulated and when their relationships are very clearly understood and uncovered. It is only when the speaker can discern a clear pattern that he or she can appreciate breaks or distortions in the pattern. A speech is often spoken of as being "crafted." That is to say, like anything that is made or built individually employing the skills of a creator, the speech must present a symmetrical and balanced whole. It must be intellectually complete. It is only when the structure is fully formed that the speaker can truly apprehend how well he or she has built a complete structure of ideas.

Form and the Persuasiveness of Ideas

We have all learned the truism that the whole is greater than the sum of its parts. What this means is that when certain individual characteristics or parts or pieces are held up and examined by an observer they may not suggest the total impression that will be given when all of these are put together. When the speaker is structuring ideas he or she should realize that the combination of ideas or the cumulative effect of ideas may be different from or greater than each idea taken individually. Consider, for example, items of behavior that might be called in and of themselves trifles: one forgets to put a stamp on a letter that is mailed, or one addresses the letter to the wrong place, or one cancels an appointment that should not have been canceled, or one sends out a letter without indicating who it is from, or one misfiles a document. These are fairly minor mistakes. When put together, however, they may give a strong impression of inefficiency or carelessness. That is, the way ideas are structured and developed may strongly suggest that a certain person or object or idea be perceived in a certain way, and that is what we would refer to as the "form" of the speech. Certain communicative forms can emerge, also, from different messages if those messages are structured similarly. For example, during 1976 President Gerald Ford's movements were reported in detail. Often these reports included some kind of physical malfunction or minor error on the President's part, such as tripping as he alighted from a plane, or falling down when he was skiing, or being a passenger in a car that collided with another car. The repetition of these incidents, and the way in which they were structured as part of the event as reported by the media tended to project a particular form. That is to say, that the idea of a fumbling or bumbling president could easily have been perceived from the structure of the individual messages. So when a speaker puts a series of ideas together he or she needs to consider not only the impact of each of those ideas but the combined impact of all of them as they appear in a single message.

The speaker uses structure to promote the persuasiveness and clarity of his or her ideas. The listener needs both to exploit and evaluate structure as it relates to his or her needs. That is, the listener must do everything in his or her power to try to understand the structure, to use it in order to follow ideas clearly, and to get from it a true sense of the speaker's purpose. The listener must also be aware of the criteria for determining a good idea: he or she must test the idea to make certain that it is clearly stated, that it is simple but not oversimplified, that it is addressed to him or her, and that it makes sense. As the listener begins to see a pattern of ideas, he or she must be prepared to evaluate that pattern through an understanding of what the pattern itself is doing. For example, although the pattern of a speech may suggest that a speaker is evaluating both sides of an argument the listener needs to ask him or herself if that really is the case, or whether a veneer of objectivity is simply being applied. Although the speaker may follow a problem solving pattern, the listener needs to exercise some caution in accepting the speaker's criteria for arriving at the best solution. While the speaker may assert that certain events are the cause of later effects, the listener must demand that such a link be proven conclusively. In other words, the listener must be aware and be actively critical of the structure of a speech and the form it suggests as he or she experiences that speech.

Summary

At this point *the speaker* should be able to generate ideas that strongly and clearly promote his or her purpose. They should be good ideas: clear, simple, sensible, and related to the situation. These ideas should be sequenced in appropriate patterns that suggest the desired form or overall impression of the speech. *The listener* can use the structure of the speech to further his or her understanding of the ideas and their relationships, but needs to be skeptical of the impact of structure on his or her own conclusions.

Of course, only discovering and stating a good idea does not prove that idea, nor does it make the idea completely clear in and of itself. The communication strategy devised through purpose and structure needs to be augmented by the right tactics. That is, ideas need to be *supported* in order to be believable and/or understandable. The next two chapters explain two sets of tactics designed to develop ideas; furthermore, these tactics suggest tests of the ideas that the listener can apply in order to sharpen his or her critical response to the speaker's message.

Select Bibliography

The following citations, and those listed in all the bibliographies, offer further practical and theoretical information related to the chapter topics, and they provide a starting point for the student who wishes to undertake more intensive study and research into the topic.

Arnold G. Abrams, "The Relation of Listening and Reading Comprehension to Skill in Message Structuralization," *Journal of Communication,* **16**(1966), 116-125.

Carroll C. Arnold, "Structure and Form," *Criticism of Oral Rhetoric.* Columbus, Ohio: Charles E. Merrill, 1974.

Eldon E. Baker, "The Immediate Effects of Perceived Speaker Disorganization on Speaker Credibility and Audience Change in Persuasive Speaking," *Western Speech,* **29**(1965), 148-161.

K. C. Beighley, "A Summary of Experimental Studies Dealing with the Effect of Organization and of Skill of Speakers on Comprehension," *Journal of Communication,* **2**(1952), 58-65.

Edward P. J. Corbett, "The Arrangement of Material," *Classical Rhetoric for the Modern Student.* New York: Oxford University Press, 1965.

R. Ehrensberger, "An Experimental Study of Relative Effectiveness of Certain Forms of Emphasis in Public Speaking," *Speech Monographs,* **13**(1946), 94-111.

Howard Gilkinson, Stanley F. Paulson, and Donald E. Sikkink, "Effects of Order and Authority in an Argumentive Speech," *Quarterly Journal of Speech,* **40**(1954), 182-192.

Milton W. Horowitz, "Organizational Processes Underlying Differences between Listening and Reading as a Function of Complexity of Material," *Journal of Communication,* **18**(1968), 37-46.

Arlee Johnson, "A Preliminary Investigation of the Relationship between Message Organization and Listener Comprehension," *Central States Speech Journal,* **21**(1970), 104-107.

Glen E. Mills, *Message Preparation: Analysis and Structure.* Indianapolis: Bobbs-Merrill, 1966.

Charles R. Petrie, Jr., "Listening and Organization," *Central States Speech Journal,* **15**(1964), 6-12.

Harry Sharp, Jr. and Thomas McClung, "Effects of Organization on the Speaker's Ethos," *Speech Monographs,* **33**(1966), 182-183.

Raymond G. Smith, "An Experimental Study of the Effects of Speech Organization Upon Attitudes of College Students," *Speech Monographs,* **18**(1951), 292-301.

Walt Stevens, "A Proposal for Non-Linear Disposition," *Western Speech,* **37**(1973), 118-128.

Ernest Thompson, "Some Effects of Message Structure on Listeners' Comprehension," *Speech Monographs,* **34**(1967), 51-57.

Frederick H. Turner, "The Effect of Speech Summaries on Audience Comprehension," *Central States Speech Journal*, **21**(1970), 24-29.

James F. Vickery, Jr., "An Experimental Investigation of the Effect of 'Previews' and 'Reviews' on Retention of Orally Presented Information," *Southern Speech Communication Journal*, **36**(1971), 209-219.

W. Ross Winterowd, "Beyond Style," *Philosophy and Rhetoric*, **5**(1972), 88-110.

PART THREE
communication tactics

CHAPTER 6 *arguing reasonably*

Supporting ideas is something that we normally do every day. When we urge a friend to see a movie that we've seen by telling the friend that it is very good we are likely to add something like, "It's your kind of humor," or "It has a lot of action," or "Harry was with me, and he thought it was great, too," or "It's as funny as a Woody Allen film." If we're recommending a particular course to someone we know it is quite likely that we'll tell the person something specific about the course like what books are required, indicating why such a course would appeal to that person. If we're explaining to a friend how to get to our house when he comes to visit over the school vacation, we'll probably draw him a map. If someone has borrowed a book and you want that person to understand that she must leave it at a place that is easily accessible to you, you might repeat the directions two or three times just to make sure that the person has it right. In other words, in our routine communication situation we develop ideas—we bring in material to make those ideas believable or understandable—when we feel that it is necessary. The necessity for the material depends on the situation, the audience, and the complexity of the idea itself.

Searching for Relevant Material

One of the major problems that faces any communicator is how to sift through the available material on any given topic and choose that which is relevant. In an evening news broadcast, for example, the editor responsible for preparing a story on a speech given by the President of the United States must select from that speech those elements that he considers to be most newsworthy. He must, in essence, characterize an entire speech of perhaps 20 to 40 minutes in a space of 2 to 3 minutes. If you were to write a letter home describing what you had done over the preceding week you obviously could not give an hour-by-hour, day-by-day description of everything; you would select those events that you think would be most interesting or appropriate for the person to whom the letter is addressed. Anyone who wishes to prepare him or herself to communicate in a public setting must engage in a process of gathering, evaluating, and choosing material that is well suited to the speech. Always remember that the principal standard for judging whether or not material is relevant to begin with is the standard of purpose: the specific purpose designates the audience response, and material that helps to achieve that response is relevant material. The speaker can find the sources of relevant material in him or herself, in others and in published sources.

A person who is going to speak will have some ideas and some knowledge and some very specific kinds of information about the topic upon which he or she will talk. In searching for relevant material, then, the speaker starts with him or herself. He or she begins to think systematically about what information is readily available from his or her own experience. Now, while this self-analysis is very important and necessary, the speaker must be very careful about relying exclusively on what he or she knows, on one hand, or on the other hand, dismissing the topic because not enough is known. Some speakers make the mistake of thinking that they already have a speech in their head and that they don't need to know any more than they do. This is usually a mistake. Furthermore, the process of preparing oneself to speak becomes something of a useless exercise if one does not grow intellectually during that process. On the other side of the coin, some speakers will discard a topic because they think they don't know enough about it. They will assume that, somehow, they should be able to get up and talk *without* preparation, and that, too, is a mistake. All this is to say *that one needs to assess one's own personal experience, but not to rely on it exclusively.*

Relevant material can also be gathered through contact with other people, either by writing to them or interviewing them. As with all other aspects of the process, it is essential that the speaker first establish a clear specific purpose before any interviewing takes place or inquiries are made. It would be foolish, for example, to go to the registrar and say, "I want to give a speech on grades, please tell me what you think about grades." That is such a vague and broad kind of request that it is liable to produce either too much information — much of which is extraneous — or no information at all. The speaker has to be prepared with specific kinds of questions designed to elicit specific information needed to accomplish the specific purpose. If the speaker has a set of tentative ideas, then what he or she is looking for is information that will help make those ideas more believable or understandable. It is also essential that the speaker address him or herself to the right person. If one wants to know about the technical problems of recording and disseminating grades then it is logical, indeed, to go to talk with the registrar. If, however, one is concerned with how a philosophy of grading develops, then other faculty members might be more appropriate as people to be interviewed. Other people can serve as important sources, then, but the speaker must be careful to choose the right people and to know exactly what he or she wants to get from those people.

Published sources will, of course, provide most of the material that a speaker needs. It is essential that anyone who wishes to prepare him or herself to speak learn to use the resources of the library. Popular periodicals—newspapers, magazines—will provide a variety of types of evidence that a speaker can use to support ideas. The speaker will need to learn to use the *Reader's Guide to Periodical Literature* and such indices as the one to *The New York Times* that prove helpful in finding information about specific topics. In addition to popular periodicals there are also specialized technical ones in a wide range of academic and technical fields that provide specialized information on specific topics. The library's card catalogue should be used to find books of general interest on the topic, and collections of special publications such as U. S. government reports also provide an important source.

One learns best how to gather supporting material by actually doing it. The more one uses the library the more one learns how to use it efficiently. In all of one's search for relevant material one should keep foremost in mind the stipulation that relevance is defined by purpose, so that the hundreds of articles or documents or books on a particular general issue should be examined and possibly used only to the extent which they promote the speaker's goal. Furthermore, as the speaker searches the relevant material there are specific kinds of evidence that will help the speaker to communicate more effectively, that is, specific kinds of support for which the speaker should look as he or she sifts through all the relevant material.

There are also intellectual and ethical considerations in selecting and evaluating sources for a speech. An article written in a magazine or periodical is *not* a speech. Simply to stand up and tell what's in a story in a recent *Reader's Digest*, for example, is, first, intellectually limiting. Retelling a printed story does not involve the speaker at all in the real process of preparing to communicate (and the audience might well have read the piece and thus learning nothing new or original that the speaker could contribute). Second, such a practice is ethically unacceptable since it is essentially plagiarism, stealing the ideas and material from the original author. And third, repeating what is in an article is not likely to be effective as communication since the article is *not* adapted to those real, specific people sitting in front of a speaker, but, rather, is addressed to a wide general audience with much more varied experiences, tastes, interests, needs, and so forth. Furthermore, relying on one article or relying on someone else's summary or digest of an article or series of articles is likely to bias the speaker in a direction that he or she might not be aware of. Only when the speaker him or herself has looked at the wide range of sources available can he or she appreciate and understand the differing points of view about a particular issue; only then can he or she begin to make independent and informed judgments. There is a saying that everyone has a right to an opinion. In a free society that is true, but it is true in the sense that everyone has the right to be stupid, or everyone has the right to be ignorant. While we all have a right to an opinion, there is no guarantee that that opinion should be regarded as sensible or should be taken seriously. Only an *informed* opinion is worth considering. The speaker has the responsibility to survey sources in such a way as to be able to form such an opinion; the listener has the responsibility to weigh opinions carefully, discarding those that are based on unreliable or insufficient sources.

Communicative Evidence

There are four major kinds of evidence that are useful in supporting ideas: *example, statistics, testimony,* and *comparisons*.

Example.   One of the very real problems faced by a speaker is how to take an idea or a concept that is abstract and make it concrete, how to take something that is generalized and make it specific. Using examples is one of the most effective ways of doing just that. Examples we use naturally in informal kinds of communication settings. When one says that a particular course was very interesting or very boring, very relevant or very removed from his or her experience, very difficult or too easy, he or she would quite normally use examples to explain what was meant. One might describe a test or the content of a lecture or an anecdote told in class or some other specific bit of information that makes the generalization clearer and understandable.

The use of the example to make abstractions real is the basis for much of the artistic and practical communication that exists. Often a novel or a play, for example, will attempt to describe how people live or how they think or how they react to crisis by creating specific kinds of characters that take on a symbolic function for a whole group of people. One can talk about the atrocities committed during World War II by indicating the numbers of people killed or imprisoned. The enormity of the crime, however, becomes more apparent through the experience of reading the *Diary of Anne Frank* or seeing the stage version of the diary. Anne Frank is not a number but a person who hid for years from Nazi persecutors only to be discovered at last and die in a prison camp. In this case a real little girl—an example, if you will—makes the abstraction of numbers a concrete thing. Charitable organizations often use the example as a way of translating the abstractions of poverty, distress, and misfortune into reality by using such specific examples as a particular family made homeless by a flood or a particular child who will not get enough to eat or a particular person stricken with a crippling disease.

There are two principle kinds of examples that a speaker might use to support ideas: a *specific example* and the *hypothetical example*. Either kind may be extended or brief. The specific example deals with a real case; it is something that actually happened that can be pointed to by the speaker directly. The following excerpt shows the use of the *specific example*.

> Fad diets not only waste your money, they can be dangerous. Last semester a girl in our dormitory tried to live on nothing but water and eggs. One day she passed out in a class and had to be taken to the hospital. Not only had the diet done her body a great deal of harm, but she had broken her arm and knocked out a tooth when she fainted and fell against a chair in the class.

A *hypothetical example* is one that represents an action or an event that could very easily and plausibly take place in the way it is described, but the example is not of any particular incident or event. While it is in a sense a "made up" example, in order to be effective it must not seem exaggerated or distorted. The following is an example of the use of the *hypothetical example*.

> Everyone has suffered from careless and irresponsible actions of others. Imagine how angry you would feel, for example, if you got up one morning, hurrying to get to an early class, only to find that someone had parked and blocked your car; or, how you would react if you got out of that somehow, managed to arrive at class just in time and discovered that the instructor didn't show up. It's when these kinds of things start happening to us that we begin to wonder if there are any unselfish people left in the world.

Because things that are real are so much easier with which to identify, the example, then, can be a very potent means of support. Accordingly, the listener has to exercise a great deal of care in evaluating arguments supported by examples. The listener, in essence, must *test* the example in order to determine whether or not it is really doing what it says it is doing. The best test of an example is the test of typicality. If the speaker is trying to support a particular generalization by the use of examples then the listener must ask him or herself whether these examples really do represent the normal course of events. If someone were to describe, as a specific example, a newspaper article that he had read in which a student was arrested for shoplifting and then argued from that example that students didn't have any values, the listener should be very skeptical. Such a specific example simply does not support such a sweeping generalization. It would be as if one argued that because a particular college professor was arrested for hit-and-run driving that all professors were criminals. Actually, it is such distortions of the use of the specific example that produce stereotyping in which an entire group is said to behave in the same way as one particular member of that group behaved on one particular occasion. It is up to the listener then to look very carefully at the relationship between an example and the conclusion to which that example leads.

As well as typicality, the listener should also feel compelled to make some judgment about the *importance* of the example. That is to say that there are times when an example will demonstrate that certain actions *can* take place, but not necessarily that they do frequently take place; yet that might be enough to support a generalization. If, for instance, one argued that a cafeteria in a dormitory should be closed pending a thorough investigation by the Board of Health, and supported that assertion with three specific examples of students who had suffered from ptomaine poisoning in a week, then whether or not those cases were typical might be a secondary consideration. Even if only 3 out of 500 were poisoned, the seriousness of the matter is more crucial than any kind of numerical representativeness.

Statistics. Statistics are a way of demonstrating how some things are related to other things. They might tell us the typicality of an occurrence and thus validate the use of the examples. In a speech dealing with the problems of rehabilitating criminals, for instance, a speaker gave an extended example dealing with the experience of a young man who left prison only to become a repeat offender and return to prison and coupled this example with statistical information demonstrating how frequently this kind of experience was repeated.

Statistics also might be used to show cause to effect relationships, or at least correlations between certain phenomena, as in a speech dealing with the relationship between smoking and health, for example, that used statistical information to show that the incidence of lung cancer increased as the number of cigarettes smoked increased.

Statistical information can be helpful in pointing out trends over time: we can appreciate better how quickly and significantly the price of building a new home has increased if we can see the year by year costs; the contention that crime is becoming a more serious problem in suburban and rural areas demands that the crime rate over a period of time be presented and specific information on the number of crimes committed contrasted; supporting the contention that medical science has made significant strides forward in the last decade calls for supporting material that demonstrates changes in such matters as life expectancy, control of communicable disease, number of hours lost from work due to illness, and so forth.

Statistics, then, are one important way of making ideas more understandable and believable; they should, however, be viewed critically by the listener. It should not be assumed that a statistic "proves" something conclusively. They are part of the total structure of evidence and should be considered in the light of other supporting material. The listener should recognize that statistics can sometimes be misleading. "Average," for example, is a notoriously vague concept even though it seems to give an air of statistical weight when it is used. Averages can be computed in different ways such as adding up a list of figures and dividing by the number of figures (the *mean*), or choosing the figure that occurs most often (the *mode*), or choosing the figure that is the midpoint between the two extreme figures (the *median*). These three methods of computing "average" may lead to quite different conclusions. Assume, for example, that there were two small businesses in a town and the owner of each was trying to get a bright young person to go to work in that business. Mr. Brown could argue, "Since the average salary at my store is $1600 per year more than at Smith's store, you had better come work for me." Mr. Smith might tell you, "My employees make, on the average, $2000 more per year than do Brown's, so you'd be better off working for me." Who's telling the truth? Well, the distressing thing is that strictly speaking they *both* are. But, they are using different methods to calculate average, and only when you find out the way they arrived at their conclusions can you begin to tell which statistic gives you a better idea of what's really happening, and who might be misleading although technically "true." Let's look at the list of salaries for each company, the first in both cases being the salary of the owner himself:

BROWN	SMITH
1. 35,000	1. 20,000
2. 10,000	2. 12,000
3. 8,000	3. 10,000
4. 7,500	4. 9,000
5. 7,500	5. 9,000
Mean = 13,600	12,000
Median = 8,000	10,000
Mode = 7,500	9,000

Mr. Brown took the *mean* as the average and therefore came out with a comparison of 13,600 to 12,000 in his favor. Mr. Smith took the *median* as his average and came out with a $2000 advantage in *his* favor. He could also have taken the *mode* and fare even better: a $2500 advantage. When you examine the data it becomes clear that Smith's workers really do better; they clearly make more money on the whole than do Brown's workers and Smith's median average seems most clearly to state the real comparison. Brown has given a mathematically accurate "average," but it is a misleading one.

The point of all this is that statistics must be approached cautiously. If the listener can ascertain where the statistics came from and how they were computed he or she will have a much better idea of how seriously to take them. If, as will be the case most of the time, this is not possible both the speaker and listener should evaluate carefully the place of statistics in the total pattern of evidence. **Testimony.** The impact that a speaker's ethos or personal appeal can have on an audience was discussed in an earlier chapter. One effective way of making ideas persuasive is, in a sense, to borrow the ethos of someone to whom the audience responds postively.

Again, this is a common practice in everyday communication settings. If you are studying for an exam, for example, with a friend and you disagree over a particular point, the disagreement could well be settled by one of you asserting that, "Jack [who is generally regarded as the best notetaker in class] let me copy this from his notes, so I'm sure it is right." In public communication testimony by authority is one of the most frequently used forms of support when controversial issues are being dealt with. For one thing, it is literally impossible for most of us to make very well informed judgments on many issues. We just don't or can't take the time to study all the available information, and we often don't have the necessary technical background or personal experience to make a reasoned judgment. In that case, we rely on those whom we regard as experts or on those in whom we have some particular reason to trust. The speaker, then, calls on the writings and statements of such persons to influence his or her audience. It is, of course, essential that the authority being quoted *be considered an authority by the audience.* It is all very well to use the testimony of a brilliant nuclear physicist regarding the future of scientific research. If, nevertheless, the audience has no recognition of the name its impact will not be very great. One has heard stories of the unscrupulous, and not very bright, debater who felt he needed a quote at a particular point in his presentation and simply asked his roommate to say, "I support this plan strongly," and then inserted in his speech, "Harry Jones says that he supports this plan strongly." This sort of verbal sleight of hand is really not very effective, as well as being dishonest, because the audience simply does not respond particularly to Harry Jones.

The listener needs to evaluate carefully testimony that is presented by a speaker. The listener evaluating testimony should raise certain questions about the nature of that testimony in order to determine whether it should or should not be persuasive.

The first question that might be asked of testimony is: *How timely is this testimony?* People's ideas change as the situation changes. It is quite possible, for example, for a political figure to have commented on the relations between the United States and the Soviet Union in 1956 in a way that would not be at all compatible with that person's views in 1976. We've probably all had the experience ourselves of finding that some initial impression we had about a person or an event or an experience in our lives changes over a period of time. You could very well find that the first few months you are at school might have been an unhappy kind of experience. If asked *then* about college life, your testimony might have been negative. A year later, as the situation changed, it's possible the testimony would be quite different. One thing, then, that a listener can do to protect him or herself from being unduly influenced by testimony is to question the situation in which that testimony was given.

The situation would include not only time, but another aspect which raises another question: *What is the context out of which the testimony comes?* Suppose, for example, a noted financial expert had written this: "Mining stocks are generally a good investment these days as long as one avoids any association with companies that have been in business for less than two or three years." It would be quite possible for any speaker, even one representing a company that had been in business for six months, to say that, according to the noted financial expert, "Mining stocks are . . . a good investment these days." Now the financial expert did indeed say this, but the context out of which it grows clearly suggests a meaning that does *not* support the speaker's contention that *his* particular company's stock should be invested in.

Perhaps the most critical factor in evaluating testimony is the nature of the authority. The listener needs to ask him or herself: *Is the person being quoted a relevant authority?* One of the most common misuses of testimony by authority in public communication occurs in advertising. Often someone who is an authority in one field is used to give testimony in a field in which he or she has no particular expert knowledge or experience. A famous tennis player, for example, may know a great deal about the best kind of equipment to use for tennis, but he or she does not necessarily know more about what kind of toothpaste is best to use or what kind of razor blade shaves the closest. This sort of shift of authority frequently occurs and should be received critically by a listener. A person might have won a Nobel Prize in physics, which would make him or her an expert in certain scientific areas and his or her testimony in those areas particularly relevant, but that Nobel Prize does not necessarily qualify the person as an expert commentator on political events. If, on the question of technical problems associated with limiting strategic arms a speaker wishes to use scientific testimony the opinion of the Nobel Laureate could be entirely appropriate; however, when the speaker calls on the views of the same scientist to support his position on whether we can or cannot trust the Russians to live up to obligations, then the question has shifted to an historical and political one, and that might be a question on which the scientist cannot give the most pertinent expert testimony.

In all these areas of concern to the listener it might not always be possible for the listener to make an informed judgment about testimony. The listener might not always be able to tell when the testimony was given or what the total context was or even assess adequately the expertise of the authority. The listener's goal, however, should be in this case as in all cases of evaluating evidence to view the evidence with some skepticism and to accept it tentatively pending more information.

Comparison. One of the principal ways that human beings learn things is by comparison. We compare the unknown to the known; we look for similarities between a new experience and an old experience; we try to see ways in which new problems that need to be solved are like old ones that have been solved.

One of the most frequent uses of comparison to make ideas more understandable or believable is by comparing the familiar with the unfamiliar. If a speaker, for example, is giving a speech in which he or she hopes to help the audience understand styles of architecture the speaker would be well advised to compare an unknown but famous architectural example with a more familiar one from among the buildings on the campus or in city or town surrounding. Or a speaker discussing certain national financial problems might well compare these with a kind of personal financial problems that are normally faced by college students. If a speaker wishes to condemn a course of action he or she might well compare that course of action with one taken in the past that led to unhappy results.

Comparisons are often made in order to simplify difficult concepts. We have all experienced traffic control first hand. We've seen, and found it relatively easy to understand, how a policeman at an intersection manages the flow of cars. In some ways this management is like certain kinds of functions performed by the brain. A speaker who wished to explain the process by which the brain controls particular action might use the comparison with the traffic policeman. Sometimes a complicated organizational system may be compared to the better known functioning of a tree with roots, a trunk, branches, leaves, and so forth.

While the listener may find comparisons very helpful and potentially persuasive he or she should be particularly careful to consider the basis of comparison. That is to say, the speaker must ask him or herself: are the things being compared really *comparable* in essential ways? It is possible that some objects, events, ideas, may be similar in certain obvious or superficial ways, but comparison on such bases could be misleading. Assume, for example, that a speaker is urging the rejection of a plan (Plan B) because it is similar to a plan the group has already rejected (Plan A). The nature of the similarities is very important if the comparison is to be a valid one. If Plan A costs $5000 to put into operation and Plan B also costs $5000 to put into operation and Plan A was rejected because no money was available for the operation, the comparison is a good one: Plan B like Plan A is too costly and therefore should be rejected. If, on the other hand, Plan A and B are similar in that both call for the expenditure of time on the part of the members of the organization, both call for quick action, and both are proposed to the group by the same people, and yet Plan B does not involve any expenditure of funds, then the comaprison is not a good one as long as financial considerations are central. The speaker who urges a particular form of government for one country by pointing out that that form of government has worked so well for another country, might be setting up a false comparison if the histories, cultures, values, and the like, of the two countries are not similar. The listener, then, must exercise great care in responding to comparisons and must always try to satisfy him or herself that the two things being compared are really similar in ways essential to the argument being made by the speaker.

Communicative Methods

In addition to the specific material used to make ideas believable and understandable certain methods of presentation of those ideas and the supporting material can be very effective. Principally through repetition and restatement and through the use of visual aids ideas can be further supported.

Repetition and Restatement.   As attractive as the prospect might sometimes be, a speaker cannot be turned off. He or she cannot be halted and moved back to repeat a paragraph nor can he or she be slowed down or speeded up by the listener. When one is reading a book one can move at his or her own pace. If the reader begins to daydream he or she can go back to the page, reread the part that the daydream obscured, or quickly scan the last few pages to remind him or herself of what is going on. With the speaker, of course, all this is impossible. So what the speaker needs to do is to provide for what is sure to be less than 100 percent attention on the part of the audience.

The speaker who wants to make sure the audience follows him or her, remembers what is said and sees the direction in which the speaker wants to go must be prepared to say things more than once and to say them in different ways. This communicative device of repetition and restatement all of us have used: for example, how many times have we given directions in which we have repeated certain crucial elements in order to make sure that the listener goes the right way? If we want him to turn right it is quite likely that we tell him to go to the corner turn right and proceed for eight blocks and turn left at the white house, and follow this with "Now do you have that—it's right at the corner, eight blocks, left at the white house." Certainly in a speech the speaker would do the same kind of thing. Take the following section from a speech as an example. Note the way the speaker presents the idea and restates it. After the idea has been developed, the speaker repeats it once more before going on to the next idea.

The best way to defend yourself from attack is by being prepared. Yes, if you know what to do beforehand, you can defend yourself.

So, we've seen that preparing for an attack is the best defense. Let's consider what you would do if actually faced with an assault.

Visual Aids.   In helping the audience to follow and to remember and in attempting to be persuasive, the speaker will do well to engage as many of the senses of the listener as possible. The fact that we talk about the audience as "listeners" indicates that the principal sense that the audience members employ is a sense of hearing. But the speaker has ample opportunities to employ the sense of sight as well. What he or she does to engage the audience visually can be very simple or very complex.

Some of the most obvious and easy to use visual aids are often neglected by the speaker. For example, every classroom and many meeting rooms contain a blackboard. The simple device of listing the major ideas on the blackboard as one talks about them can be a help to an audience; such a process can simply make it easier for the audience to follow as the speaker moves from one point to the next. The blackboard can also be very useful when one is trying to demonstrate how a particular process works and wishes to do this by adding one step at a time as the process is explained. It should be noted, however, that using the blackboard takes a certain amount of skill and that the speaker who ends up talking to the blackboard rather than the audience distracts from rather than adds to the communicative effect. It is probably better to make some preparations beforehand, and the very simple and easy to prepare chart is most likely the best technique. Often an example can be made more dramatic through the use of a visual, statistics can be made more clear and more vivid through the use of a chart or a diagram, and comparisons can be made clearer when they are represented visually. Following are examples of visual materials that have been used in student speeches. They were presented very simply on a chart or a blackboard and proved very helpful to the speakers (Figures 7 to 13).

SMOKING EFFECTS YOU!

- SMOKING CAN KILL YOU
- SMOKING CAN BE DANGEROUS TO YOUR ENVIRONMENT
- SMOKING CAN TURN PEOPLE OFF YOU
- SMOKING COSTS YOU MONEY

Figure 7

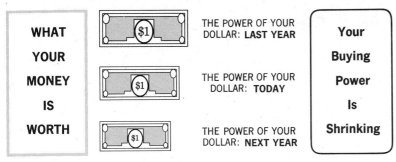

WHAT **YOUR** **MONEY** **IS** **WORTH**	[$1] THE POWER OF YOUR DOLLAR: **LAST YEAR**	**Your**
	[$1] THE POWER OF YOUR DOLLAR: **TODAY**	**Buying** **Power** **Is**
	[$1] THE POWER OF YOUR DOLLAR: **NEXT YEAR**	**Shrinking**

Figure 8

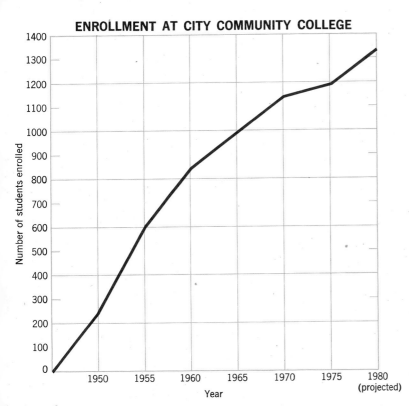

Figure 9

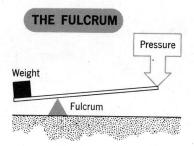

Figure 10

THE PISTON

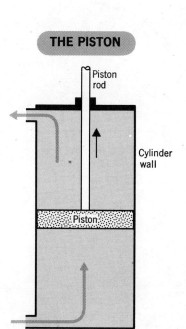

Figure 11

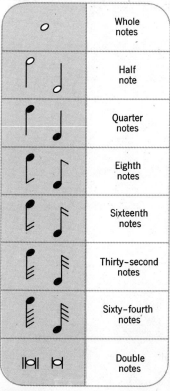

Figure 12

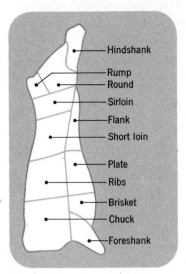

BEEF CUTS

- Hindshank
- Rump
- Round
- Sirloin
- Flank
- Short loin
- Plate
- Ribs
- Brisket
- Chuck
- Foreshank

Figure 13

More complex and more technical means of representing ideas and their support visually are available in some cases. There are times that certain kinds of technical equipment is absolutely necessary if a speech is to make any sense and have any impact at all. If, for example, a speaker is talking about the history of jazz in America, it is inconceivable that he would not play a tape or phonograph recording of examples of the music. A speech on how films are made certainly seem to call for some use of films during the speech. Other kinds of equipment such as slide projectors, opaque projectors, and overhead projectors all provide ways of presenting material visually to an audience. In some cases even videotaping facilities are available, and videotape may be used. The point is that ways of visualizing ideas, whether very simple or very sophisticated, should be incorporated into the speech whenever it is appropriate to do so. What often happens is that speakers do not fully exploit the potential of visual material and do not realize how important it is and how frequently it can be used. There is almost no speech that would not benefit from some kind of visual aid and the speaker should always keep this in mind.

There are, however, certain common sense rules that ought to be followed when using visual aids. First, visual aids should be used because they support an idea directly and never used just for effect. The visual does have the added benefit of adding interest and attention, but it should never be used for this alone. A visual that does not support an idea can end up confusing, misleading, or distracting an audience. Second, the visual should be as simple and as clear as possible. Visual material should never be cluttered with unessentials.

Only what is important to the speech should be part of the visual. And the speaker must always keep in mind that no visual is useful if an audience cannot see it and understand it. Speakers have actually gone in front of an audience and held up for their inspection a piece of ruled notebook paper with a diagram in pencil on it and expected this to help the audience to understand the point. Third, a visual should not in any way distract the audience from where its attention should be. A visual aid that is put before an audience too soon, for example, can be distracting. A chart put up for an audience to look at long before it is necessary might engage their attention when the speaker wishes them to focus on what he is saying. Furthermore, the chart is rather dull and uninteresting when the speaker finally does get to it. The problem of distraction is also the one inherent in handouts. When someone passes a picture or an article around in the audience it usually engages each individual auditor's attention as it is received thus distracting the listener from the point the speaker is making at the time. In order to be effective, handouts ought to be given out in enough copies for everyone and used as soon as everyone receives a copy. The point is that the speaker needs to think very carefully about the impact of his or her visual material on the audience so that it promotes rather than hinders clear communication of the idea. Fourth, the speaker should certainly *practice* using his or her visual aid before doing so. Equipment can malfunction, finding a place on a phonograph record or a tape can be difficult, referring to a chart while one is speaking is not always an easy or natural thing to do. Practice in using material will enhance both the speaker's confidence and skill in handling visual aids.

Determining the Quality of Argument

We all know that there are good and bad arguments; too often we tend to decide which is which on the basis of how closely those arguments match our own opinions or beliefs: a "good" argument is one that we agree with. Of course, anyone who stops to think about it knows that he or she is not always right or that he or she has been convinced that something should be done only to find that it was the wrong thing. All of us have been "talked into" something that proved to be disappointing, or unhappy, or even disastrous. The process of "talking someone into something" is the process of argument. Accordingly, the ultimate judges of whether or not an argument is good are the speaker and the listeners. But, since listeners can be actuated on the basis of an argument that leads them in a direction they did not wish to take, it is important to realize that there can be things wrong with arguments that *seem*, on the surface, to be sound ones. For an argument to be a good one, then, there must be a recognition of its worth by the participants in the rhetorical situation as well as by the neutral observer testing the "logic" of the argument.

The Rhetorically Sound Argument

An argument moves from a premise that an audience can accept through a variety of kinds of evidence to a conclusion. Let us consider each of these parts of the argument.

The *premise* is an acceptable generalization that grows out of the context in which the public communication occurs. The first test of the premise is whether or not it makes sense to an audience. There are certain values in our culture or our particular group that are supported without much serious question. But, such fundamental ideas are audience specific: in our society most listeners might agree that everyone is entitled to fair and equal treatment under the law, other societies might assume that power and rank automatically assure one of the right to circumvent the law. We might feel confident that an audience in our society would accept the idea that individuals were important as human beings and should be protected in their rights, whereas others might not question the assumption that individual rights had to be sacrificed for the good of the whole community. And even within our culture, certain listeners will need no proof for the assertion that education is important for everyone, whereas others are not at all convinced that education is worth spending time or money on.

Quite often the premises are not even stated by the speaker; they are invisible underpinnings like the pilings sunk into the ground to support a bridge. But, like the pilings, they need looking after, inspection to make certian they can sustain the weight. The speaker has a responsibility for testing the firmness of these foundations. Indeed, the speaker, unless he or she is very careful, might not even be aware himself or herself of what these premises are. Such a lack of awareness is probably a mistake. For certainly part of what the speaker wants to do is to be absolutely sure of the integrity of his or her own thinking. Similarly, the speaker, as well as the neutral observer, should seek to know and question the premise. Take, for example, the following excerpt:

> I have consistently argued for a reduction of the budget. Five years ago, it was the committee that I headed that was responsible for reducing a variety of social service payments and costs by almost 20 percent. The Citizens for Tax Relief have judged my performance to be an outstanding one. There can be no doubt in anyone's mind that I have always stood for good government.

Now that argument is based on a certain premise. The premise could be stated something like this: good government is that which is economical. The speaker in this case is obviously arguing that his frugality is the critical ingredient in determining whether he is for "good government." The listener, in his or her efforts to uncover this premise, hopes to bring to light the foundation of an argument, and then to question whether or not such a foundation is solid. The speaker in this case is arguing as if such a premise is beyond question. Many, however, *would* question economy as *the* basic ingredient of good government.

Assuming the validity of a premise, the conclusion of an argument rests on the strength of the supporting material. We already discussed in this chapter the principal kinds of communicative evidence and ways to test them. It is important here to say that a sound argument is one in which the evidence is both qualitatively and quantitatively adequate. That is to say the evidence passes the tests (the examples used are representative, the statistics accurate, the testimony by an authority, the comparisons of objects or ideas that are indeed comparable, and so forth), and are quantitatively sufficient to provide ample justification for the conclusion. Perhaps the best way to summarize and conceptualize the structure of an argument is to look at it operationally. Many students of the communicative process and of the reasoning process have done this. It might be most advantageous here to consider a simplified diagram that grows out of what we have been saying: there is a premise that comes out of the total context; on the premise is built specific items of evidence and these items of evidence in turn support the conclusion of the argument (Figure 14).

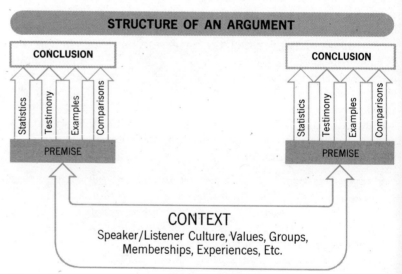

Figure 14

The best argument, then, is one in which the conclusion is most adequately supported by the evidence and which grows out of an intellectually and emotionally acceptable premise. Of course, be noted that the best argument is not always the most effective one, just as the best product is not always the one that sells the most. Unhappily, consumers—consumers of products and consumers of arguments—can be and are being duped. Incensed by the fact that our foods can poison us, that extremely expensive machinery wears out in a short time, that gadgets fall apart in our hands, that services are promised us which are never performed, we as consumers have begun to rise up against the hucksters who would exploit us. Intellectual hucksters are just as harmful, and probably more dangerous to us. The absolute responsibility of the speaker is to apply carefully the principles that demonstrate the proper use of evidence, and that of the listener to evaluate carefully and critically the relationship between evidence and conclusions.

Reasoning and Rationalizing

We have all been in a situation where our real "reason" for doing something is not the reason we publicly express. We might, for example, go to meetings or participate in activities that we say we are interested in; in reality, our attraction to postage stamps or travel or bowling or scuba diving might be caused by the fact that a *person* in whom we are very interested happens to have an attraction to those activities. Similar kinds of situations abound in our lives: we might, for example, buy something that is very expensive because we want it, because we like it, because we want to indulge ourselves, and then later explain to a friend or parent that we bought it because it will save money in the long run. We've all probably told ourselves that taking a break in the middle of studying by going to a movie we want to see is really therapeutic—it will help us study better in the long run. Or we may have decided that we just had to study tonight because we really did not want to go out with a person who asked us to go. A popular cartoon once showed a character—a young boy— writing a letter to a medical school. After going through a long section in which he attested to his desires to help others, his feeling of being useful in society, his need to serve the community, he ended up with something like, "and besides all that I really want to make a bundle." Most of us are not that candid, but most of us do have the experience of dressing up our real reasons and motivations in clothing that will be more acceptable to the outer world or even to ourselves.

Public communication, of course, affords numerous examples of this process at work. Speakers, for example, will often give lofty, highly principled and highly abstract reasons for promoting policies or plans that are less idealistic than they sound. There have been times in our past when speakers have appealed, for example, to the purity or integrity of the constitution or have urged us to launch a campaign to check the rising tide of crime in the street, or who have urged us to adopt policies that promote self-help as opposed to government aid. Sometimes these speakers have been honest and straightforward in their arguments, at other times, at the other extreme, such arguments have been used to mask the most determined kind of racism: law and order could be translated into "zap the blacks." Speakers have been known to promote schemes to reform taxes or to guarantee that everyone pays a fair share, or to preserve the rewards of one's labor—all commendable kinds of things; but these are sometimes merely acceptable ways of arguing on behalf of those who want to pay as little as possible to support the needs of society. Advertising, of course, provides other examples of substituting acceptable reasons for real ones in public communications. A mother, for example, may want to buy a certain kind of cereal for her child simply because that child likes to eat it since it is coated in sugar and tastes good. But she must be assured by that manufacturer that it is also good *for* the child, that it is fortified with vitamins, that it is part of a balanced breakfast, and so forth.

Interestingly enough, advertising also provides examples of the awareness on the part of the persuasive communicators that real reasons exist, and that these might better be appealed to. One of the most fascinating examples is advertising toothpaste. It seems fairly clear that brushing one's teeth is primarily a way of preserving and protecting those teeth. Advertising that is directed largely to parents appeal for this reason: they argue that such a brand of toothpaste reduces cavities, keeps teeth healthy, and so forth. As the advertising begins to aim at a more mature audience it seems to recognize that brushing one's teeth for health purposes is somewhat secondary to brushing one's teeth for social purposes. Some ads recognize the dual purpose and discuss how their toothpaste will both make one attractive to the opposite sex as well as keeping one's dentist happy. In this case it might well be that the real reason is being attractive to the opposite sex, whereas keeping one's teeth healthy makes the toothpaste respectable by adding to its cosmetic value a health value. In some cases, however, toothpaste is frankly advertised as making one's teeth white so as to make one's mouth more sexy. Here, the real reason has emerged most blatantly.

The process that we have been discussing—that of finding good or acceptable reasons for taking action or believing ideas that one is inclined to do in any case—is called *rationalization*. Another way of saying it is that rationalization is adding stated reasons in place of the underlying real reasons. Why do we rationalize? We probably do so because of the way we believe certain public arguments will affect our images, images that we have of ourselves and images that others have of us. If we like, for example, to think of ourselves as practical and hardheaded, we may not wish to admit, even to ourselves, that we bought a new car because we particularly like the color. In that case, we will want to be armed with the salesman's arguments about gas mileage, record of repair, and comparative costs. This way we can preserve for ourselves our image of ourselves. Or, we may have bought that car so that we can show off in some way, perhaps gloat a little that it's a better car than the one owned by a neighbor or a friend; it will enhance our perception of our own prestige. Of course, it would be rather awkward to admit—perhaps to ourselves, but certainly to others—this real reason for buying the car. So, again, the salesman's arguments are necessary for us.

It's also quite conceivable that people will want to do things that they perceive as in contrast to the norms or practices of the group with which they identify, and so will try to find reasons for that behavior that are acceptable to that group. One professor, for example, who identified himself with what he considered to be the moderate-to-liberal intellectual community decided to vote for a gubernatorial candidate who was rather conservative, decidedly not intellectual—some even said exceedingly dull—and whose outlook was extremely parochial. The real reason for this choice may well have been that the opposition candidate was personally distasteful to the professor and/or that the professor was really much more conservative than he would admit. And so he justified his action by asserting that the candidate of his choice was a great friend to education in the state. Judging by the candidate's support of the basketball team this was very true; by almost any other criterion it was not. In this example, of course, there is no way of saying whether or not the particular candidate should or should not have been elected. The point is that the professor perceived his vote for the candidate as something that had to be justified in terms of the accepted norms of the group to which he perceived himself as belonging. Sometimes a person might rather go to a play than go bowling or go bowling than to a play, and find it difficult to justify such a decision in light of the attitudes and behaviors of his or her group. In that case the person will feel pressured to say that the choice is based on the necessities of the moment or parental pressure or pressure from a teacher, on the demands of certain of one's friends, on mistaken information, and so on, preferring to hide the reason that this is just something that he or she would rather do.

This process of rationalization has the most profound and far reaching implications for both speaker and listener. For the speaker, as has been pointed out in a previous chapter, one important task in understanding the audience is understanding the kinds of allegiances, loyalties, and associations that audience members have and subsequently the kinds of motivations and pressures to which they might be subject. As the speaker prepares to speak he or she must be aware that audiences may well demand a good sound argument not only to be convinced or to be motivated—they may be that already—but, in a sense, to be armed with weapons necessary to defend their decisions. The lifelong Democrat, for example, may be ready to switch parties because he feels this would be in his best economic interest; yet he hesitates to abandon long professed principles for what he is afraid might appear crass or selfish reasons for taking such a political step. In short, a speaker recognizes that rationalization is likely to take place and that it is his or her responsibility to provide the audience with a good, sound, sensible argument.

The most important fact about rationalization for the listener is that he or she does it. Rationalization is simply a part of our behavior. It is a way that we manage the world around us. There are times when we must rationalize in order simply to cope with our lives. But in a public communication situation the more we can understand about our own reactions to messages the better off we are bound to be in judging and acting upon those messages. As we respond, we should make every effort to understand the basis of our response. Ultimately, we may decide that it is not politic, or polite, or safe to explain to others the real reasons of our actions; we may never want to tell someone that we bought a car because it was fire-engine red. Nonetheless, we can make more informed kinds of decisions if we at least recognize ourselves the basis of that decision. It might just be that if we say honestly to ourselves, "I really want to buy that car because of that color," we might give ourselves a chance for internal rebuttal, a chance for another part of ourselves to say, "Is the color worth the gas guzzling?" How we resolve that question can depend on many factors, such as perception of environmental problems, our commitment to improving the ecological situation, our realistic assessment of our own finances, or our basic value system. Rationalization is, after all, a way of smoothing over conflict. The listener who would make the best decision often must encourage conflict within himself.

Undoubtedly, any discussion of rationalization raises ethical questions. On the most basic kind of level there can be really no question posed such as: Is rationalization right or wrong? Rationalization simply *is;* it is a psychological process. The real question is whether or not it can be misused or misdirected by speakers and listeners in the public communication situation. All of us recognize that there can be times when people are offered what appeared to be "good reasons" in order to encourage them to do things that are harmful or socially undesirable. There are times when people tend to act on the basis of prejudice, ignorance, and narrowmindedness, grasping at more "respectable reasons" for doing what is essentially wrong. There are other times when people have basically good instinctive feelings which direct them in a way that is beneficial to the community in which they live. These people may need to be assured that their instinctive responses are, indeed, the right ones. The resolution of such issues will hinge on how a speaker or a listener sees him or herself and the world in which he or she lives. That is, one's personal values will ultimately be the determinant of the way in which rationalization is used. But, in the context of this chapter there is one rule that seems a sensible one in connection with ethics and rationalization and within reasoning generally. That is simply this: a sound argument is one that is clearly thought out, well developed and supported by evidence, and reaches a sensible conclusion. An argument that is clearly an effort to promote reasonable and logical thought could hardly be conceived as unethical. However, an argument that is unsound, that is based on faulty or insubstantial evidence, and that comes to a conclusion that is misleading or myopic obviously does not promote rational thinking and is clearly an unethical way in which to participate in the process of public communication.

Summary

The speaker who has considered his or her audience and the situation in which public communication occurs and has determined a reasonable purpose is then ready to invent and develop the ideas of the speech. From a search of the relevant material, the speaker will generate clear, complete ideas and uncover communication evidence—principally in the form of examples, testimony, statistics, and comparisons—that make the ideas more believable or understandable. The listener who eventually hears the evidence, as well as the speaker who gathers it, should be aware of ways to test the evidence to see if it does truly support the conclusions being reached. Along with the evidence, methods such as repetition and restatement and the use of visual aids will further enhance the ideas.

The speaker and the listener should be able to make some judgment about the quality of an argument, understanding the premise and its relationship to the final conclusion reached through the process of presentation of evidence. The process whereby people find or use reasons to support decisions made or conclusions reached through a less obvious chain or reasoning can be called rationalizing. This process, which is usual for everyone to engage in, suggests to the speaker that listeners will often want good, sensible reasons for taking actions that they might already be disposed to take, and to listeners that the sources of their actions may not always be the ones that are out in the open.

This chapter has been concerned with reasoning tactics designed to promote ideas to an audience. Other closely related, and overlapping, tactics may be designed to involve the listeners in the communication event and are therefore relevant to the speaker and listener alike. They are considered in the next chapter.

Select Bibliography

The following citations, and those listed in all the bibliographies, offer further practical and theoretical information related to the chapter topics, and they provide a starting point for the student who wishes to undertake more intensive study and research into the topic.

Carroll C. Arnold, "What's Reasonable?" *Today's Speech,* **19**(1971), 19-23.

William E. Arnold and James C. McCroskey, "The Credibility of Reluctant Testimony," *Central States Speech Journal,* **18**(1967), 97-103.

Samuel L. Becker, "Research on Emotional and Logical Proofs," *Southern Speech Journal,* **28**(1973), 198-207.

Robert S. Cathcart, "An Experimental Study of the Relative Effectiveness of Four Methods of Presenting Evidence," *Speech Monographs,* **22**(1955), 227-233.

Lane Cooper, ed., *The Rhetoric of Aristotle.* New York: Appleton-Century-Crofts, 1932.

Vernon E. Cronen and Nancy Mihevc, "The Evaluation of Deductive Argument," *Speech Monographs,* **39**(1972), 124-131.

Gary Cronkhite, "Logic, Emotion, and the Paradigm of Persuasion," *Quarterly Journal of Speech,* **50**(1964), 13-18.

Jessie G. Delia, "The Logic Fallacy, Cognitive Theory, and the Enthymeme: A Search for the Foundations of Reasoned Discourse," *Quarterly Journal of Speech,* **56**(1970), 140-148.

John Dewey, *How We Think.* New York: D. C. Heath, 1910.

Douglas Ehninger, "Argument as Method: Its Nature, Its Limitations, and Its Use," *Speech Monographs,* **37**(1970), 101-110.

W. Ward Fearnside and William B. Holther. *Fallacy: The Counterfeit of Argument.* Englewood Cliffs: Prentice-Hall, Inc., 1959.

Helen Fleshler, Joseph Ilardo, and Joan Demoretcky, "The Influence of Field Dependence, Speaker Credibility Set, and Message Documentation on Evaluations of Speaker and Message Credibility," *Southern Speech Communication Journal,* **39**(1974), 389-402.

John A. Kline, "A Q-Analysis of Encoding Behavior in the Selection of Evidence," *Speech Monographs,* **38**(1971), 190-197.

John A. Kline, "Dogmatism of the Speaker and Selection of Evidence," *Speech Monographs,* **38**(1971), 354-356.

John A. Kline, "Interaction of Evidence and Readers' Intelligence on the Effects of Short Messages," *Quarterly Journal of Speech,* **55**(1969), 407-413.

James C. McCroskey, "The Effects of Evidence in Persuasive Communication," *Western Speech,* **21**(1967), 189-199.

James C. McCroskey, "The Effects of Evidence as an Inhibitor of Counter-Persuasion," *Speech Monographs,* **37**(1970), 188-194.

James C. McCroskey, "A Summary of Experimental Research on the Effects of Evidence in Persuasive Communication," *Quarterly Journal of Speech,* **55**(1969), 169-176.

Gerald R. Miller, "Some Factors Influencing Judgments of the Logical Validity of Arguments: A Research Review," *Quarterly Journal of Speech,* **55**(1969), 276-286.

Glen Mills, *Reason in Controversy.* Boston: Allyn and Bacon, 1964.

Robert P. Newman and Dale R. Newman, *Evidence.* Boston: Houghton Mifflin, 1969.

C. Perelman and L. Olbrechts-Tyeca, *The New Rhetoric: A Treatise on Argumentation.* South Bend, Ind.: University of Notre Dame Press, 1969.

William J. Seiler, "The Conjunctive Influence of Source Credibility and the Use of Visual Materials on Communication Effectiveness," *Southern Speech Communication Journal,* **37**(1971), 174-185.

Stephen Toulmin, *The Uses of Argument.* New York: Cambridge University Press, 1958.

Victor D. Wall, Jr., "Evidential Attitudes and Attitude Change," *Western Speech,* **36**(1972), 115-123.

Karl R. Wallace, "The Substance of Rhetoric: Good Reasons," *Quarterly Journal of Speech,* **49**(1963), 230-249.

Jack L. Whitehead, "Effects of Authority-Based Assertion on Attitude and Credibility," *Speech Monographs,* **38**(1971), 311-315.

Russel R. Windes and Arthur Hastings, *Argumentation and Advocacy.* New York: Random House, 1965.

CHAPTER 7 *audience involvement*

Quite frequently, students of the communication process tend to be suspicious of emotion. We have all heard the comment that a speech we listened to or a story we read in the newspaper or a comment reported by the news media was not very "logical." We probably have all had the experience, in conversations with others, to accuse others of becoming too "emotional" as they become excited or highly involved, or, most especially, when they begin to disagree strongly with us. One of the sexual stereotypes preserved over the years was that women were emotional and men were logical. As was generally true of such stereotypes, they were designed to define women to some inferior role since emotion was seen as inferior to logic. Indeed, a general conception exists that logic and emotion are two mutually exclusive entities—that one must be *either* logical *or* emotional. Furthermore, emotion is sometimes confused with bombast; the shouting, sweating, arm-waving speaker, lacing his message with appeals to fear or prejudice or superstition is seen as the ultimate "emotional" communicator. Such skewed perceptions of emotion tend to obscure the very important realization that *emotion, whether its effects be good or bad, is absolutely essential to successful public communication.*

Emotion is, after all, an experience of strong feeling. It is being roused from an impassive, impersonal state to one of *involvement*. We've all probably had the experience of being in a communication situation in which we had no emotional involvement at all. Television commercials, for example, for products we couldn't possibly use or aren't remotely interested in, as insistent as these messages may be, usually fail to gain our attention and, consequently, do not motivate us to absorb information or take action. It's possible that you've sat in lectures and wondered why on earth you were taking that particular course, anyway. Feeling completely detached from the content of the message, you found it very difficult to understand and retain information. If you were asked to give money to a cause that neither interested nor affected you, if you were asked to vote in an election whose outcome you believed could have no bearing at all on your life, if you were asked to learn a precise and technical procedure for repairing a piece of machinery that you had never even seen or heard of or anticipated using, if you were asked to spend time engaging in an activity that you believed simply did not form a part of your experience, if you were asked to do any of these things and you perceived them as somehow apart from you and your life, then you would not do them. For someone to take the time or expend the energy or make the effort to understand, or to believe, or to act, *that person must have some feeling of identification with or involvement in the recommended knowledge, belief, or action.*

Much has been said concerning the evils of apathy. Apathy certainly is one of the primary forces that works against successful public communication. And surely apathy is the reverse of emotion; it is a lack of any strong feelings—it is simply just not caring. The communicator who would successfully implement the strategy that grows from his or her purpose and the overall structure of the speech, must plan tactics that appeal not only to the reason of the audience but that also involve the audience emotionally.

Reason and emotion should not be thought of as incompatible. A speaker does *not* have to choose one or the other. The speaker is under the obligation to himself and to his listeners to make as sound an argument as possible. But, he must recognize that even the soundest argument is of little persuasive or informative potential unless it is attended to. Listeners will not be motivated to respond to planned purposes if they perceive the desired response as irrelevant to them. A speaker, for example, who would hope to have his or her audience understand the operation of a rocket engine needs to consider seriously ways in which he or she can point out to an audience *why* such information is important to *them*. The speaker who would urge his or her audience to take action against pollution needs to make certain that the audience feels strongly that such effects are a direct and personal threat to them.

The question that the speaker faces, then, is how to involve directly the listeners with the topic. The ways in which a speaker can promote emotional involvement on the part of the receivers of communication are varied—the following specific ways in which the listeners may be emotionally involved will be discussed: by meeting the listener's needs, by appealing to a listener's beliefs and values, by directly engaging the emotions of the listener, by capturing the listener's attention, and by establishing common ground between the speaker and the listener.

Meeting Listeners' Needs

The psychologist, A. H. Maslow, has described basic human needs in terms that will be helpful in understanding and developing tactics for listener involvement. Let us consider here those that are relevant to this discussion.

Satisfying Basic Physical Needs

Basic to all human life is the need to be physiologically secure. We all need food and drink, clothing, shelter, and sexual gratification if we want to feel comfortable and to avoid the discomfort of pain, sickness, injury, and so forth. These needs are "basic" because, in a sense, they preempt or obliterate all other needs if they are not met. Groups such as the Salvation Army long ago recognized that those who are in the deepest and most serious distress can hardly be called on to live up to their full potential as human beings if their most basic needs are not met. And so such organizations will provide food, clothing, and shelter and only then make an appeal to people to fulfill other kinds of needs. Most of the audience, however, to whom most of us will normally talk will be audiences whose basic needs have been or are being met. Freed from the preoccupation of satisfying these needs, most listeners will be more successfully appealed to on the basis of the "higher" needs.

Assuring Their Personal Safety

People like and need to have a safe environment in which to live. That is, we all need a secure and predictable world. A certain amount of routine, order, or predictability protects us from dangerous, surprising, and unfamiliar situations that threaten our safety. This does not mean that people have a basic drive for dullness; even the mountain climber wants the security of knowing precisely how his or her equipment will function; the scuba diver does not want to be surprised by an unexpected flow of the tide. However, just as physiological needs do not unduly preoccupy most of those who would be members of our audiences, so do the needs for safety rarely dominate listeners' minds. There are routine ways in which safety is guaranteed in any sort of organized society. We have a police force to protect us from crime, we have a fire department to protect us from a disaster, we have a host of departments and agencies dedicated to make sure that gas lines do not blow up, that electric wires do not break, that buildings do not crumble beneath our feet, or that highways do not disintegrate under our automobiles. There is a "Defense Establishment" designed to protect us from potential enemies abroad, and government bureaus to protect us from being poisoned at home. Our safety is the concern of many people and groups. Most of us go through most of our lives assuming our own safety. It is only in periods of crisis, such as war or natural disaster, that we seriously question how safe we are. Nevertheless, there are times and places when our personal safety does appear to us to be seriously threatened and such apprehension may be a predominate psychological factor in the makeup of an audience. In many large cities, for example, people, and particularly older people, feel very unsafe. In this case, both their physical preservation from attack and their financial social security are perceived as definitely threatened. In such a setting, a speaker who would like information to be understood or action to be taken or beliefs to be modified would be well advised to consider how such purposes would meet the very important safety needs of the audience.

Feeling Love and a Sense of Belonging
The love that exists between people—a father and a son, a husband and a wife, between two lovers—fulfills a very important human need. Furthermore, in a larger sense, there is a distinct human need to be loved or at least to be accepted, wanted, or identified with groups. People join clubs, or they maintain close family or ethnic ties, or they associate themselves strongly with some church or religious movement, or they take great pride in their nationalistic feelings toward their country. All these things help meet the need to be an accepted and cared-for part of some identifiable group. Listeners are likely to be more emotionally involved when they believe, for example, that a speaker is advocating a proposal that will be of direct benefit to those whom they love, or a proposal that will reduce the listener's feeling of isolation or help to make him or her a secure part of an admired group.

Feeling Confident in Themselves and Appreciated by Others
These "esteem needs" stem from a person's desire to feel of some worth and importance. People like to have the feeling that they control to some extent their destiny, that they are not constantly under the thumb of other people, and that they are in some way recognized as good or important human beings by others. We all like to have some attention paid to us and be thought of as "good" in some way or another. This need can frequently be translated into a desire for status, a desire to be better than other people, and the symbols of status the indicators of what makes one person "better" than another are of a real significance. In many ways this need for prestige can be seen as the most obvious one appealed to in much public communication. Assuredly it is the basis of much advertising that would have us believe that smoking a certain kind of cigarette or driving a certain kind of car or wearing a certain brand of shoes will help us acquire the status we long for by being looked up to as people fashionable and wealthy enough to do just the "right" thing.

Striving to Realize Their Own Potentials
This need for "self-actualization" recognizes that human beings want to make the most of themselves. Most people are in the process of becoming. We tend to strive for something; we tend to have goals toward which we work. Most people, if they feel striving is worth it, will continue to do so and will probably never be completely self-actualized. Not everyone of course will have the same ideal or the same ambition. Nevertheless, the speaker who realizes that people do want to achieve the full extent of their capabilities will appeal to this very important need.

Any tactic or set of tactics designed to help an audience meet their needs is bound to promote emotional involvement, and will thus contribute toward the achievement of the purpose. Yet, along with needs to be met there are also beliefs and values that will shape the nature and degree of emotional response in an audience.

As we go about our daily lives we are constantly called on to make decisions. We make these decisions on a variety of bases. We have, in other words, a set of standards that shape our behavior. These standards, or values, we carry around in our heads, and they provide a means whereby we can make decisions in situations in which these standards apply. The standards could be moral or ethical ones that will help us decide matters relating to such things as our sexual behavior, the kind of political candidates we might support, and the extent to which we will use other people or other people's work in preparing what is supposed to be our own original work. Standards that we internalize might also help us make practical kinds of decisions, so that if we value efficiency and commonsense we will tend to value those solutions that seem to us to best exhibit corresponding characteristics.

Listeners derive their values and beliefs from many sources. Certainly the country we live in, or the part of the country, or the city, or rural area all effect our value systems; our religious affiliations, our political allegiances, the kinds of clubs or organizations to which we belong, and the kinds of friends we have all shape our values and beliefs.

In the 1950s and 1960s, for example, when blacks were struggling to achieve civil and economic rights, Martin Luther King, on August 28, 1963, gave what was to be his most famous speech, the "I Have a Dream" speech. In this speech Dr. King asserted that his dream was "rooted in the American dream." What Martin Luther King attempted to do in that particular speech was to show that what he and other black leaders were asking for was nothing more than the same rights, same opportunities as other Americans. He appealed to what he hoped were commonly held values in America—the values of fair play, of equality under the law, of equality of opportunity. But as King and other black spokespersons knew appeals to such values did not automatically bring positive responses. Just because it was pointed out that there were great disparities between the values we professed and the practices we engaged in didn't mean those practices would be immediately or radically changed.

The values of our country or our group or our individual selves may not always be very easy to live up to. Indeed, we may never live up to some values that we profess to hold. The whole situation is complicated by the fact that values can often be in conflict with each other; we can hold at the same time two values that simply don't fit together. Americans, for example, have long been under the strain of trying to live up to a whole set of ethical or moral ideas while at the same time experiencing the very strong urge to succeed. Americans are often thought of as expedient people. In our politics we generally tend to promote *compromise* in order to get along, and we end up with 2 major parties and not 12 or 15 splinter parties—as often happens in political situations where principles aren't flexible. At the same time we seem to want to succeed, to get ahead to *compete* successfully with others. One famous football coach was supposed to have observed that the reason football was so popular was because "Football is life." In many ways that might be true, Americans are supposed to be able to show a certain amount of stamina, determination, and enthusiasm in order to score and to win the game. Sometimes, winning might also involve punching someone in the face when the referee is not looking. A lot of young people are very upset or puzzled because they seem to see in the world around them people telling them that to behave in a fashion that is fair, honest, and equitable is the right thing to do, and yet they see behaving very unfairly people who seem to be rewarded by material success.

Another obvious way in which Americans are pulled in opposite directions is over our feelings about individuality and conformity. If one looks at or listens to much public communication one can get the feeling that we believe that each individual has certain rights and privileges, we believe that individuals ought to be protected by the government and not sacrificed by some larger good. In short, individual people are all—each and every one—of some real worth. At the same time, and again this is evident in the content of public communication, one quickly realizes that there are strong pressures in this society to conform. On the one hand, we are urged to make up our own minds, to be our own masters, to determine our own fate; on the other hand, we are urged to be part of the team, to cooperate, to do what everyone else is doing.

Anyone planning a message to be delivered in a public communication situation needs to bear strongly in mind the fact that there are commonly shared values to which members of his or her audience will react strongly and feelingly, and at the same time these values may be in conflict with each other. As the speaker attempts to engage emotions, as he or she tries to develop tactics that will make the listeners *care about the message* and *identify with the message* and *be associated with the outcome of the message* and *be interested in the results of the message*. As the speaker plans such tactics he or she must make some estimate of the intensity and importance of the values held by the audience.

Much of this goes back to what was previously discussed concerning ways in which one should explore the nature of the audience. And we return to the point that all listeners are not alike, and a speaker can never assume that all listeners are like him or her. The speaker needs to think very carefully about how what he or she has to say bears on the kinds of standards that the culture develops, or that the region develops, or that the listeners' group associations develop. Take, for example, the question of the nature and role of higher education. For a long period of time those who urged that colleges and universities should receive more financial support based much of their argument on the recognized value of success and maintained that going to college would help someone who did so make more money as a result. Earning a college degree would also contribute to the person's success by enhancing his or her ability to move onward and upward in a chosen profession. When the economic realities changed drastically, the rationale for higher education became rather shaky. Indeed, the success value seemed to be working against college graduates, and against increased support for educational institutions. Or take, for example, the speaker who urged that certain zoning changes be made in a community so that a section of town could be torn down and a new shopping center put up. That speaker had to contend with a variety of conflicting values — probably held with different intensity by different listeners — as he or she went about trying to accomplish the purpose. Some people, for example, may value progress highly and feel that building new buildings is progress. Others might value efficiency and practicality and say that the land would be much more useful developed as a shopping center. Others, and particularly those in the neighborhood, might stress their individual rights to privacy, peace, or simply the right to keep their own property and live where they have always lived. It is precisely because such values become engaged in these kinds of controversies that they do become so emotionally charged to those who participate in them.

Listeners responding to public communication cannot fail to respond emotionally if their values are truly engaged. This means that consumers of public communication will, if they are truly touched by the message, tend to measure its effects against their value structure. They will have to cope with the problem of incompatible values that are sure to arise. This is another situation in which the listener's ability to be open with him or herself is of paramount importance. An intelligent response demands that the listener order his or her priorities, that he or she recognize conflict and deal with it in a way that is most honestly compatible with his or her own feelings or beliefs and with his or her own judgment of the reasonable aspects of the case as well.

Listeners, then, have needs to be met and they have values to which they adhere. The question naturally arises, what sorts of techniques or procedures can be employed in public communication that best relate these needs and values to the communication event by actually engaging the emotions of the listeners.

The speaker who would hope to engage the emotions of listeners must begin with his or her own emotional involvement. Listeners tend to respond to a speaker in an emotional pattern similar to the

Engaging Listeners' Emotions

speaker's. The speaker sets the *mood,* as it were, for the speech. One of the speaker's most basic assessments must be of his or her own feelings. The speaker who hopes to excite an audience, to interest an audience, to direct an audience's anger against an injustice or to fill them with pride over a laudable kind of practice or program will have a very difficult time in doing so unless he or she feels such emotions him or herself. It is always best for the speaker to choose to speak about those things for which he or she can generate genuine feelings; it is absurd to try to feign emotion. There are, of course, highly skilled professional actors who are able to project emotional states. But for most of us engaged in the public communication process to attempt to do such a thing would be futile and foolish, to say nothing of unethical. It is always best to be genuine, sincere, and honest with an audience; indications that this is not the case sensed by the listeners are bound to destroy any efforts to communicate successfully. All of this does *not* mean that the speaker shows no emotional restraint. The nature of the audience, the setting, and the total situation dictate certain limitations on both the speaker's and listener's emotional responses. In one public speaking class, for example, a student was talking about the destruction of certain wilderness lands by some commercial industries. The student felt very strongly on this matter and during the course of the speech became very angry, repeatedly pounding his fist on the lectern. In the small classroom with a small audience his reaction seemed much too extreme. The audience literally jumped each time he pounded the table and soon became uncomfortable and restless. The genuine emotion had deteriorated into excessive emotionalism, and that distracted from rather than contributed to the message. Another speaker in a beginning public speaking class suddenly stopped in the middle of her speech and said, "I can really see that nobody here seems to be terribly interested in what I am saying. It's probably because I haven't convinced you about how important and how real and how terrible the disease I'm talking about is. As a little girl I watched my grandmother die. Recently I learned that my sister also has this disease. This is a very real and very terrible thing to me, and the only reason I am talking about it is because it could happen to you. I'm not talking about something rare or unique. I'm talking about something that I've had to cope with and something you might have to cope with." It is possible that such an insertion in the speech, if it had been an "emotional outburst" could have been embarrassing or disruptive. In this case it was so genuine, and yet so calmly stated, that it deeply impressed the audience. When the speech was over one of the listeners said, and many of her fellow listeners agreed, that "This was the first time I really concentrated on what was going on in a speech, I really heard it, she made me stop thinking about what was going on in my life and think about what was going on in hers. She really made me *feel* that it could be me."

Listeners' emotions may be engaged when the premises of argument are clearly recognizable as need or value based. There are some kinds of controversies that seem to generate a great deal of emotion, and these arguments apparently do so because they are perceived by an audience as directly relevant to an audience's deepest interests. For example, there often are heated controversies over the selection of textbooks in public schools. These controversies are so emotionally engaging because arguments often are based on premises such as these: "Schools should reinforce the prevailing religious views of the community," or "The role of the schools is to expound *the* truth," or "The role of the schools is to promote and equip students for free inquiry." All of these premises engage important values for different segments of the audience. They also relate to human needs such as those that deal with the listener's self-actualization, with his or her need to be appreciated by others, with his or her feelings of love and protection for others and, even, in some cases, with some listeners' real fears that arise from what is perceived as a threat to personal safety. In order to understand the basis of emotional response and to stimulate emotional response the premises of arguments need sometimes to be made explicit if they are not obviously so in the content of the controversy. In this particular example, listeners might not tend to get involved in this issue if they perceived the argument to be a purely pedagogical one, that is, one that centers on a question such as: Is a particular textbook employing the most worthwhile techniques for promoting learning? The tendency in such a situation might be to feel, "Leave it to the experts." Whereas, if the listeners perceive the issue to be related to a very basic premise dealing with religious values, then they could well be expected to respond with deep and intense emotional reactions.

Listeners' emotions may be involved when needs and values are related to the stability and comfort of the known. Change can be a very frightening thing. All of us experience some degree of stress when we are put in new and different kinds of situations. Often we have a tendency to defend ourselves against the distressing feelings that change can provoke by looking back on what has been and trying to recapture it. In 1933, for example, when President Franklin Roosevelt was inaugurated, he faced a country in the throes of a disastrous economic depression. Everywhere the world seemed to be going to pieces and each change brought more bad news. Under these circumstances the President was about to ask for many, many more changes, changes that would come in rapid and surprising succession. In his efforts to rally the American people, he foretold these changes in the context of a *return* to that which *was* good. "We face the arduous days that lie before us," he said, "with the clear consciousness of seeking the old and precious moral values." Sometimes the appeal seems couched in escapist terms; the urge is to return to "the good old days" that somehow seem so much safer than the present. In other words, as is true in almost any aspect of public communication, such a method may be useful and legitimate direction of our emotions in order to make the most of what we have, or it may simply be a way of using our emotions to delude us.

Listeners' emotions may be engaged through the language used in public communication. This topic will be touched on again as we discuss style and language, but it is important to point out here that the words that a speaker chooses to use can trigger emotional responses. Words do not, in and of themselves, have meaning; they only have meaning as we put that meaning into them. A word in a foreign language that we do not understand might simply be to us a collection of sounds. Translated, that same word could insult, amuse, anger, or excite us. Stories are often told of people being given something to eat which they report to be quite good, only to become physically ill when some name or label is attached to it (rattlesnake, or candied fisheyes, for example). Little children may chant that while sticks and stones will break their bones words will never hurt them, but words *do* hurt. Language can be a weapon. The use of epithets to taunt people can make them angry. The use of soothing and loving words can make people feel good. The words we choose reflect perceptions we have, and a speaker's choice of words can influence the perceptions that a listener forms. A person whose ideas usually, when expressed, lead to an extended discussion in the group, could be described by his or her superior as "provocative," or as "one who raises important issues." The same person could be described as "quarrelsome," or "a troublemaker." In both cases the actual behavior might be the same but the person initiating the message obviously *interprets* that behavior differently and *communicates* a different interpretation.

Speakers have been known to use language in place of argument, to dismiss the idea not by dissecting it, or by analyzing it, or by examining its weaknesses or strength, but simply by *calling* it something that is undesirable: the idea is too "socialistic;" the idea is too "radical"; the idea is too "conservative." Sometimes, a speaker can use language that has a strong negative emotional connotation for a listener, and the speaker may not be at all aware of it. In an interview, for example, a young man walked in and said to the interviewer, "That dude that just left said I should come in next." As it turns out the interviewer reacted very negatively to the word "dude." He associated it with nonbusinesslike slang. He perceived it as a kind of country-and-western "hick" way of speaking that prejudiced him against the interviewee immediately. Some listeners are extremely offended by what they take to be obscenities or "bad" language. They find the message obscured by their identification of the speaker with the contravening of important values. The speaker and listener both must recognize that language in context can produce strong associations with needs and values and thus arouse emotion. To be unaware of that can lead the speaker to blunders and it can lead the listener to act on the basis of emotionally triggered responses to language alone.

The listener's emotions are often engaged through the vivid description of pleasant or unpleasant situations. The use of the specific example was discussed earlier, and that discussion is relevant here. It was pointed out that telling a story about real people tends to promote identification between the audience and the subject. The simple telling of a story can make us feel ashamed or angry. A student, for example, once began a speech by describing in vivid detail an automobile accident. She went on to explain how the victims of the accident were rushed to the nearest hospital and how one of the victims was examined very quickly and without much attention put on a stretcher and left in a hallway. She described the patient's condition as the hours passed, and how doctors and nurses hurried by, some occasionally stopping for a quick look and then going on. As she told this story the sense of frustration and surprise and anger in the audience was apparent. Everyone wondered why on earth something wasn't being done for that patient. She concluded her story by explaining that the accident, which took place several years ago, involved a black woman who had been taken to a white hospital. Actually, the example was so vivid and the emotions aroused so real that the speaker had very little more to do to finish her speech. There is no doubt that listeners who are exposed to a careful and detailed narrative description have a strong likelihood of identifying their own needs and values within the context of that description and thereby respond immediately (Figure 15).

So far, we have been talking about listeners' emotions, their relationship to needs and values, and some tactics designed to engage these emotions. It remains for us to discuss two other important tactics designed to involve the audience: the tactical procedures associated with *attracting attention* and those associated with *establishing common ground*.

ENGAGING EMOTIONS

- Be emotionally involved.

- Develop argument on need/value–based premises

- Relate needs/values to the familiar.

- Use appropriate language.

- Use vivid descriptions.

Figure 15

Attracting Attention

There are several factors of attention and interest that can be used to heighten the involvement of an audience in a particular topic. Let us consider the most important of these.

1. *Listeners attend to things they perceive as vital.* A worker who has heard that his plant might close down within a few days throwing him out of work will go to a union meeting and listen carefully. He will attend to what's going on because what's going on is very important to him and he knows it. A student who wants to find a part-time job and goes to listen to a career officer talk about immediate openings will be likely to give full attention to the speech because what is said is so critical to him or her. Sometimes there are matters that are just as important to listeners but listeners are not as fully aware of the importance. Under those circumstances the speaker's job is to promote attention by stressing the importance of the topic.

2. *Listeners attend to the novel and to that which arouses their curiosity.* One student speech, for example, was exceptionally well received by an audience that listened very carefully because the speaker succeeded in arousing curiosity. He began by describing in vivid detail the way a traveler would have first have come onto the pyramids along the Nile. The speech, which was an informative one, was designed to promote understanding about the construction of the pyramids. This is not a topic that would seem on the surface to be greatly important to students or one that they would feel a great need to know about. It was, however, very interesting in and of itself and succeeded in satisfying the listener's curiosity about these engineering miracles.

3. *Listeners attend to messages that are characterized by conflict and contrast.* As anyone who reads the newspaper or watches a television news program knows, conflict is a basic element in much of what is reported. Vivid, dramatic interactions capture and hold our attention. They also tend to contrast with our normal daily routine. If we walked down the street in the summertime and saw someone coming toward us wearing a large fur-lined coat and hood, with corduroy pants and high boots we would undoubtedly notice that person; he would certainly draw our attention. If we were walking down the same street in January that person might pass us scarcely noticed. In the first instance his clothing would be in such contrast to everyone else's and in such conflict with the needs of the environment that we would attend to him. A wise speaker would not wish to provoke conflict between himself and his audience anymore than he would want the audience to feel that the speaker's ideas, behavior or attitudes were in direct contrast with the listeners'. What the speaker does hope to do is to enhance the dramatic or conflicting elements within his material, to demonstrate to the audience that the topic at hand is one that provokes different and intense reactions, for example.

4. *Listeners attend to messages that tend to resolve conflict.* Just as conflict interests us, we are also interested in establishing a kind

of equilibrium in our lives. If things are somehow unbalanced or somewhat out of phase or incomplete, we like to find ways of bringing about some balance, some completion. A speaker who carefully and clearly recognizes and identifies a problem that his listeners sense, or a void that they need filled, and proposes to resolve this difficulty is most likely to be assured of attention.

5. *Listeners attend to messages that afford them some measure of enjoyment.* The speaker who begins the speech with an anecdote or a story that is truly funny and then relates that story to the message that follows usually captures the audience's attention. There are dangers inherent in the use of humor, however; humor is a very difficult thing to carry off. Often, what seems very funny to one or two people might not seem so in an audience setting. A student once, for example, decided to report in an advanced speech class on an important historical parliamentary debate by describing it as Howard Cosell would describe it. That probably sounded very funny to him the night before, his roommate most likely agreed that it was an hilarious idea. But at 8:30 the next morning in a class of fairly serious students, and a very serious instructor, the humor was extremely strained and leaden. Some people think they should begin a speech by "telling a few jokes." Even if the jokes are funny and well told, if they don't relate to the speech they will only serve the most fleeting use as attention getters. For if they don't have anything to do with the speech they will become ends in themselves; it is quite possible listeners will only listen for other jokes and not for any more serious kinds of message. Nevertheless, we do attend to what we find enjoyable, to what helps us escape from realities that we may find depressing, that which might release us from current concerns or worries. Although this method of gaining attention must be approached cautiously, it is evident that listeners do attend under such circumstances (Figure 16).

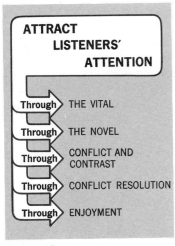

Figure 16

Speakers and listeners tend to become involved with others as they perceive similarities between them. Such similarities can promote understanding. When the speaker and the listener speak the same language, have the same kind of cultural background, share the same social and educational experiences it is quite natural that they would understand each other better. In such cases the speaker would use examples that involved either people or experiences with which both speaker and audience would be familiar, the speaker would understand what kinds of comparisons would be most appropriate for the listeners, the speaker would tend to rely on the same authorities to bolster arguments as would listeners.

Furthermore, we tend to find people who are similar to us attractive. In spite of the old adage that opposites attract, in reality, listeners often find themselves more attentive and more involved with speakers when they perceive themselves to be like them. We might even tend to minimize differences and exaggerate similarities when such attraction results. And people that we find less attractive we tend to respect and trust less.

Now, for all these tendencies for listeners to be involved with and respond positively to a source of communication that they perceive to be similar to themselves, it must be kept in mind that everyone is not always moved to act or to believe or to understand simply because the communicator is like the listener. Nevertheless, it is very important to realize that perceived similarities tend to facilitate the kind of communicative response that is desired. The process of establishing common ground involves both recognition of similarities and the use of those similarities in the preparation of the message. Similarities in experience and background that are relevant to the topic, for example, the speaker may wish to emphasize as he or she begins to talk. The speaker may wish to point out clearly what substantive similarities exist: that is to say, either the values or the ideas or the specific kinds of proposals on which both the speaker and the audience agree. Most likely the speaker will want to take his or her listeners a step further than they now are. He or she will either want to change or reinforce positions that these listeners now hold. It is likely that he or she will encounter areas of disagreement with the audience, but, if the common ground can be first established then areas of disagreement occur within a general context of agreement. It is a way for a listener to say to an audience, "We are not opposite people. We do not see the world in an entirely different way. Instead, because we are alike, because we share the same kinds of concerns, and because we want the same kinds of things, we can work out a good solution to our problems or come to some kind of agreement on what the best way is for us to proceed together."

Common ground is also promoted when membership ties are exposed. The speaker who belongs to the same kind of groups (social groups, political groups, ethnic groups, economic groups, and so forth) as does his listeners may promote a responsiveness on the part of the listeners depending on the extent to which such memberships are considered relevant.

Common ground, then, grows out of a shared experience between the listener and the speaker. The speaker should think very carefully and thoroughly about specific ways to establish common ground. This does not mean, however, that commonalities that don't exist should be created or false impressions given. Such ground would be very shaky indeed. As well as being totally unethical, such a practice would be very dangerous to the communicator if an audience sensed his insincerity. At its best, the establishment of common ground is an effort to bring the speaker and the listeners together as well as to bring all the potential listeners themselves together. One of the earliest examples of the attempt to establish common ground in American speechmaking was Thomas Jefferson's inaugural address. After a long and bitter political campaign Jefferson hoped to promote unity among those who had lately fought each other so doggedly and determinedly. The whole tone of his speech was one of conciliation. It was largely an attempt to establish common ground as is exemplified in the memorable passage: "But every difference in opinion is not a difference of principle. We have called by different names brethren of the same principle. We are all Republicans. We are all Federalists."

Involving the audience with the speaker and the speaker's message is, of course, a process that goes on throughout the entire speech. But it also does take on particular significance as the speech is introduced and as it is concluded. Let us now consider those tactics that could prove most useful in promoting the listeners' identification with the speaker and the speech as the message is begun and as it is ended.

The principles that govern audience involvement have already been discussed in this chapter. It is helpful here, however, to consider them as specific tactics to be used in the introduction. Of course, all these methods will not be used in every speech, but the speaker should consider the entire range of possibilities as he or she plans a message.

1. *Listeners can be told of the significance of the topic.* Basically, listeners' attention can be elicited by answering the question: To what extent and in what ways will the content of this message meet listeners' needs? The speaker needs to consider the ways in which his or her topic will promote the listener's well-being: financial, social, and emotional. If what the speaker is about to say will save the listener money then the listener should be made aware of that right away. If what the speaker has to say will make the listener healthier, then the listener ought to know that. The speaker's responsibility is to consider very carefully the ways in which his or her topic will touch on the lives of the listeners and make sure that the

listeners do understand these ways. Of course, the wise and careful listener will both help the speaker by trying to discern the ways in which the topic can influence the listener's life, and, will evaluate carefully whether or not the significance suggested by the speaker is real or strained simply to fit the case.

2. *Listeners can be challenged by a striking rhetorical question.* The unusual and the arresting, can immediately capture listeners' attention and make them want to hear more. One student, giving a speech on the need for universal safety and first aid training began his speech with the question, "Have you ever sat hopelessly by and watched your best friend die?" He went on to say that this is exactly what happened to a young man who had pulled his drowning friend out of the water, but then didn't know what to do to save the friend's life. It should be clearly understood that every question is not necessarily striking or interesting. Just raising a rhetorical question does not automatically engage an audience's interest. The speaker who began his speech with the question, "Did you have breakfast this morning?" probably felt that he was using an acceptable device to start his speech. Such a question, as important as it might be to the speaker or to what will follow, is hardly striking. Also, in raising questions as in every other aspect of the speech, the speaker needs to remember that the speaker's and the listeners' interests are not identical. One speaker, beginning his speech with a question, totally ignored the fact that everyone in the audience was not caught up, as he was, in a particular sporting event. The result was slightly ludicrous when he began his speech by saying, "I suppose why you are wondering: how would I go about pole vaulting?" The significant question is one that challenges the audience to respond; one that starts listeners thinking and feeling about the subject.

3. *Listeners can be drawn into the topic through the use of an extended example.* Speakers who begin with a story, whether it is humorous, exciting, or horrifying, usually gain attention immediately and lead the audience into the speech itself. Of course any example or story used needs to be relevant. A good story is not good at all if it doesn't make precisely the point the speaker hopes to make. This is why just telling jokes is not a good way to introduce a speech. One student, for example, began her speech by telling a very pertinent story of her friend Craig. In detail, she explained how Craig had a serious financial problem and was afraid he would have to drop out of school. She told of the day in which Craig went to register and asked for a deferred payment only to be told that he had to have a voucher from the student aid office in order to do this. She explained Craig's long wait to see the student aid officer, his recounting his problems, and the student aid officer's response: certainly Craig could get a voucher promising financial aid as soon as he produced his enrollment cards that demonstrated he was a student! Craig's travels between the registrar and the student aid officer were elaborated as the speaker continued in her opening story. By the time

she finished the audience was both amused at the foibles of the bureaucracy as well as indignant that a student should have been put through such difficulties. Listeners had begun to identify with the student and certainly to be interested in both the nature of the problem and the way it might be solved.

4. *Listeners can be interested by provocative quotations or statements.* There are times when someone has stated a thought particularly well, or when someone has made a statement that is bound to grasp the audience's attention, or when someone with whom the audience strongly identifies has commented on the topic at hand. In all these cases, one sensible tactic would be to begin the speech with the appropriate quotation. One speaker, for example, began her speech to a largely black audience with this quotation from Malcolm X: "So, I'm not standing here speaking to you as an American, or patriot, or flag-saluter, or flag waver, no, not I. I'm speaking as a victim of this American system. And I see America through the eyes of the victim. I don't see any American dream; I see an American nightmare." Such a quotation served the dual purpose of coming from someone with whom many in the audience may have strongly identified, and also served as a quite unusual, interesting way of expressing the strong sense of frustration felt by many members of the audience. Another student speaker began a speech in which she used statistical information to form a provocative statement, pointing out that psychiatrists predicted that 1000 college students would kill themselves in the following year, that another 9000 would try and fail, and that 90,000 would threaten to commit suicide. She added that the suicide rate for college students was 50 percent higher than that for the general population. Bearing in mind that all material used must be relevant, the speaker can select carefully either from the words of others or from unusual or different kinds of information that which will help to engage an audience's interest and attention and involve them with the topic of the speech.

5. *Listeners can be reminded of a specific situation out of which the speech grows.* Obviously the goals of an organization sponsoring the meeting at which a speaker appears, or the reason for calling the meeting, or the national, local, or campus situation out of which the speech grows can all be referred to in order to interest the audience. Furthermore, in the *immediate* situation, such things as the content of previous speeches may also be incorporated into the introduction. One student speaker, for example, combined the emphasis on the significance of the topic with the use of immediate situation when he began his speech by saying, "All of you have sat here for the past several class meetings patiently and politely listening to speeches. Many of you, I'm sure, would have rather been somewhere else, some of the time. I appreciate the fact that you've all come to listen to my speech even though you don't have a speech of your own to give. I hope that today your patience and endurance is really going to pay off for you. Because today I'm going to tell you something

that is going to save you money—a lot of money, and it's going to begin saving you money right away."

6. *Listeners can be prepared for the content of the speech.* Listeners can sometimes listen and follow a speech much better if they have some idea in advance about what's going on. For example, the speaker could, in the introduction of his or her speech, help the audience to understand and follow the message, and therefore help the audience become more involved, by either stating the main point of the speech and or by presenting some kind of initial summary of the speech in which the major points are laid out. Such a "preview" of a speech should help keep the listeners with the speaker as he or she progresses through the speech itself.

Concluding Messages

The conclusion to the speech is the speaker's last word. This is his or her final chance to leave a positive impression with the listeners. Essentially there are three important considerations for the speaker to keep in mind as the message is brought to a close.

1. *Listeners should be left with the overriding feeling of the speech.* The speech has, hopefully, created strong feelings or a mood that the speaker hopes they will feel. For example, the speaker who began her speech with the story of Craig's battle with the bureaucracy wanted to leave her audience with a feeling of indignation. She ended with the story of what happened to Craig when, as a result of red tape, he finally gave up his college education and found himself in real difficulties getting a job. Feelings that a good person was wasted, that technicalities upset someone's life, left the audience angry about the system and insistent that something ought to be done to change it. It is important to realize here that just as the mood of the speech can be sustained, it can also be completely destroyed. Some speakers seem not to conclude but just to stop. This often leaves the audience with the feeling that somehow the speech hasn't been closed properly. Many television programs will end with a short epilogue of sorts, which in a few minutes resolves the loose ends of the story and reinforces the tone of the program. Many viewers would feel disoriented if this final short session did not occur, just as listeners would feel if the speech was not properly concluded. A weak, ineffectual, or rambling ending, as well as no ending at all, will contribute to the destruction of the feeling the speech should project.

2. *The listeners should be left with a clear idea of the content of the speech.* After all the points have been made the speaker can help the listener considerably by going back and either restating or reiterating the major point, or summarizing and reviewing the main ideas. The conclusion is not the place to introduce new and different material; this can be confusing and misleading for an audience. It may well be the place for the speaker to tie the whole thing together by a quick review of what has been said already. It is well to remember here the point that was made earlier—that a listener does

not have the opportunity to stop a speaker and go back as he does to stop himself while he's reading and go back to the previous page. The listener must depend on the speaker alone to fill in any gaps in comprehension and to emphasize what the speaker wants emphasized. A concluding summary is usually very helpful in doing just this.

3. *The listener might be left with concrete suggestions for action.* If the speaker has successfully aroused the concern of listeners, if he or she has convinced them that there is a certain wrong that needs to be righted or that there is a good solution to an important problem, the listener will naturally look for something to *do* about it. The last word the speaker leaves with the audience, in those situations where it is appropriate, could well be a word of direct suggestion. The speaker would then give the audience some way to follow through on the message that has been delivered.

Summary

We have considered here the task of finding ways to involve the audience so as to promote the communicative purposes of the public communication message. The speaker needs to consider as he or she gathers and assembles evidence, that material that will demonstrate to listeners how their needs might be best met, and that will appeal to their values and beliefs. The speaker through his or her own emotional involvement, through identification of the needs and values with argumentative premises, through demonstration of stability, through proper language choice, and through the vivid description of experience may engage the emotions of listeners.

In devising tactics to increase attention and interest, the speaker will try to show the vital relationship of the topic to the listener, make use of the novel, uncover elements of conflict, point to ways to resolve conflict, and search for that which the audience will enjoy.

As shared experiences are exposed and presented, common ground between the speaker and listener can be created. Listener and speaker alike need to be wary of commonalities that are falsely created and search for genuine ties that bind the participants in the public communication process. The introductions to speeches can be designed to involve audiences further by stressing significance, challenging through a rhetorical question, using an extended example, stimulated by provocative quotations or statements, or reminded of the specific situation out of which the speech grows. Conclusions should leave the audience with the overriding feeling of the speech, a clear idea of the content, and suggestions for action.

As we looked at the public communication process thus far, we have considered the audience and the speaker and their relationship, the design of a strategy of purpose, and a strategy of form, along with tactics designed to promote successful communication by making ideas believable and understandable to listeners. Now it is time to consider in more detail the means whereby the speaker can integrate strategy and tactics as he or she prepares to communicate: the process of outlining.

Select Bibliography

The following citations, and those listed in all the bibliographies, offer further practical and theoretical information related to the chapter topics, and they provide a starting point for the student who wishes to undertake more intensive study and research into the topic.

James R. Andrews, "Reflections of the National Character in American Rhetoric," *Quarterly Journal of Speech,* **62**(1971), 316-324.

Samuel L. Becker, "Research on Emotional and Logical Proofs," *Southern Speech Communication Journal,* **28**(1963), 208-218.

Samuel L. Becker, "Research on Emotional and Logical Proofs," *Southern Speech Journal,* **28**(1973), 198-207.

Dalbir Bindra and Jane Stewart, eds., *Motivation.* Baltimore: Penguin Books, 1966.

Charles N. Cofer and Mortimer H. Appley, *Motivation: Theory and Research.* New York: John Wiley and Sons, 1964.

Lane Cooper, ed., *The Rhetoric of Aristotle.* New York: Appleton-Century-Crofts, 1932.

Richard E. Crable and John J. Mukay, "Kenneth Burke's Concept of Motives in Rhetorical Theory," *Today's Speech,* **20**(1972), 11-18.

Gary Cronkhite, "Logic, Emotion, and the Paradigm of Persuasion," *Quarterly Journal of Speech,* **50**(1964), 13-18.

Joel R. Davitz, ed., *The Communication of Emotional Meaning.* New York: McGraw-Hill, 1964.

Walter R. Fisher, "A Motive View of Communication," *Quarterly Journal of Speech,* **61**(1970), 131-139.

Alfred A. Funk, "Logical and Emotional Proofs: A Counterview," *Speech Teacher,* **17**(1968), 210-216.

Peter H. Knapp, ed., *Expression of the Emotions in Man.* New York: International Universities Press, 1963.

Abraham H. Maslow, "A Dynamic Theory of Human Motivation," *Psychological Review,* **50**(1943), 370-396.

Abraham H. Maslow, *Motivation and Personality.* New York: Harper & Row, 1954.

Abraham H. Maslow, *Toward A Psychology of Being.* New York: Van Nostrand-Reinhold, 1962.

Ivan L. Preston, "Relationships among Emotional, Intellectual and Rational Appeals in Advertising," *Speech Monographs,* **35**(1968), 504-511.

Milton Rokeach, *Beliefs, Attitudes and Values.* San Francisco: Jossey-Bass, 1968.

Milton Rokeach, *The Nature of Human Values*. New York: Free Press, 1973.

Herbert W. Simons, "Psychological Theories of Persuasion: An Auditor's Report," *Quarterly Journal of Speech*, **57**(1971), 383-392.

Raymond G. Smith, "Motivation and Communication Theory," *Central States Speech Journal*, **15**(1964), 96-99.

Edward Steele and W. Charles Redding, "The American Value System: Premises for Persuasion," *Western Speech*, **26**(1962), 83-91.

Otis Walter, "Toward an Analysis of Motivation," *Quarterly Journal of Speech*, **41**(1955), 271-278.

W. Weiss, "Emotional Arousal and Attitude Change," *Psychological Reports*, **6**(1966), 267-280.

PART FOUR
communication skills

CHAPTER 8

outlining: a synthesis of strategy and tactics

A beginning speaker introduced his first classroom speech by saying, "How many times have you either gone to class in the morning, or to work, and heard somebody say, 'Boy, I must have slept on the wrong side of the bed last night, my neck is killing me.'" The introduction thus dispensed with, the speaker went on to raise the rhetorical question, "What is Super Marvel?" and answered it with the information that Super Marvel was a mechanical muscle relaxer that had been on the market for 53 years. He continued by explaining that Super Marvel, unlike other treatments for aches and pains, was not a greasy cream or ointment and needed only an electrical source to operate. Producing a Super Marvel from a bag, the speaker asserted that it could be used for mechanical muscle massage or converted for an electrical impulse treatment. He concluded, "The next time you go to the store looking for relief from common body ache, don't ask for a cream or an ointment, ask for the Super Marvel." *Would you?* Probably not; as most of the speaker's listeners probably would not. There is a lot wrong with that speech; the strategic considerations of purpose, structure, and form do not appear to have been given much thought; the tactical choices designed to make ideas understandable and believable and to involve the audience are severely limited. The speaker obviously did not prepare himself well. He took some time (but not very much) and he made some effort to put a message together. The fact that preparation is inadequate is demonstrated by the following outline.

The Super Marvel

Specific Purpose
To introduce the audience to one of the most successful treatments of the common body (muscle) aches.

Introduction
How many times have you either gone to class in the morning (or work) and heard somebody say "Boy, I must have slept on the wrong side of the bed last night, my neck is killing me."

Body
 1. What is the Super Marvel?
  A. A mechanical muscle relaxer
  B. Has been on the market for 53 years
 2. Advantages of the Super Marvel over common treatments of aches and pains
  A. No greasy ointments or creams involved
  B. No side effects
  C. Only need an electrical source to operate
 3. Demonstration of the Super Marvel
  A. Showing muscle massage
  B. Showing electrical impulse treatment

Conclusion
The next time you go to the drug store looking for relief from a common body ache, don't ask for a cream or ointment, ask for the Super Marvel!

Bibliography
No sources but myself.

It should be obvious to anyone who has read this book that the Super Marvel outline is evidence of poor preparation. The point to be emphasized here is that it is the *preparation* that is being faulted, because the outline should be the *result* of the way the speaker prepares him or herself to speak, and *not* just a division of the speech into some sets or categories.

Outlining, then, is a process. The outline grows as the speaker gets ready to speak. The outline is *not* something that one does as the final link in the chain of events leading to the speech. Nor is it a set of notes to be assembled just before practicing for the speech. It should *emerge* as the speaker goes along. Let us consider the Super Marvel outline in some detail as an example.

The first strategic choice involves purpose. As the speaker develops his or her purpose, he or she will be creating the first, crucial determinant of the outline. You will remember that it is from the purpose that structural strategies emerge as the speaker decides what ideas will further the purpose and how they should be put together. Strategically, it is apparent that the Super Marvel speaker made initial errors. First, he did not formulate clearly his purpose in terms of audience response. "To introduce the audience" to something does not describe the response. Accordingly, there is some confusion about whether the speech is essentially an informative or a persuasive one. This initial ambiguity helps to explain the problem in conceptualizing the main ideas and forming them into a coherent structure. The first idea should not be a question, "What is a Super Marvel?" but, rather the *answer* to the question, something like, "Super Marvel is a mechanical muscle relaxer." *If* the purpose is, "I want my audience to understand what a Super Marvel is," then that is probably a good first idea.

The second idea is not correctly stated either; it is a heading for a list of advantages and not what the audience should believe or understand. Again, there is a problem here because the purpose is not clear. What the speaker probably has in mind is a persuasive purpose, such as, "I want my audience to agree with me that the Super Marvel will improve their health," or "I want my audience to buy Super Marvel." These purposes could generate different structural and ideational strategies. If the purpose is to get audience adherence to the proposition that the device might improve health, the first idea should most likely deal with the relation of the device to well being, such as, *"Pain resulting from tension or muscle fatigue can be reduced or eliminated through electric massage."* The same idea could begin a speech with the second purpose, buying the device, but would more likely result in a set of ideas that *stress* the advantages the speaker mentions along with several others that should be devised dealing with matters of cost, safety, and so forth.

The speaker planned, as his third point, a "Demonstration of the Super Marvel." Now that is *not an idea.* What purpose does the demonstration serve? The idea might be that *the Super Marvel is easy to use,* and one way to make that idea believable is to show the audience. But whether or not this is an idea that should be in the speech at all depends on the strategic considerations of purpose and structure, and in this case these considerations are too vague. So the fault with the outline at this stage is a fault in *preparing.*

The outline illustrates preparation problems related to tactical concerns as well. A quick examination of the outline shows that there is almost no effort made to make ideas believable and/or understandable through the development of those ideas, nor is there conscious effort to involve the audience in the subject. Of course, the tactics are dependent on the strategy, so if there is no clear purpose and structure, it will be impossible to provide enough supporting material, or even to know what kind of supporting material should be provided. But if one takes what is in point II and restates it as an idea, *Super Marvel is the most effective way to treat common aches and pains,* then it is plain to see how inadequately the speaker has planned to support that idea. One appeal is obviously to cleanliness since no messy creams and ointments are used. There is a reference to "no side effects," but that makes one raise the question of what side effects are caused by *other* remedies. And what *are* the other remedies, anyway? The only common treatment mentioned is the use of creams and ointments. The final piece of support given the idea is that it needs only an electrical source. But, since creams need no electricity at all, and thus could be used anywhere, as well as calling for no expenditure of energy, a need for an electrical source might be said to be a *disadvantage.*

This illustrative discussion of the outline should indicate that things went very wrong as the speaker got ready to speak. The communication process itself may be seen as constructing and applying a model of information and appeals—the construction and use of strategy and tactics—that the outline evidences. So one does not *do* the outline as if it were an additional technicality to satisfy some critic. *One builds an outline as one prepares him or herself to speak.* The result is concrete; not only something for an instructor to criticize and react to, but also a tangible map of experience that a speaker can use him or herself as a tool for self-criticism and self-regulation as he or she prepares for the public communication process.

Learning to Evaluate Preparation

An excellent way to begin to see and understand preparation problems and avoid them as one participates in the communication process is by developing an awareness of and sensitivity to what a good outline is like. This is often very hard to do just by looking at samples in textbooks. The remainder of this chapter presents two real outlines—those turned in by beginning speakers in a public communication class—and illustrates some of the ways an instructor might point out their shortcomings and suggest improvement. This is followed by a statement that lays out in summary form the guidelines for evaluating outlines (and, hence, preparation). Finally, several additional samples of real outlines are presented, without analysis, for your own investigation and evaluation.

Outline 1. The Zodiac

Specific Purpose
To explain how zodiac signs got their names.

Introduction
  I. The Zodiac is an imaginary belt in the heavens that extends for several degrees on either side of the path of the sun.
    A. This path is called the ecliptic
      1. The ecliptic is divided into 12 sections of 3 degrees
      2. These sections are known as the Houses of the Zodiac
    B. The sun takes a year to travel through the 12 houses
      1. These months are not the ones we are familiar with
      2. They are periods from the 21st of our months to the twentieth of the next (approximately)
    C. The beginning of the zodiacal year is when the sun enters the house of Aries
      1. From this time the days are longer than the nights and are increasing in length

Body
  II. The first sign is Aries
    A. The constellation of Aries is a group of three very bright stars visible to the naked eye
      1. The brightest is referred to as the Ram

B. The Babylonians and the Chinese gave great prominence to Aries
   1. Aries was believed to have occupied the center of the heavens
   2. The symbol for Aries is the Ram
   3. In early religions the symbol of sacrifice was the ram
III. The second sign is Taurus
   A. This constellation is a beautiful cluster of stars
      1. The constellation's name is *Hyades* from Greek meaning "rain"
      2. Its influence is believed to be conducive to rain
   B. Taurus was named after the seven daughters of Atlas
      1. Because of their great virtue and purity were rewarded by a place in the heavens as a constellation of stars
      2. The symbol of Taurus is the bull
IV. The third sign is Gemini
   A. In the earliest zodiacs this house was symbolized by two kids
   B. The Greeks substituted twin children
      1. The sons of Jupiter, Castor and Pollux
   C. The myth of Castor and Pollux
      1. Castor was killed in battle, and Pollux, overwhelmed at his loss, asked Jupiter to restore his brother to life or make them both immortal
      2. As a reward and in recognition of their noble deeds when on earth, Jupiter turned the two brothers into the constellation Gemini
V. The fourth is Cancer
   A. Cancer, the crab, was placed in the heavens as a reward
      1. The goddess Juno rewarded Cancer for the sacrifice of its life, which it lost in an attack on Hercules, in her service
VI. The fifth sign is Leo
   A. In Greek mythology the lion is said to represent the monster who was the terror of travelers in the forests of Nemaea
      1. He was slain by Hercules in battle
      2. To commemorate the great combat Jupiter gave it a place amongst the stars
VII. The sixth sign is Virgo
   A. In mythology Virgo was represented by Isis
      1. She was the goddess of harvests and fruits
      2. She is said to have invented the arts of husbandry
      3. Previous to this humanity existed on a diet of acorns
VIII. The seventh sign is Libra
   A. Libra is symbolized by a pair of scales
   B. Libra was not included in the earliest zodiacs and it has not yet been determined how it got its name

IX. The eighth sign is Scorpio
   A. According to Greek mythology the scorpion was placed in the heavens by Juno Queen of the gods
      1. Scorpio carried out Juno's wishes by stinging Orion
      2. Orion had offended the goddess by boasting that he could subdue the wildest and fiercest beast
      3. Orion died from the effects of the sting
X. The ninth sign is Sagittarius
   A. This sign is named after Chiron the son of Saturn
      1. Chiron studied medicine and became a skilled physician
      2. Chiron was also a famous astronomer and scientist
      3. He was the instructor of Achilles and Hercules
   B. Chiron became a zodiac sign by accident
      1. Chiron dropped one of Hercule's poison arrows on his foot
      2. Being born of immortal parents he could not die
      3. He was released from his pain by becoming a Zodiac sign
XI. The tenth sign is Capricorn
   A. Capricorn is usually seen as half goat and half fish
   B. This is explained by an adventure of the god Pan
      1. Pan while feasting on the banks of the Nile was attacked by the monster Typhon
      2. In order to escape Pan jumped into the river and took the form of a fish for the lower body and a goat for the upper half
XII. The eleventh sign is Aquarius
   A. It is not really known how Aquarius got its name
      1. It is believed Aquarius gots its name from the ancient Chinese but no one is sure
XIII. The twelfth sign is Pisces
   A. In ancient Grecian mythology it is recorded that two fishes were placed in the heavens by the goddess Minerva
      1. To commemorate the escape of Venus and her son Cupid from the monster Typhon
      2. To escape, Venus and Cupid transformed themselves into fishes and plunged into the river which took them to safety
XIV. There are a lot of books on zodiac mythology
   A. It makes for very enjoyable reading

Bibliography
William Thomas and Kate Pavitt, *The Book of Talismans, Amulets, and Zodiac Gems*. London: Rider & Company, n.d.

Outline 1. The Zodiac
The purpose of this speech is *not* stated as audience response. "To explain" is a speaker-centered description and not an audience-cen-

tered one. Probably, the speaker hopes to have the listeners understand how the zodiac signs were named. Given this purpose, the structure that has been used is a very poor one. Each sign is named as an "idea," giving 12 "ideas" that don't help to accomplish the purpose. Looking at the main ideas will not provide many clues as to *how* the signs were named at all. The structure that is suggested by the purpose should be one that would help the audience first to know just what the zodiac signs are, the differences between "signs" and "constellations," and then to see relationships between the signs and their names. The "Introduction" to the speech seems really to be the first main idea, one that tries to explain what the zodiac is. The ideas that follow, however, do not promote understandings of the *origin* of the names. As the speaker was preparing himself he should have asked: Did the signs get their names in different ways? What were these ways? In fact, the outline taken as a whole makes it very difficult to see exactly *how* any got their names. The speaker probably was thinking about "saying something interesting" about each one of the signs instead of focusing on the audience's response. It appears that some of the signs were named for animals and some for gods or goddesses in Greek mythology, but *how* were they named? Were they named because they *looked* like particular figures to observers? The signs are often represented somewhat like the "connect the dots" games that children play, suggesting that by drawing lines connected the stars one can produce a picture that looks like a bull or a crab.

To develop the purpose as restated here, the main ideas for the speech might be:

I. Some signs were named because their configuration looked to observers like the shapes of certain animals.
II. Some signs were named because their configuration suggested to some observers the shape of mythical characters.
III. The origin of the name of one sign is obscure.

Such a group of main ideas seems more likely to promote the specific purpose of the speech than the listing of 12 signs.

Of course, the tactics used to develop the ideas would now be different from those in the outline. The speaker would need to uncover and arrange those materials that make the ideas more understandable and believable. In this kind of speech, examples would probably be the most frequently used form of support. Thus, Leo looks like a lion and Cancer looks like a crab. Yet, if you will look carefully at the original outline, you will see how careless preparation leads to difficulty as we attempt to reconstruct the outline. The speaker must know more about the subject than we, the critics, do, and so should be able to determine the accuracy of certain information and its best place in the scheme of the speech. The speaker in this case has not supplied enough information for us to decide if the shape came first, and then a story was made up to explain it, or if there was a story to explain the constellation and then the "symbol" was taken because of shape. Look at Taurus. The speaker has not really prepared to deal with how that name came about. Probably there are seven stars (a fact not mentioned) and mythology accounted for this fact more than for the fact that a line drawing would come out like a bull. So this is somehow different from Leo or Cancer, the *names* for lion or crab. And then there is Aries, whose "symbol" is the ram, but the *origin of whose name* is never mentioned.

The organizational pattern that is suggested here might not be the best one if the speaker's purpose was not the one we hypothesized. It becomes obvious that there is a lot of anecdotal material, examples of how Greek mythology accounted for the constellations, that doesn't fit into this new outline that is devoted exclusively to the *names of signs*. What becomes apparent as we examine the outline in detail is that the speaker's preparation was governed by a deep misconception of purpose; the speaker seems to have come across a book about the Zodiac and is going to use it to tell the audience something about each sign. As a result, the speech will be very difficult to follow, and generalizations very hard to remember, while a few assorted, but not integrated, facts may remain. Furthermore, there is no planned introduction or conclusion. How can listeners be made interested in this topic? Does it relate in any way to their needs or values? There is no consideration here of the methods suggested for identifying the audience with the topic and helping them to follow what will come. And in the conclusion there seems to be only a quick reference to a book. The speaker has not wrapped up this speech and not left the listeners with the overriding theme or mood of the speech.

This analysis should show more than that the speaker "has not put the ideas together" correctly. It demonstrates that the preparation began with a poor conception of purpose and form, and proceeded with a very limited and not appropriately focused set of tactics.

Outline 2. From Sugar to Honey
Specific Purpose
To persuade listeners to give up refined white sugar and to use honey as a substitute when necessary.

Introduction
After a nice weekend did you ever wake up on that first day of the week with a disease called the "Monday morning blues"? Well you may think the sole reason is because you have to be in class at 8:00 A.M., but there may be another reason that can easily be eliminated if you would just give up refined white sugar and use natural sugar such as honey. I'd like to tell you just what refined sugar is and how honey can benefit you, also how to substitute honey in your cooking.

Body
    I. Refined sugars are stripped of their nutritional value during the refining process

A. Grapes as an example on why this is done
   1. Will keep practically forever
   2. Could have them in condensed form to put on the table
   3. Could flavor food with their sweet taste summer and winter
B. Result of refining process is a vitamin B loss
   1. Vitamin B is necessary to burn the sugars in digestion so it steals vitamins from vital organs, nerves, muscles, liver, kidneys, stomach, heart, skin, eyes, and blood
   2. Results of Niacin deficiency: will make a strong courageous person cowardly, apprehensive, suspicious, mentally confused and depressed
II. Honey, as a nutritious, natural sugar, contains protein calcium, phosphorus, sodium, potassium, and 9 of the 10 amino acids necessary for human nutrition, and vitamins B and C
III. Calorie content of honey is less in proportion to sweetening power of sugar
A. Need half as much honey as sugar
B. Save 33 percent of sweetening calories
IV. How to substitute honey for sugar
A. Use half as much honey as sugar
B. Dark honey
   1. Better on breads
   2. As syrup on pancakes
C. Light honeys
   1. Come from early spring crops
   2. Suited for cakes, cookies, light breads, fruits, tea
D. Use more flour or less liquid to get right consistency.
E. Oven temperature when making cookies and breads is 25 degrees less, because will brown faster.
F. Cakes and cookies cooked with honey are moister and fresher.
G. In jams, jellies, and preserves use half as much honey as sugar that the recipe calls for.
H. Thin honey before adding to beaten egg white
   1. Meringue
   2. Cake frostings
I. How to thin honey
V. It is easy to store in refrigerator
   1. Becomes hard to pour
   2. May crystallize and get grainy
      a. Just thin to return to normal state
      b. Will not hurt quality of honey or alter consistency permanently

Conclusion
I'm not suggesting you deliberately add honey to your diet, because honey is a carbohydrate and most of us get too much carbohy-

drated food in comparison to our protein consumption. But if you feel you need a sweetener on cereals or on fruit by all means use honey instead of sugar, it is a healthy food which is easily substituted for sugar. Also you need half as much so you save half the calories. You might like to know that when craving sugar that that is a natural way of getting us to eat vitamins and minerals, since they are tasteless; you wouldn't eat them if they weren't put in a sweet form, so when you are craving sweets it is craving sweets because it needs those vitamins and minerals that come in the sweet form, and remember with sugar cane, they stripped away all the vitamins so you get calories and nothing else, so get sugar the way nature meant for us, eat foods with sugar that still have vitamins and minerals, and if you need sweetener use honey, and wake up on Monday morning with a smile.

Bibliography

J. I. Rodale, *Health Builder.* Emmaus, Pennsylvania: Rodale Press, Inc., 1959.

"I'll Take Honey, Thank You." *Prevention,* pp. 132-137.

Outline 2. From Sugar to Honey

The speaker's purpose in this case is fairly clear; she calls for direct action on the part of the listeners by giving up refined sugar and substituting honey in its place when it is necessary to use sweetening at all. (The purpose, however, could be somewhat more precisely stated in line with the suggestions offered in this book by phrasing it: "*I want my audience to* give up refined white sugar and to use honey as a substitute when necessary.") But the purpose is fairly clear and direct in this case.

To further that purpose, the speaker has come up with five main ideas. The first idea (*refined sugars are stripped of their nutritional value during the refining process*) is obviously designed to show that refined sugars are harmful. This, of course, makes sense; if the speaker hopes that we will stop using the product, she certainly needs to make us believe that it is good for us to do so. The idea that the nutritional values are gone is supported by an example (which is not very clear as it appears in the outline and makes one wonder if the speaker is *sure* of the point to be made), and by an assertion that vitamin B is lost in the refining process. The loss of vitamin B is further amplified as the speaker describes what happens in the body to get necessary vitamin B, and gives one example of what can happen to someone who suffers a niacin loss.

There are many problems with the planning of this idea. It is certainly a good and useful enough one given the purpose, but it seems inadequately and incorrectly developed. II. B. reads, "Result of refining process is a vitamin B loss." But the material that supports this assertion is a claim that, since Vitamin B is necessary to burn sugar *in the body,* Vitamin B is stolen from vital organs. Yet what happens in the body is not a way of making clear how vitamin B is removed during the refining process. The material necessary to support B. is that which contributes to our understanding and belief that the vitamin is removed during refining. What B.1. suggests is that there is some harm to the body by the depletion of Vitamin B caused by the body's attempt to burn sugar. That point is larger than the matter of loss of nutritional value. What is needed here are two main ideas: I. *Refined sugars are stripped of their nutritional value during the refining process*, and II. *Refined sugars can be directly harmful to the human body*. Now the speaker needs to consider how well she has planned to support each of these ideas. The first point is supported only by the grape example, and the second point only by the assertion that sugar "steals" vitamins from vital organs. Obviously, for an audience to be convinced, more is needed. Testimony of nutritionists could be brought to bear on the question of the results of the refining process, and of nutritionists and medical authorities on the point of its damage to the body. Examples in the form of medical case studies or hypothetical descriptions of what could happen could be used to assess the effect of sugar on the body. Statistical information indicating the extent of the problem could be adduced. Comparisons between the effects of other harmful substances and sugar could be made. Indeed, if the speaker really hopes to get an audience to change its behavior, considerable preparation must go into amassing enough evidence to make a case beyond merely telling each listener that a substance is bad for him or her. The point B.2. has not been considered so far. This point suggests that there is another main idea that the speaker should explore and develop: III. *Refined sugar could, by creating certain imbalances, cause undesirable changes in behavior*. This is a point that would require additional evidence of a medical and psychological nature. The important point being made here is that the speaker tried to cover in a very quick and superficial way what was really important in helping to bring about the change she desired.

The same criticism can apply to points II and III. These are totally unsupported statements that claim that honey, as concentrated with refined sugar, is good for you. Perhaps the two points fit together as one: *Honey is a natural sugar and, unlike refined sugars, is good for you*. This point could then be developed by a much fuller elaboration of the nutritional values of honey and the advantages in terms of caloric intake. Here, too, the speaker would need statistical, testimonial, and comparative support, as well as specific examples that would further involve the audience in the extent and nature of the problem, *as a problem to them*.

The main ideas IV and V both relate to the ways in which honey can be used as a substitute, and could profitably be combined into one idea. IV. *How to substitute honey for sugar* is not a complete sentence and, perhaps, a simple, short list of reminders that touched on quantities, light versus dark, ways to store, and so forth. Given the nature of the audience—a beginning public speaking class of undergraduates—the specific details on baking might better have been eliminated.

The speaker has made an effort here to plan an introduction that relates to the feelings of the audience and gives a brief summary of what will happen in the speech. But more is needed to involve the audience if they are to believe that this is a serious health matter. Perhaps some striking medical testimony, or a surprising statistic that dramatically illustrates the extent of the problem, or a specific example of a medical incident would serve the purposes of involvement. The conclusion includes an attempt on the part of the speaker to effect closure by going back to the opening through the "Monday morning" reference. But there is a very jumbled quality that is partly a result of the initial problems in the ideas of the speech, and a careful summary of the ideas as revised, coupled with a final word in the form of a quotation or an example, would end the speech on a sounder note.

Guidelines for Evaluation

From all that has been written thus far, and from the examples of ways in which one might begin to evaluate preparation just presented, let us construct a set of summary guidelines to help you as you analyze the sample student outlines that follow and, subsequently, your own preparation.

1. *In evaluating preparation consider the purpose.* The purpose should be clearly stated as a response desired from the audience.
2. *In evaluating preparation consider the main ideas and their relationship to the purpose.* The ideas should be those that serve to promote the purpose by moving the audience in the direction desired by the speaker.
3. *In evaluating preparation consider the adequacy of supporting material.* The ideas need to be developed through the use of ample forms of communicative evidence such as examples, testimony, statistics, comparison, and through sufficient motivational material to involve the audience in the topic.
4. *In evaluating preparation consider the ways in which the message is introduced and concluded.* The speaker must plan to engage the audience's interest immediately and to help them follow what will come in the speech; he or she must end on a note that ties the speech together and leave the listeners with an appropriate sense of closure.

Anyone who has been reading this book carefully knows that to do the above things is not simple. And its not always simple to know how well others have done them. As you study the outlines that follow try to improve your ability to spot problems that the speaker had in preparation. These outlines are, remember, not made up for this book; they are real ones that beginning students like yourself turned in. Chances are, you may share some of the same problems with them. If you can learn to tell what's wrong with their preparation and to give suggestions for improving preparation, then it is likely that you will be able to look at your outline, diagnose your own problems, and improve your own preparation the next time you speak. Furthermore, if you can begin to see what's wrong with preparation by examining an outline, it will sharpen your skills at identifying what's wrong with a speech as you hear it, thus making you a better and more critical listener.

Title. Child Abuse

Purpose
To get my audience to understand the intensity of the problem of child abuse; also, to make them aware of what they can do if they suspect a certain person.

Introduction
One of the most common causes for permanent physical injury and death of young children is child abuse, amounting to some 60,000 cases per year. Most of these children are under three years of age. Almost half of them are under one year of age. They are totally defenseless.

Many people don't want to get involved, they think it's not their business, but it is. Child abuse causes children to be bitter, hostile, and harsh toward the world. It has been diagnosed as one of the reasons for the following person's behavior:
1. Lee Harvey Oswald
2. Jack Ruby
3. Charles Manson

These people have been a threat to our society.
  I. Majority of all criminals were victims of child abuse.
 II. Child abuse is detrimental to protect child and each one of us.
III. Our world is what we make it, by molding ourselves, our children, and our society.

Body
  I. An example of one poor woman who beat her children
    1. One child disobeyed
    2. Mother beat her over her head with a frying pan and killed her.
 II. Stepmother kills step-daughter
    1. Stepmother would beat step-daughter
    2. Then bathe her in bleach
    3. Take her out and swab her wounds with an SOS pad
    4. The girl got gangrene and died.
III. One man killed his son over a poster.
    1. The child tore the posters

2. The father tied it to an electric cord and swung it around the room.
IV. What are the parents like?
1. Nine out of ten parents are considered normal.
2. Child abuse is inflicted by those who were abused when they were children.
3. The parent identifies with authority yet takes out anger and wrath on child.
4. Symptoms of the parents
One woman came to the hospital
1) chest pains
2) headaches
3) weakness
4) dizziness
Yet there was no apparent reason for all of the following.
5) finally a psychiatrist examined her to find out she had beaten her two daughters and threw them up against the wall.
5. "Child abuse reflects the folklore of a prejudiced society. What most people think they know about the battered child syndrome isn't so." (*The Nation* — March).
a. its not peculiar to black parents
1) most mothers in California prisons are white
b. not only the lower class but all classes
1) lower class cases are more likely to be reported
c. in New York in more than 1/2 the families, were under suspicion before the deaths.
V. What can be done to eliminate child abuse?
1. Understand that child abusers are not criminals but people in need of help.
2. Be aware of agencies you can contact.
VI. Every member of the community has a responsibility to report to the appropriate agency in his area any suspected cases of child abuse or neglect. Every member should not be afraid to get involved, we must intervene for the sake of the child.
A. Places to contact for assistance
1. Municiple child protective unit
2. Parents Anonymous
3. counseling programs
4. specialized homemaker facilities
5. day care centers
6. foster parents program
7. other organizations depending on your community.

Conclusion
If we all take action and report child abuse we will make this world more fit and safe for ourselves and our children. That's why it's so important for each one of us to take part *now!* Hopefully we will be

eliminating the production of individuals like Charles Manson. It's not difficult to take action just pick up the phone and dial one of your local community centers the next time you suspect a child battering (abusive).

We will insure a safer environment for ourselves and most important our children.

Bibliography
1. *Nation,* pg. 293, March 6, 1972.
2. *Newsweek,* pg. 66, January 24, 1972.
3. *Newsweek,* pg. 32, January 16, 1973.
4. *Parents,* pg. 20, March 1973.
5. *Parents,* December 1975
6. *Red Book,* January 1974.
7. *Science Digest,* October, 1974.

Pyramid Power

Specific Purpose
To have audience gain a better understanding of what pyramid power is and where it comes from.

Introduction
Wouldn't it be nice to buy a cheap bottle of Boone's Farm Wine and then be able to turn it into something that tastes like Mateus Rosé? Or how about being able to buy a cheaper cut of meat but still have it be as tender as the finest porterhouse steak?

There is such a device around today that some claim will actually do these things and more, like purify water, preserve food, cause plants to grow faster, wounds to heal speedier, and even heighten meditation and sexual experiences.

The devise is a pyramid and it utilizes a mystical energy called "Pyramid Power."

A recent example of the use of pyramid power was during the 1976 Stanley Cup Playoffs. Coach Red Kelly, of the Toronto Maple Leafs, was able to make a sudden improvement in his team's game when he placed several pyramids under the team bench. Consequently they won 3 games over the Philadelphia Flyers.

And team captain, Darryl Sittler, scored 5 goals in one game after 8 scoreless games after standing under a pyramid for 10 minutes before playing. This all was a definite upswing for the Toronto team but, unfortunately, they still lost the championship to the Flyers — 4 games to 3.

Well now, what is it that causes these strange phenomenon and where did it come from?

Body
    I. Pyramid power was "fathered" by Antoine Boris.
       A. Initial discovery made during his exploration of the Cheops pyramid near Cairo in Egypt.

1. Found Pharoah's chamber to be unusually humid yet dead animals inside were dehydrated and mummified.
2. Thus he thought maybe there was more to Egyptian mummies than a fantastic, unique embalming method.

B. Boris experimented with pyramid
1. Boris built a scaled-down replica of Cheops pyramid according to exact dimensions.
2. Located his pyramid on North-South magnetic axis, like Cheops, and placed a dead cat 1/3 way up from base and in exact center of pyramid—the location of Pharoah's chamber.
3. Thus, Boris experimentally reproduced the same results he found in Cheops.

II. Karen Drbal, a Czechoslovakian scholar at Prague further experimented with pyramids.
   A. Drbal conducted the popular razor blade experiment.
   1. He placed a razor blade in his own model of the Cheops pyramid and nothing happened.
   2. So Drbal used the razor blade until it was dull.
   3. He then placed it back in the pyramid and a few days later it was sharp again.
   B. In 1959 Drbal obtained a patent from the Czechoslovakian patent office for the "Cheops Pyramid Razor Blade Sharpener."

III. There is a scientific explanation for Drbal's razor blade experiment.
   A. Razor blades are made of crystals along the edge which can replace themselves under the right conditions.
   B. The pyramid either focuses energy or collects energy to build a magnetic field to provide the necessary environment.

IV. There are many pyramid products on the market.
   A. The pyramid tent heightens whatever takes place inside.
   B. Energy generator affects whatever is near it or on it.
   C. Table top pyramid has a base and affects what is put inside it.

Summary

Many believers are now using such devices faithfully and finding new uses for them. Although some nonbelievers feel the only power a pyramid has is the power to increase the wealth of those who produce and distribute them.

Sources

1. *New York Times,* September 12, 1976, Vol. VI, p. 95, Bruce L. Bush.
2. *New York Times Magazine,* August 20, 1976, p. 24-25.
3. *Vogue,* May 1976, p. 124, Leslie Kenton.
4. *Mechanix Illustrated,* April 1977, p. 150-3, B. Miller.

Cancer and Nutrition

Purpose
For the listener to understand the need for raw fresh fruits and vegetables in their diet, in the control and prevention of cancer.

Introduction
I am sure most of us have heard of someone who has had an operation and had their cancerous tumor removed and had been cured of cancer. The fact is they were not cured of cancer. There is no cure for cancer. Cancer is not a medical problem, it is a problem brought on by our poor lacking diet, by which we poison and destroy our bodies.

Body
I. Two examples of cancer control by diet
   A. Robert W. Stickle
   B. Dr. Max Gerson
II. Diet for the cancer victim
   A. Proper diet
      1. Low animal protein, high in raw fresh fruits and vegetables
      2. High potassium content
   B. Improper diet
      1. Stimulants
      2. Refined foods
      3. Canned and frozen foods processed in any way.
III. Consequences of not following diet precisely.
   A. Value of eating in the raw state
   B. Vitamins, minerals, enzymes, and hormones function in assembly line process.
IV. How the diet affects the body
   A. Quote from an article written by Dr. Gerson: "Diet and medication serve the purpose of restoring potassium and the minerals of the potassium group to the tissues until they are completely saturated and, conversely, of reconveying sodium and its group out of the cells and into the circulatory fluids, the connective tissues and other tissues where they belong. The retentive surplus of sodium must be eliminated. It is only on this basis that further recovery of the organs can take place."
   B. Liver restoration
   C. Restore metabolism
V. Preventing cancer with sensible diet
   A. Eat foods close to natural state
   B. No processed or refined foods
   C. Avoid spicy foods, narcotics, and stimulants

Conclusion

I know it seems impossible to follow the rules I have pointed out above, it takes all the fun out of living, but we can do the best we can at eating things as close to their natural form as possible. Why not eat an orange instead of drinking orange juice, there can't possibly be as many vitamins and minerals in that juice as there is in the orange itself, it may be convenient but not nearly as healthy. Our bodies are a powerful machine and can take more abuse than a mack truck and can be built back from the most devastating torment imaginable, now we can torment it but don't kill it, let's give it the food it needs, live food, the food mother nature gave us, because we can cheat now, but once we have cancer there is not room for cheating. When we get to that point we may be able to bring it back to a healthy state and we may not, we could only hope to be as lucky as Robert Stickle, because at this point one out of every three of us will get cancer and the ratio is still climbing.

Tornado Spies Use Skywarn Spotters Network to Find Funnels

Specific Purpose

To describe the importance of tornado spies using Skywarn networks to locate tornadoes.

    I. How good are your chances of survival without tornado spies using Skywarn networks?
        A. The question may be asked "What are Skywarn networks?"
            1. The definition of Skywarn network is as follows.
            2. The people who are involved as tornado spies are volunteers.
        B. The Skywarn networks are an aid to the National Weather Service.
            1. Most of the volunteers of tornado spies goes and assumes positions on hills to report weather conditions to the National Weather Service.
            2. The tornado spies are the backbone of the tornado warning service.
    II. The importance of tornado spies and Skywarn networks are for three reasons:
        A. To alert the local communities to seek shelter in case of threatening weather conditions.
        B. They help to save lives in the local communities.
        C. They advise the National Weather Service of Indianapolis of weather conditions in this area.
    I. During the course of my speech I would like to do three things.
        A. First, explore briefly the origin of tornado spies using Skywarn networks in Bloomington.
        B. Second, to tell the necessary equipment and location for tornado spotters.

C. Third, explain what happens when a tornado spy spots a tornado.

II. Prior to the Spring of 1975, there wasn't a network system of Skywarn in Bloomington.

 A. In 1975, Nick Carder, employee of WTTS, Mr. Bud Lynch,

  employee of Indiana University as emergency coordinator for Department of Environmental Health and Safety, local police, state police, local fire department and Red Cross got together to form a network to warn Bloomington residents of approaching tornados.

 B. There are no rules and regulations to set up a Skywarn system, only to have volunteers to participate.

III. The necessary equipment is simple and the location is practical.

 A. The equipment consists of a compass, a pair of binoculars and a walkie talkie, which has a telephone on it.

 B. The location is a high point of ground.

IV. The steps in reporting a tornado as a spy are as follows.

 A. The tornado spy gets in touch with a police operator and WTTS and WGTC radio.

 B. The tornado spy tells where, what direction and the speed of the tornado.

 C. Then the police operator gets in touch with the man in charge over the watch to set off the warning system, while the DJ's announce the warning over the radio.

V. So, the next time you see threatening weather conditions here in Bloomington, be thankful for tornado spies with the use of Skywarn networks.

 A. They could be a help in saving your life.

 B. They may also be able to give you sufficient warning to save your possessions.

Sources

Mr. Nick Carder, volunteer of Skywarn of Bloomington.

IDS, Wednesday, March 9, 1977.

Tornado, U.S. Department of Commerce/National Oceanic and Atmospheric Administration.

Tornado Preparedness Planning, U.S. Department of Commerce/ National Oceanic and Atmospheric Administration, National Weather Service, October 1970.

Why Don't You Buy a Horse?

Specific Purpose

To persuade audience to buy a horse.

 I. Introduction

  Have you ever envied anyone that owns a horse? Well instead of envying them why don't you buy a horse? There are several reasons to buy a horse so let me tell you about a few of them.

II. Reasons to buy a horse
   A. Hobby
      1. After work
      2. Take pride in animal
   B. Exercise
      1. stubbornness
      2. lifting tack
      3. legs
   C. Get to go outdoors more often
      1. trail rides
      2. fresh air
   D. Competitive
      1. shows
      2. training
III. Bad points of buying horse
   A. Boarding
   B. Cost
      1. Boarding
      2. Feed
      3. Hay
   C. Time
   D. Resale
IV. Conclusion
   In conclusion I would like to review some of the main points of why you should buy a horse: first, very competitive; second, a good hobby; third inexpensive and finally it doesn't take a lot of time. So think of these points then make a decision—should you or shouldn't you buy a horse.

Saccharin

Introduction
   I. Saccharin has been safe since its discovery almost 80 years ago.
      A. Why then does the FDA want to ban saccharin.
      B. The reason for this ban on saccharin is that the Canadian government experimented with saccharin and came to the conclusion that it could cause cancer in humans.
      C. So the FDA was forced to ban saccharin due to the Delaney Clause.
         1. The Delaney Clause states that any food additive which causes cancer in animals must be removed from the market.
   II. The main reason for the widespread opposition of the ban on saccharin is the hardship that it would place on many millions of people who depend on saccharin as an artificial sweetener.
      A. The people who this ban would affect the most are:
         1. The 10 million people who suffer from diabetes.

2. The millions of heart patients.
3. The 40 million or so overweight people who must control their weight to decrease their chances of becoming heart patients.

B. For these people saccharin is a necessary part of preventive medicine.
1. The only way to help these people who are trying to keep their good health is stop this ban on saccharin.

III. There is a lot of evidence disputing the finding that saccharin causes cancer in humans.

A. The most valid evidence, in the view of the FDA and the National Cancer Institute, is what we call epidemiological evidence.
1. The most recent study was a study of the incidence of cancer among diabetics in England in 1976.
2. In this study 5,971 diabetics were analyzed, and it was found that instead of the 213 tumors that were expected, based on the population at large, only 189 tumors were found.
3. These numbers refer to the sum of all cancers not related to smoking.
4. This is the best available evidence.

B. The National Cancer Institute estimates that if you reduced the dosage on the rats down to the comparable order of the normal human intake of saccharin, the number of tumor cases would be 4 in 10,000.
1. This means an increase of .04 per cent in the chance of any human getting a tumor during a lifetime of normal use of saccharin.

C. The study of Dr. Philippe Shubik of the Eppley Institute for Research in Cancer at the University of Nebraska
1. Dr. Shubik concludes that the rats were fed a commercial diet that was already contaminated by small amounts of carcinogens.
2. Dr. Shubik also states that rats of all groups tend to have bladder problems.
3. This raises the question about the vulnerability of the rats' urinary tract.

D. Whatever the rat experiments show, there is still no evidence that saccharin causes health problems in humans.
1. Three years ago, two British scientists compared the histories of nearly 20,000 diabetics with those of equal number nondiabetics and found no difference in the occurrence of cancer.
2. Despite the fact that the diabetics consumed much more saccharin than the nondiabetics.

E. A very interesting study by Dr. Frederick Coulston of Albany, New York on Rhesus monkeys.

1. Dr. Coulston gave Rhesus monkeys, which are much closer to humans than rats, saccharin for over 6½ years, relatively high doses six days a week.
2. After examining the monkeys Dr. Coulston found nothing wrong.
3. The monkeys were perfectly normal.

IV. Reason for why the ban on saccharin should be halted if not stopped.
   A. Most sugar substitutes are hard to find.
      1. Most sugar substitutes, including saccharin, have been discovered by accident.
      2. This is because experts know very little about the mechanism of taste.
   B. There are a number of other sugar substitutes being tested.
      1. The main problem with these substitutes are that they will not be ready for five or six years.
      2. The ones that are ready have very bitter aftertastes.
      3. Most other sugar substitutes have a few calories unlike saccharin which has no calories.

V. The risks of denying saccharin far outweigh the risks of providing it.
   A. It has been found that over the last 10 to 15 years diabetics and heart patients are much more likely to stay with their diets with saccharin than without it.
      1. If saccharin is taken off the market these peoples lives will be reduced considerably.
   B. A hypothetical example of what the ban on saccharin could cause.
      1. Picture a young diabetic who has been accustomed to using artificially sweetened desserts, cookies, cakes, and soda pop.
      2. Now after this ban on saccharin takes place, this diabetic youngster who goes to a school party will either have to stand in a corner or eat what everyone else does.
      3. Chances are he will eat what everyone else does.
      4. Which could cause him serious health problems.

VI. What is really needed to settle this saccharin controversy is to readjust the Delaney Clause.
   A. A growing number of congressmen now believe that it is time to update the 19-year-old Delaney Clause.
      1. With our improved technology carcinogens can now be detected at very low levels that may not necessarily be harmful to humans.
      2. It is believed that legislation should be drafted which would give the Secretary of Health, Education, and Welfare the authority to weigh the values and the risks of a food additive, such as saccharin, and then decide whether or not it should be banned from the market.

B. Change won't come about easily, because it forces congress to address a sensitive question.
   1. How far should the government go to protect the public from the risks of cancer.
C. If you want to keep the diet products on the market, and believe the Delaney Clause needs improvement, I urge you to write to your Congressman as soon as possible.

Bibliography
Time, March 21, 1977.
Newsweek, March 21, 1977.
New Republic, March 26, 1977.
U.S. News, March 28, 1977.
Business Weekly, April 4, 1977.
U.S. News, April 4, 1977.
Time, March 28, 1977.

Save the Whales

Specific Purpose
To obtain action from the audience on behalf of the rapidly vanishing whales by informing them as to the existing conditions and by showing them two simple methods by which they can help.

Introduction
This morning I'm going to talk about a problem I'm sure you have all heard at least a little about. Last year I.U. hosted a symposium on saving the great whales from extinction and the campus abounded with enthusiastic support. Now that enthusiasm has died down, but the problem remains grave. Today 100 great whales will die—one every fourteen minutes. I hope to convince you of the senselessness and waste of those deaths and to enlist your support in alleviating the situation. In achieving this I will present information about some whales themselves, the industry that is destroying them, why they should be protected, and what you can do to help.

Body
  I. Whales are fascinating creatures worthy of man's awe and admiration.
    A. They range in size from the mammoth blue whales to their mansized cousins the dolphins.
      1. The larger whales are the most severely threatened, especially the sperm, right, bowhead, humpback, gray, and blue whales.
      2. As stocks of the larger whales diminish, whalers turn to larger catches of ever smaller species.
    B. The blue whale will serve as an example of these magnificent creatures now on the road to oblivion.
      1. The blue whale is the largest creature ever to have lived on Earth. It can:

      a. reach lengths of over 100 feet

      b. weigh 150 tons

      c. swim at 20 mph

      d. blow water 30 feet into the air

      e. yield 10,000 gallons of oil when slaughtered

2. The largest of all creatures eat the smallest creatures.

      a. A blue whale eats krill and plankton, minuscule crustaceans never reaching more than 2½ inches.

      b. They can eat three tons of this a day be drawing in millions of cubic meters of sea, filtering out the water, and swallowing the fish.

3. The blue whale has an extremely long reproductive cycle.

      a. A female is only able to conceive once every four years.

      b. She must be three quarters grown to bear a calf.

      c. Reduced populations has made finding a mate at the proper time difficult.

II. Modern whaling bears little resemblance to the romantic and prosperous days of Captain Ahab.

  A. The equipment used is extremely efficient, resulting in massive kills.

    1. A fleet of high powered catcher boats serve a gigantic factory ship where the whales are processed.

      a. A factory ship can reduce a 90-foot blue whale to unrecognizable products in 30 minutes.

    2. The whales are spotted by the use of sonar, radar, and helicopter scouts.

    3. The whales are caught by the use of harpoon cannons with explosive heads.

    4. These sophisticated techniques spell extinction.

      a. In 1930, 42,000 whales were killed of which 30,000 were blues.

      b. By 1962, 66,000 whales were killed of which only 400 were blues.

      c. No full grown blue whale has been reported since 1951.

      d. Although fully protected since 1965, the blue whales have been unable to increase their population which now stands between 600 and 2000 — down from an original population of ½ million.

  B. Whaling is no longer an economically sound industry.

    1. Whale meat for human consumption could never contribute significantly to the world's food market due to the already faltering herd populations.

    2. Synthetic substitutes exist for every whale related product, drastically decreasing demand.

    3. Therefore, no new whaling ships are being built, not even by Japan or Russia the two largest whaling na-

tions, because they are no longer a worthwhile investment.
    4. The whalers' single intent is to make as much profit as
       possible before their present fleets become obsolete—
       not caring if the whales run out first.
III. Why should whales be protected?
    A. We are not yet sure what role whales play in the ecological
       cycle.
        1. Whales are intimately related to the plankton population,
           which is at the very base of the oceanic food chain.
        2. Whales are evolutionary wonders.
            a. They are the only land mammals to have successfully
               returned to the sea.
            b. Their bone structure still shows traces of legs and five
               digits.
    B. Medically, the whale might hold the key to some important
       questions.
        1. Of the countless whales dissected by whalers over the
           centuries, no malignant tumor has ever been found.
        2. Whales dive to terrific depths and surface instantly
           without getting the bends.
        3. The whales' brain is second only to man's.
            a. They communicate with one another.
            b. They have sensitive sonar capabilities.
            c. They are now being trained for undersea rescue and
               location.
IV. What can you do to help?
    A. You can contribute to Rare, Inc., a nonprofit organization
       devoted to obtaining a complete moratorium on whale
       killing: Rare, Inc., 950 Third Avenue, New York, New
       York 10022.
    B. You can join the five million other Americans who actively
       boycott Japanese and Russian products.
        1. The United States now has a ban on importation of any
           whale products.
        2. However, some products reach U.S. markets through
           "back door" methods.
            a. The transmission fluid in Japanese cars comes from
               Whales.
            b. Many European perfumes, for example Chanel, con-
               tain ambergris, obtained from sperm whales.

Conclusion
In conclusion I should like to reiterate some key points: All species
of great whales are in immediate danger of extinction. Why?—intensive commercial whaling. Whales are not killed to feed hungry people. Their bodies are processed into cosmetics, luxury soaps, car
wax, lubricants, automatic transmission fluid, margarine, fertilizer,

cattle feed, and pet food. Yet, adequate substitutes at reasonable prices exist for all whale products. Whaling is not economically important to any nation. In fact, all large-scale whalers expect to cease operation within a few years because all whales worth chasing will be commercially extinct. This mass butchering must be stopped now or the whales will not be commercially extinct — but truly extinct. In the words of Nicholas Rosa, a leading whale advocate, "It is going to be a dull and lonely place when the only intelligence left alive here is ours. Such as it is."

Sources

"Boycott to Save Whales." *Audubon,* 76 (July 1974), 120.

Cousteau, Jacques-Yves. *The Whale: Mighty Monarch of the Sea.* Garden City, New York: Doubleday and Co., Inc., 1972.

Hill, David O. "Vanishing Giants." *Audubon,* 77 (June 1975), 56-88.

Reiger, George. "The Mathematics of Extinction." *Field and Stream,* 80 (February 1976), 30-31.

Rosa, Nicholas. "What is Leviathan's Future?" *Oceans,* 7 (May 1974), 48-53.

Rosa, Nicholas. "What Price Whales?" *Oceans,* 8 (September 1975), 68-69.

Van Note, Craig. "Japan, Soviet Union Under Whaling Gun." *Audubon,* 78 (September 1975), 123-124.

"Whaling Industry Harpooned by IWC." *Science News,* 107 (5 July 1975), 5-6.

What's Wrong About IQ Testing?

Purpose

I want my audience to believe that the public schools and society on the whole place too much emphasis on IQ scores. Also, in order to understand the issue, I want my audience to understand what an intelligence quotient is.

Introduction

Maria migrated to New York City from Puerto Rico at age six. Like many island children she carried a special burden because she could speak only Spanish. She began public schooling at P.S. 85 and was recalled favorably by her fifth-grade teacher Mrs. Olive Decker. Although Maria was the best student in her class, she was removed to a class for Children with Retarded Mental Development (C.R.M.D.) because of a low IQ test score.

I. What is the Intelligence Quotient?
   A. We tend to believe it is a measure of innate intelligence.
   B. It is a number expression of specific units.
     1. Chronological Age (CA) is a person's age in months and years.
     2. Mental Age (MA) measures mental maturity in terms of that possessed by children of corresponding CA.

3. IQ equals MA divided by CA and multiplied by 100. (IQ = 100(MA/CA)).

II. IQ testing has a dismal history.
    A. Alfred Binet developed the first tests to help isolate persons who needed special classes.
    B. Lewis Terman developed the Stanford-Binet Test.
    C. The U.S. Public Health Service used IQ tests to isolate feebleminded immigrants.
    D. During W.W. I, IQ tests showed that blacks had lower IQ scores than whites.
    E. Cases like Maria continue today.

III. IQ testing presents many problems.
    A. The tests often measure trivia instead of important life skills.
    B. The format of the tests is confusing.
    C. The tests and their results are dehumanizing.
    D. The interpretation of scores is culturally biased.

IV. There are evaluative alternatives to IQ testing.
    A. Teachers' comments about students' work provide valuable insight about academic potential.
    B. Contracting and specific criterion are accurate ways of measuring achievement.
    C. Parent-teacher conferences can aid the learning experience.
    D. Grades (A, B, C, D, F) are easier for most people to understand than IQ scores and may be useful measurement tools.

Conclusion

We have seen that the IQ is a numerical expression and that IQ testing has a dismal history which presents many problems. However, there are alternatives which offer hope as shown by the example of Ned, a boy with an IQ score of 90 who successfully attended Harvard Law School because a teacher recognized his potential and helped him to utilize it.

Bibliography

Fine, Benjamin, *The Stranglehold of the IQ*, Doubleday and Co., Inc., New York, 1975.

Ross, C. C., *Measurement In Today's Schools*, Prentice-Hall, Inc., New York, 1954.

Davis, Allison, *Intelligence and Cultural Differences*, The University of Chicago Press, Chicago, Ill.: 1951.

Rosenthal, Robert and Jacobson, Lenore. *Pygmalion In the Classroom*. Holt, Rinehart and Winston, Inc., New York: 1968.

Black, Hillel. *They Shall Not Pass*, William Morrow and Co., New York, 1963.

Smith, Fred M. and Adams, Sam. *Educational Measurement For the Classroom Teacher*, Harper and Row, New York, 1972.

Lavin, David E. *The Prediction of Academic Performance*, Russell Sage Foundation New York, 1965.

Cohen, Daniel, *Intelligence — What Is It?* M. Evans and Co., Inc., New York, 1974.

Smoking: A Hazard to Your Health

Specific Purpose

I want the audience to become more aware of the many hazards of smoking and the outcome which usually occurs from smoking. Hopefully, those who smoke might consider (or reconsider) quitting and the nonsmokers will remain nonsmokers. My main purpose is to persuade them to be against smoking.

Introduction

If someone asks you if you mind them smoking by you, by all means you should say "yes, I do mind." The smoke they exhale from their cigarette endangers your health just as they are endangering their health — even more. Those gases and poisons they are exhaling are pure and they are polluting the air you breathe.

Seventy-five years ago cigarettes weren't recognized as an important threat to public health. They were not a major article of consumption. Things have changed since time has passed. Cigarette consumption has shown a general *upward* trend in recent years. What is ironic about this is, in spite of new knowledge about the hazards of smoking, for one reason or another, people are risking their good health and possibly their lives by smoking.

To broaden your knowledge on the subject of smoking and to hopefully persuade you to keep your distance from it, I plan to cover several areas of importance and interest.

1. Diseases associated with cigarette smoking.
2. Comparisons of death rates between smokers and nonsmokers.
3. Opposing viewpoints or pros and cons.
4. Reasons why people smoke.
5. Advertising, how companies get their sales.

Body

I. Research studies strongly indicate that tobacco smoking, and particularly cigarette smoking is associated with a shortened life expectancy.
   A. Some 300,000 Americans die prematurely each year from diseases related to smoking.
   B. Cigarette smoking is a major cause of several diseases.
      1. lung cancer
      2. heart disease
      3. emphysema
      4. chronic bronchitis
      5. strokes
      6. other circulatory diseases
   C. In most disease related to smoking, the health hazards are directly proportional to 3 things.
      1. The number of cigarettes smoked per day.

      a. Even one cigarette increases blood pressure.
   2. Earlier the age at which smoking was started.
      a. Younger age—long period of time to smoke-greater risk.
   3. The number of years smoking has continued.
      a. Most smoking diseases develop over long period of time.
      b. People who quit or slackened off have greater chance than nonsmokers.

II. Looking at death rate of smokers, we can divide them into 3 categories.
  A. These 3 categories are mild, moderate, and heavy smokers.
   1. Mild = seven times as likely to die of lung cancer as nonsmokers.
   2. Moderate = twelve times as likely to die of lung cancer as nonsmokers.
   3. Heavy = twenty-four times as likely to die of lung cancer as nonsmokers.
  B. If you smoke you can probably place yourself in one of these 3 categories.
  C. In the study I used, which was taken from the book "Tobacco and Your Health" the total death rate, from all causes combined, is far higher among cigarette smokers than among nonsmokers or pipe and cigar smokers and the death rate increases in direct relation to the number of cigarettes smoked.

III. Even though doctors and scientists have experimented for years and come up with facts and proof that "smoking is hazardous to your health" there are some people who still oppose or ignore these facts.
  A. Spokesmen for the tobacco interest keep saying: "There is no scientific proof that cigarette smoking causes any human disease or in any way impairs human behavior."
   1. Same spokesmen responsible for misleading TV commercials and magazines and billboard ads.
      a. Implications: robust health, vigor, charm, and romance.
  B. This theme is a way of selling their product—it is a farce. However, people are unconsciously persuaded by it.
   1. What would happen if:
      a. Athlete coughing—short of wind?
      b. An older aged man shown coughing his head off?
      c. Picture of a smoker's lung: caption or narrator saying: "This is what our cigarettes will do for you!"
   2. Of course if this would be the site of commercials and ads, there'd be no sales or very few sales. Lets face it, these captions are truer pictures of what actually happens. Commercials and Ads are propaganda.

C. In opposition to these spokesmen of the tobacco interest we also have statements made by medical experts.
   1. Dr. Luther Terry, a doctor with many credentials stated: "The period of uncertainty is over. There is no longer any doubt that cigarette smoking is a direct threat to the user's health. . . ."
   2. Dr. Charles A. Ross, a doctor in a cancer institute says: "Cigarette smoking is the most serious public health problem this country has ever faced."
      a. Difficult, frustrating, and frequently discouraging problem to many people.
IV. Smoking can be learned to relieve any negative effect and to evoke any positive effect.
   A. Some people smoke to reduce feelings of distress, fear, shame, or disgust. In these cases cigarettes are being used as sedatives.
   B. Some people smoke because of nervousness. By smoking a cigarette they have something to do with their hands. Some even smoke because they like to see the smoke come out of their mouth.
   C. Some positive affects people get from smoking are when people use smoking as a stimulant, to experience the positive effects of excitement, and smoking as a relaxant, to experience the positive affect of enjoyment.
   D. In regards to smoking and the youth, children begin to smoke because of parental example. Children have the habit of following what their parents do.
      1. Fathers influence their sons, while mothers influence their daughters.
   E. Another reason youth begin to smoke is because of peer pressure.
V. Tobacco Industries and Advertising Agencies use many tactics to get people to buy their products. They turn on the charm to catch peoples attention.
   A. Magazine articles and advertisements put catching pictures with their brands.
      1. A picture of a handsome male will catch the female interest. A picture of a pretty female will catch the eyes of the male population.
      2. Colorful sceneries catch the public's attention.
         a. Some ads have rainbows, waterfalls, countryside scenes. One ad went so far as to put the Statue of Liberty along with their product.
      3. Sporting scenes are often seen along with cigarette brands advertisements. Many outdoors scenes are used.
   B. Various adjectives are used to describe cigarette taste. Some examples are: 1. "mild"
      2. "the most satisfying taste"   3. "a full tobacco flavor"

4. "menthol soft taste"   5. "a full fresh taste every time"

Conclusion

If you'll just think awhile about your health, or your friends health, you should be able to comprehend the potential dangers of cigarette smoking. Smoking increases your susceptability to diseases and it also shortens your life span considerably. These two areas deal with each person here, smokers and nonsmokers alike. It is my hope that what I have said will assist you to come to that inescapable conclusion that it is high time to quite smoking, to reduce your smoking habit or to just make a personal decision never to start.

Bibliography

Harold S. Diehl. *Tobacco and Your Health: The Smoking Controversy*. Copyright by McGraw-Hill Book Co., 1969.

George Madis. *Smoking, Life and Health*. Copyright by George Madis, 1964.

Alton Ochsner, M.D. *Smoking: Your Choice Between Life and Death*. Copyright by Alton Ochsner, 1970.

Smoking: Facts You Should Know. Pamphlet in the information file in UGL.

The Use of Solar Energy for Heating

Specific Purpose

To show you how to capitalize on the sun's energy and save.

Introduction

  I. I don't know how many of you now own or plan to buy homes, but how would you like to heat your house for only $12/month? This can be a fact and I hope to be able to prove this to you.
    A. The rising cost of residential heating fuels.
    B. Methods of installing in old or new structures.
    C. The environmental impact of the use of solar energy.

Body

  II. The rising cost of residential heating fuels.
    A. Examples of the cost of electric-oil-gas fuels.
    B. My personal dealings with electricity.
    C. Cost of using solar energy by Harry Thomason.
 III. Methods of installing in old or new structures.
    A. How to install in a new home.
    B. How to install in an old home.
    C. The use of the heated water for a swimming pool.
 IV. The environmental impact of the use of solar energy.
    A. Less pollution of the air.
    B. The savings of our natural resources.

Conclusion

  V. With all these factors figured in I feel that solar heating will be as common as the automobile. Just keep this in mind the next time you adjust your thermostat.

Bibliography
Mechanix Illustrated, May 1974, Pgs. 13-15; 132.
Popular Science, September 1974, Pgs. 104-105; 146.
Popular Science, April 1977, Pgs. 110-113; 142.

Law Without Justice

The specific purpose of this speech is to convince the students that civil rights are violated in the United States just as often as in other countries. I also want to convince them that the government lies to the public by covering up this type of activity. I will also attempt to show that this type of activity must be brought to the attention of the public before it is too late to do anything about it.

Introduction

Imagine this setting: A young man is lying in his bed reading at 1:30 in the morning. Suddenly the door bursts open and two men rush into the room with drawn guns. They drag the young man out of bed, throw him into a closed car and drive him for miles through the dark night. When the cars stop the young man is marched through dark hallways into a room that has only one light, shining right in his eyes. A man sitting in the darkness behind the light says, "You are accused of writing treasonous material." He is then thrown into a cell in solitary confinement where he is held for two weeks without ever seeing another person, much less a lawyer. After a trial during which he is never called to the stand, he is convicted and sentenced to 10 years at hard labor. While in prison he is not allowed to write to his family or friends, nor is he allowed to receive letters.

I can hear you say "So what, that is a rather common tale from Russia or some South American country.

Well, this episode happened on an American military base. This is not an isolated case, it happens all the time, not only on military bases but in cities and towns all over the U.S. This must be stopped before it is too late.

Body

 I. In the example I opened with, the young man was the editor of an underground newspaper that was attempting to tell the truth about the high level theft in the N.C.O. club.

  A. He was warned by the top NCO in his unit to lay off.

  B. When he refused he was given an article 15 by his unit commander.

   1. An article 15 is a minor type of punishment given out by a unit commander. It can be a fine or loss of rank.

   2. In this instance it was both.

  C. Finally he was arrested and the aforementioned activity took place.

 II. One other example of this type was a young man accused by his unit commander of being a drug dealer.

  A. He was arrested in the middle of the night.

1. He was held without being formally charged.
2. He was also held in solitary.
B. His girlfriend found out about the incident from his German landlord.
    1. She got word to a civilian lawyer who managed to get him released.
C. There was absolutely no evidence against him.

III. These are examples of Military law. This is law without justice.
A. Under military law, a person is considered guilty until he can prove himself innocent.
B. There is no writ of Habeas Corpus in this system.
C. In many instances military lawyers are told that the person will be convicted irregardless of the evidence.
D. A person who is once accused of something, even though he is completely exonerated, still has an entry put in his permanent file that he was once considered guilty.

IV. This type of law system is allowed to exist because the Government does not let this type of information be released to the general public.
A. The Government controls the news media, so that only the information they want to be seen is released.
B. The general public is apathetic to a very marked degree.

V. If nothing is done by individuals to find the truth and make it widely known, this law system will one day become the national norm.
A. There are many groups who are trying to do just this.
    1. They are labeled as Commie or wierdo extremists or just plain ignored.
    2. Apathy is the greatest enemy to this project.

Conclusion

Let me sum this up by saying that if we are to continue as a free society, we must have access to the truth. The truth sometimes hurts. But a truly honest man seeks the light, it is only the dishonest who seek the shadows. If we are apathetic and just sit back; fat, dumb and happy, and let this atrocity continue, then we deserve what we inherit from the society that we have allowed to come into existence.

If you no longer want to be fooled and lied to, it is up to you as the new, upcoming generation to seek the truth, and expose this evil for what it is.

Transcendental Meditation

I want my audience to attend a meeting for transcendental meditation (with the realization that it could help them both mentally and physically in handling everyday stress and minor problems).

Introduction

A 67-year-old alcoholic states "I thought my life was over but now I feel its just beginning. I stopped being a fifth-a-day drinker."

A 22 year old student at California says, "I no longer have a need for drugs. I've become a respectable member of society. My confidence and self-respect have returned."

Mayor General Franklin Davis states "My blood pressure went down 10 points. My wife says my disposition improved and minor stresses and strains around Washington didn't bother me anymore."

And Joe Namath states, "I felt I wasn't doing anything for myself. I wasn't growing. So then I started and it made me feel like I'm helping myself, and that it has done so much for my whole togetherness."

What is this that they are all talking about? This that can help anything from drug abuse to anxiety, to sex problems. It is transcendental meditation or TM.

I. Basic knowledge of Maharishi and his methods to worldwide fame.
   A. Introduced in the U.S. in 1959 by Maharishi Mahesh Yogi.
   B. Stated as not a religion, but a scientific discovery from India.
   C. Worldwide exposure in 1967 with the acceptance by the Beatles.
   D. The basic concept is that it makes the mind more orderly, gives the body deep rest, and improves the coordination between the two.
      1. It is not concentration which is the rigid fixing of the mind on one particular point and holding attention on this point as long as possible.
         a. It avoids concentration for it does not allow to submerge into deeper levels of consciousness.
      2. Biofeedback is where a person learns to control some aspect of his body function which is usually not under conscious control, as breathing, heart beat, etc.
         a. TM is effortless and happens spontaneously
         b. TM produces more than 1 specific change, produces spontaneous state of deep rest and alertness for body and mind

II. The TM technique and its effects
   A. Defined as "TM technique is a simple natural, effortless process that allows the mind to experience subtler and subtler levels of the thinking process until thinking is transcended and the mind comes in direct contact with the source of thought."
   B. Acts to remove tension, frustration and worry.
      1. Process based on fact that man stores his feelings of stress inside him, and this stress forces him to act in certain, often antisocial ways.
      2. These pockets are released enabling him to enjoy a much freer more fulfilled life.
   C. Process is natural, thus easy and effortless.

1. Each is assigned a nonsense syllable called a mantra.
    a. Each individual pulsates in a certain rhythm and this word is specifically selected by a trained teacher for its ability to pulsate with that particular, quite individual rhythm.
    b. One does not try to define the meaning of the word but rather repeats sound.
    c. Sit comfortable, close eyes, and repeat sound to begin process.
2. Let mind go wherever it wants, when let to drift freely it will drift in direction that pleases you greatly.
    a. In theory, the mind travels to more refined levels of mental activity, reaching the so called "source of thought."
    b. This experience enables the individual to expand his awareness and understanding about the workings of his own intelligence, and making more of his mental potential available for use.
3. When ended sit 2 or 3 minutes, then open eyes slowly, don't come out all at once.
D. Rest is the basis of all our activity
    1. We evolve into 2 cycles—period of rest (night) and activity (day and evening).
    2. TM adds 2 periods of revitalizing rest.
    3. Chart shows change in metabolic rate.
    4. Adds a fourth stage of consciousness to other 3 (Deep sleep, dreaming, awakefulness)—restful alertness.
        a. body is resting deeper than sleep
        b. body is resting but mind is awake
    5. Dr. Herbert Benson, Assistant Professor at Harvard Medical School, states TM provides more deep sleep in 1-20 minute period than 6 hrs. of sleep, and in 2 periods more than whole night.
        a. proven by the use of the electroencephagraph (EEG).
III. This provides 5 fundamentals necessary for progress and success in life—stability, adaptability, purification, integration, and growth.
    A. The state of being is the deepest state of meditation. It is the place in your mind where energy, intelligence, stability, and happiness have there beginning.
        1. Since no stress or tension it is called pure.
    B. We must use from 5-15% of our mental capacity, TM comes in contact with the 85-95% of the mind not using.
    C. It increases intelligence—chart-adaptability.
        1. Increased intelligence of H.S. and college students over 16 month period.
        2. Increases response to new situations with greater adaptability, creativity and comprehension.

D. It increased recall chart
  1. Tm improves ability to learn to learn
  2. Problem-solving increase chart.
     a. The efficiency of problem solving increase
     b. Organization of memory continued to stabilize even when the mediators were engaged in problem solving
     c. Increases clarity and efficiency of the conscious thought processes and at same time improves unconscious process.
  3. Overall academic Perf-chart.
     a. GPA increased sharply
     b. systematic development of creative intelligence.
  4. On the job scene it:
     a. increases productivity
     b. improves job performance
     c. increases job satisfaction
     d. improves relations with supervisors
     e. improves relations with co-workers.
E. It increases stability chart.
  1. Spontaneous skin resistance shows greater resistance to environmental stress, psychosomatic diseases and behavior instability by stabilizing nervous system.
  2. Increases reaction time in alertness, coordination, perception, and performance.
  3. Improves performance as driving a car, hitting a target, and many sports.
  4. Reduces heart beat thus reduces the work load of the heart.
  5. Also effective in helping high blood pressure and aids in hypertension and cardiovascular diseases.
  6. Increases perceptual ability in the auditory discrimination.
F. It increases purification
  1. Decreases blood lactate which results in muscular relaxation.
  2. Increases inner control, in essence, decreases anxiety measured by the Rotters scale-locus of control.
  3. Gives greater relief from insomnia by relieving deep seated stress from the nervous system.
  4. Decreases anxiety—can be expected to be accompanied by greater availability of individuals inherent resources.
  5. Has beneficial effect on bronchial asthma by helping psychological stress.
  6. Gives faster recovery from sleep deprivation by dreaming, which is thought to be a form of stress release.
G. It increases growth chart.
  1. Changes in full independence by: greater ability to structure experience, greater organization of mind and cogni-

tive clarity; improved memory, greater creative expression, stable internal frame of reference, greater creative expression; stable standards, attitudes, judgments, and sentiments.
>   2. Development of self-actualization as openness, receptiveness, cheerfulness, good humor, positive thinking (Northridge Development Scale).
> H. Integration increases chart.
>   1. Tourance test of creativity thinking shows creativity thinking increases by fluency, flexibility, and originality of ideas.
> IV. Solutions through TM
> A. Found TM can help in rehabilitation of criminals, reduction of drug abuse, reduces use of alcohol and cigarettes, increase tolerance in high school students, and general crime rates.
> B. Only stipulations to use
>   1. Must go to 4-2 hour sessions to learn technique. Then practice 2-20 min. periods a day.
>   2. Fee charged of $65 for college students—non-profit organization.
>   3. Cannot take any nonprescription drugs, 15 days before meditation, except alcohol and cigarettes due to fact that drugs alter perception.

Conclusion

Virginia Cook, researcher at University of Pitt. says, "You are swimming in the stormy Atlantic. The rough choppy sea batters you until you feel like Joe Frazier sparring partner. You are bruised and exhausted, but suddenly you dive to the very bottom of the ocean floor.

"All is quiet there, all is serene. You see fish and plants, more beautiful than women at opening night. Finally, you swim into the intoxicating blackness of the ocean deep.

"When you surface the storm is over and the sun is shining. You are deeply rested from the quiet of the ocean, and you are excited because you have touched unknown depths. You swim easily now the concrete water beneath supporting you."

Bibliography
The TM Book, Denise Dennison, 1975.
"Transcendental Meditation: What's it all About?" *Readers Digest,* Dec. 1975.
Tranquility Without Pills, Jhan Robbins, 1972.
"How TM changed our Family Life," *Ladies Home Journal,* Nov. 1975.
Herbert Benson, "A Wakeful Hypometabolic Physiological State," Introductory lecture on TM, first semester of this school year.
Friends of mine who've taken TM.

CHAPTER 9 *communicating in public*

Style is a very hard term to define. One reason it is so difficult to give a good definition is that we use it in so many different ways. We can refer to a person as having "style," and the context of our references will tell whether we mean that person dresses particularly well or sings in a unique way or plays basketball with some special skill or flair. When we talk about the communicator's style we similarly may mean many different things. One might say that a speaker's style is the unique or particular kind of image he or she creates for the audience: an image that is perceived through the speaker's use of language, his or her movement and gestures, the way he or she looks on the platform. Of course, style in its largest sense really covers much that has been discussed in this book. For certainly a person's style is influenced by the way he or she thinks, by the way arguments are put together, by the way the speaker relates to the audience. Also, what listeners have heard about a speaker or know about a speaker or think they know about a speaker can create for them certain kinds of expectations. These expectations often lead listeners to expect that the speaker will exhibit some striking qualities which they might call "style." So, in a sense, while all we have been discussing so far would contribute to your personal style as a speaker, the focus in this section is particularly on language—how to choose it and how to use it. That is to say, then, that we will consider style for the moment to be *your use and choice of language.* This consideration will be followed by an examination of the qualities of delivery, a process that many consider also to be a part of style. In this chapter we look at style in its relationship to understanding messages as well as style in its persuasive dimensions.

One thing that is difficult for a speaker to appreciate is that he or she and the listeners do not always speak *exactly* the same language. All of us, for example, may speak English. But we do not use and choose language in the same ways. For one thing we may come from different cultural backgrounds that provide us either with different words or different meanings for words. Black English for example, is often rich in linguistic patterns and usage that are different from certain other forms of English. Often these uses are absorbed by the rest of the culture, so that by now most speakers and listeners would at least comprehend what was meant if they were urged to "be cool," or told that one of their friends was really "bad." Yet these meanings are not universal and are known to different people and different times. And as with black English there are regional uses of English, ethnic uses of language, generational uses of language, that can be confusing to those outside of the linguistic group. Sometimes, there are language uses that are very specific and very unusual. For example, at one New Jersey college what was normally called in other places "making out" or "necking," was called "grouching" there. People who attended that institution would know what "grouching" meant and might even go so far as to say that someone had given them a little grouch when they meant they had been given a little kiss; no one else, however, would have the slightest idea of what such a reference meant — indeed, the normal listener would probably assume that the term referred to someone who was very grouchy or someone who was grumbling or complaining in some way. Of course, language is not always or even usually so extremely specific or limited. The point, however, is that no speaker can assume that his or her language choices will inevitably or automatically be those that are natural to his or her listeners. As in all other aspects of communication, the speaker needs to consider who his or her audience is. Given these basic kinds of considerations the speaker needs to choose and use a language to promote the following characteristics.

Language Should Be Clear To Listeners

In all aspects of the speaking situation, the speaker needs to keep in mind that a speech, being oral, is very different from a written presentation. This is especially true when it comes to the language chosen. You know that if you are reading a page and you come across words that you have never seen before, you will either figure out the meaning from the context (which might require rereading the paragraph a couple of times), or you will go and look up the word in the dictionary. A listener can't stop the speaker and get him or her to run through a section of the oral message again, nor can the listener stop the speaker and go look up a word. The speaker needs constantly to keep in mind the kinds of problems that the audience might face in relation to his or her language.

One way to promote clarity is to be sure to use words with which the audience is familiar. Once the author of this textbook was giving a lecture in which he described a particular political speech that had recently been broadcast over television as "pedestrian." After the lecture was over one student came up to talk to him; the student was somewhat puzzled and frustrated at not being able to understand precisely the instructor's evaluation of the speech. "I thought a pedestrian was someone who walked across the street," the student said, "how can a speech be pedestrian?" This is an extreme example. One should be able to assume that a college student would know the meaning of "pedestrian" in this context. Nevertheless, the instructor might have said, "This was a very pedestrian speech, one that had nothing unusual or striking or interesting about it; it was very ordinary." Such a restatement tactic would have explained the unfamiliar word and reinforced the idea.

The speaker should remember particularly that technical words may be unfamiliar to an audience. Sometimes we are so wrapped up in our own experience and in our own interests that we forget the terms we use on a regular basis might be quite unusual to someone else. A chemistry major will have no difficulty understanding what a reagent is and an accounting major in understanding a trial balance. For someone training to be an auto mechanic a sparkplug is an ordinary object and its use and function is readily understood. A nutritionist knows what carbohydrates are, a lab technician what a blood sample is, a teacher what a lesson plan is. In other words, technical language doesn't have to be words such as aerodynamics, quantum mechanics, iambic pentameter. Technical language is any language that has a very precise and definite meaning within a particular field of endeavor. It's easy, therefore, for us sometimes to forget that language we consider to be ordinary an audience might think technical. The same, of course, is true of technical or specialized abbreviations or substitutions for longer words or titles that are used commonly in particular contexts. The best example of this is the way in which we use letters to stand for names or titles. Anyone who is interested in broadcasting will know what is meant by the FCC regulations, whereas other members in the audience might not know that this refers to the Federal Communications Commission. Many college students will know a GPA whereas their parents, friends, or others not associated with the university might not know the reference is to a grade point average. Anyone in the medical or paramedical field will know that a GP is a doctor who does not have a specialty, but, is, rather, a general practitioner. The speaker, then, needs to be conscious of the fact that his or her language grows out of his or her experience and knowledge and needs at times to be translated for the experience and knowledge of the listeners.

Words that are chosen for their concreteness and their specificity increase clarity. Telling an audience, for example, that they must exert increased effort or that they must be very active, is not really telling them what they are expected to do. The vagueness of those words will not leave a clear impression in the minds of the audience. On the other hand saying to an audience that they could appear at the student union building at nine o'clock in the morning to distribute handbills is saying something *specific*. Asking an audience to vote for a candidate because he is in favor of enlarging educational opportunities is vague. Asking an audience to vote for a candidate because he or she supports an increase in the federal loan program for students is specific. Describing someone as a humanitarian does not make that person's contribution clear to an audience; but describing him or her as someone who has voluntarily gone into prison in order to teach inmates how to improve their educational skills does tell the listener something.

Individual words must be chosen to promote clarity, but they must also be used together to promote clarity. This means that words have to be put together in as straightforward a way as possible so the sentences that they form are direct and easy to follow. Clarity of oral style as opposed to clarity of written style might demand more repetition than a writer would use; things might have to be repeated and restated in order to be clear. Even so, the speaker aims to talk in a way that will promote the audiences' efforts to follow, to remember, to understand. One thing that helps promote a clearer style is the use of transitional language that continually points the audience in the proper direction. So that as a speaker amplifies a particular point, for example, he or she might say, "I've been telling you that a diet that is not properly supervised can be very dangerous for you. Let me give you an example of just how dangerous by telling you about a college student named Joan." The move by the speaker from the generalization to the specific example is thus clearly delineated through the use of specific transitional language. Probably the best advice that can be given to anyone to help him or her use language clearly is to be sure that one's *thinking is* clear. If the speaker first understands him or herself what the idea is then it will be much easier to convey that idea to an audience. When a speaker who has not thought out an idea clearly, when the speaker is vague about the concept, then the result is likely to be confusion for the listeners.

Language Should Be Interesting To Listeners
Factors of attention and interest have already been discussed earlier in this book. Nevertheless, there are some special observations that can be made regarding language. One of the things that always interests us is *action*. The way we choose language and the way we put it together can create a kind of action for our listeners. We can create the illusion of action and help the listeners to understand more precisely what the speaker has in mind in several ways. One of the best things for a speaker to keep in mind is that simple and precise words and sentences help contribute to an active speech. Consider, for example, the way Winston Churchill described to the U.S. Congress events in North Africa in the early days of World War II. Things had not been going well for the British in Europe or for the Americans, who had entered the war just a few weeks before, in Asia. Churchill hoped to create a sense of forward movement and give hope of success. There are no exceptional or unusual words in the passage, no particularly unique sentence construction. But here is clarity and forcefulness that gives a good picture of what is going on.

"For many months we devoted ourselves to preparing to take the offensive in Libya. The very considerable battle which has been proceeding for the last 6 weeks in the desert has been most fiercely fought on both sides. Owing to the difficulties of supply on the desert flank we were never able to bring numerically equal forces to bear upon the enemy. Therefore we had to rely upon a superiority in the numbers and quality of tanks and aircraft, British and American. Aided by these, for the first time we have fought the enemy with equal weapons. For the first time we have made the Hun feel the sharp edge of those tools with which he has enslaved Europe. The armed force of the enemy in Cyrenaica amounted to 150,000 men, of whom about a third were Germans. General Auchinleck set out to destroy totally that armed force; and I have every reason to believe that his aim will be fully accomplished."

Style also promotes the feeling of action when it is lively. Language that gives the most realistic and vivid description of events or people or ideas is the most lively. To meet an assignment in a speaking class, for example, two speakers each described a teacher that he had had sometime in the past. Consider in the following two examples which is the more lively.

"When I first went into class a tall man with a slightly grey hair sat at the front of the room on the desk. He smiled and handed me a card to fill out. When I gave it back to him, he smiled again and said, Thank you, in a quiet voice. But it was a funny thing, I knew somehow that that quiet voice was a powerful one, too, one that I was going to like to listen to, one that would sort of fill the room, but not batter at your ears. He looked relaxed sitting there, but I could tell he was watching everyone that came in, studying them, sizing them up. This was a lit class, and I figured there was going to be a lot of BS about books that nobody had really read. But as I watched this guy I got a feeling that phonies were not going to get away with anything, that you had to know what you were talking about here. When he got up to talk, I actually felt excited, like something was going to happen. I was a little scared, scared that this guy would be tough, but more scared that maybe he wouldn't be, maybe I was wrong. English always bored me, but I really hoped maybe this time it would be worth it. When he started to talk he looked right at me and at everybody. He made some kind of joke. But then he started to talk to us, right to us, and I thought to myself, 'My God, this might be OK after all.' "

"Mr. Harrison was an excellent teacher that I had in high school. He was always well prepared and tried to enlighten the class when he had the opportunity. He tried to understand student needs and the values we held and to adapt accordingly to

our experiences. He was certainly a good teacher and served as such a role model for me that I decided to become a teacher, too."

The first example is clearly more real, creates more suspense, is more specific and as a whole, accordingly, more lively.

Language that is in and of itself striking or impressive can create interest for an audience and contribute to the audience's understanding of the ideas. Literally, for centuries students of rhetoric have studied what are called figures of speech; these are special ways of using language to heighten the beauty of expression or the clearness of the idea. It is not important for the beginning student of public communication to understand and identify all the technical names for the different kinds of figures of speech. But there are some special ways of using the language that the listener and the speaker would both be aware of. These special ways of using the language offer some additional opportunities to increase the interest and clarity and so could prove very helpful. Most of these are usual figures in public communication.

Language should be used in a special way to compare things. A direct comparison can be made between things that the audience might not see as similar. (This kind of comparison is called a *simile,* and the word "like" or "as" always appears.) "A day in the life of the college student," one student began her speech, "is like a day at an amusement park. You have ups and downs; you can get spun around; you can do new things you've never done before; you can have a lot of fun; and you can end by throwing up." Another kind of common comparison is the *metaphor* in which two objects that the audience might think of as quite dissimilar are compared. (The technical distinction between metaphor and simile is that "like" or "as" does not appear in the metaphor.) One freshman college student at the end of her first semester, facing her first set of finals described her feelings through metaphor: "I think I understand the principles of swimming, but I'm about to find out by jumping into the deep end of the pool; I just hope I don't drown." Because these images not only arouse interest but also create feelings and moods they can make an important contribution to the audience's total understanding of the communication.

Language can be used to make contrasts. The special device known as an *antithesis* is a way of putting two things together that have sharply contrasted meanings. This is a way in which the language can reinforce the idea; by strong contrasts in words or phrases strong contrasts in thought are also suggested. One student speaker, for example, argued that "Forces of life and personal sacrifice are contending with the forces of death and personal profit right here on this campus." This speech was one that attacked those who would risk the effects of pollution in order to make money. The antithetical language construction in the example pits life against death and sacrifice against profit in such a way that those who put money first are allied with death.

There are a wide variety of other stylistic devices that are used to enhance the ideas and thus to make them more believable or understandable. Through *irony,* a speaker can imply a meaning that is really the opposite from that stated: "As we all know, doctors, who have taken the Hippocratic Oath care a great deal about their patients and don't care anything at all about how much money they can make." Using *alliteration* a speaker employs a repetitive pattern of sound that can hold the audience's attention and reinforce the idea: "For some the university, instead of being a passport to plenty, is the doorway to doom." Through *personification* the speaker gives the characteristics of human beings to non-human forms or things: "This city can be a very hostile place. It can ignore you, it can frighten you, and it can punish you very severely if you ignore its unwritten rules." Through *eptamorthosis* a speaker modifies by making some kind of retraction a statement that he or she has just made: "This is a great school, by that I mean this is a great faculty. This is a great school, no it doesn't have the most beautiful buildings and maybe the equipment is not as extensive or as new as we would like, but this is a great school because it has great people working in it." There are literally dozens of other devices that could be listed, but the point is that language can have a force of its own. It can be interesting, clarifying, and persuasive for an audience when used properly. The important thing for the speaker to keep in mind is simply this fact: The language that is chosen and and the way it is used can make a difference in the way the audience responds, so it is of primary importance to the speaker to become conscious of language and of all the possibilities that are afforded in its use.

Language Should Be Appropriate To the Situation

If you give the matter any thought it will become apparent to you that we all use different language in different kinds of situations. One of the most dramatic examples ever seen of contrasting uses of language is that demonstrated by the publication of the famous Watergate tapes. These recorded conversations illustrated the startling differences between the public and private choices of language made by the President and many of his advisers. All of us know that there are conventions in the use of language that apply to people and contexts. We all know that the words we choose when talking to our friends tend to be vastly different than the ones we choose when talking to our parents or our employers or our teachers. We know that a conversation in a dormitory might involve different kinds of language from a conversation one might have with the parents of a roommate who are visiting. One of the things that was most terribly shocking to some people in the Watergate transcripts was not so much the use of particular expletives, but the fact that those words were used by the President of the United States in the Oval Office of the White House. Somehow their use in that setting did not seem fitting to many people who had surely heard the language before and perhaps even used some of those expletives themselves.

Of course, what is being discussed here is much larger than the issue of when one uses certain words that may or may not be socially acceptable or unacceptable. The real issue is much broader, and that is: What language is best suited to the context in which the public communication occurs? The speaker him or herself is an important element within this context. The speaker must deal with the fact that the language to be used is different from his or her normal conversational language, but yet remain true to one's self. That is, a speaker will probably think more carefully and choose more carefully and use more carefully language in a public communication setting than he or she would in a private setting. Nevertheless, he or she is not going to "fake" language in order to sound like something he or she is not. For example, it would be absurd and inappropriate for a well-educated speaker to assume some kind of poor grammatical construction or coarse language choice that he or she felt was called for by the nature of the audience. Such an action would probably be seen by the audience as condescending and insulting rather than adaptive. It would probably be unwise for someone to whom the language use was not natural to assume the slang and special cultural or technical languages of a group when such language choices did not come naturally to the speaker. The other situational aspects —the audience, topic of the speech, and the occasion setting in which the speech takes place—also have an impact on language choice.

When Martin Luther King, for example, addressed the famous rally in behalf of civil rights in Washington, D.C., on August 20, 1963, he gave a speech that is probably the best example of language that grows out of all the constituents of a situation that can be afforded. His first words in the speech itself are, "Five score years ago a great American in whose symbolic shadow we stand today signed the Emancipation Proclamation." Standing as King was on the steps of the Lincoln Memorial this opening was the epitome of situational factors guiding language choice: it was well calculated to remind the audience most vividly of Lincoln and his Gettysburg Address and, by extension, the entire long and bloody struggle over slavery and racial prejudice. Most of us do not appear in public communication settings that are as dramatic or as overriding as the setting in which King found himself. No matter where we are, however, we need to ask ourselves what the audience knows and thinks about the topic, what level of linguistic sophistication the audience holds, how serious or how casual are the constraints of the setting, how formal or informal the situation is, what the physical limitations and relationships between speaker and listener are in the situation. In short, the speaker must ask him or herself what the audience expectations are and how they will affect his or her choice of language. A commencement speaker, for example, might begin his rather formal remarks with some kind of greeting to all those distinguished persons on the platform, naming the president of the university, the president of the board of trustees, various other guests, the graduating class and so forth. It would be absurd in a public speaking class for someone (someone who is not burlesquing the form) to get up in front of the audience and begin by saying, "Professor Jones, Chairman of the day Mr. Smith, fellow speakers . . ." and so forth. The public speaking class is a much more informal kind of situation. It calls for, among other things, different stylistic choices. The wise speaker is one who thinks carefully about what an audience expects of him or her and adjusts to meet those expectations. In a public speaking class one speaker conveyed a certain message in this way: "I'm planning to say something today that is very important. I hope you're going to see how important it is, but what is really vital to me is that what I'm going to say is larger than this situation we find ourselves in. What I'm going to say is of great interest and importance not only to us but to people everywhere, and I just hope I can say it in a way that is fitting and proper." Conveying much the same idea a minister in a church preceded his sermon with the old prayer, "May the words of my mouth and the meditations of my heart be always acceptable in thy sight, O Lord our strength and our redeemer." Quite obviously reversing those two openings would be inappropriate, even though the essential conception or thought might be the same.

Style, then, can make a real difference in substance. It makes a difference because the way we use language can influence the way the audience receives and perceives our public messages.

It should be apparent from reading the foregoing section that style can have a strong impact on listeners almost apart from the ideas being expressed. That is, the way in which the ideas are expressed can be as important as the ideas themselves in forming listener reactions. Words, for example, have both denotative and connotative meanings; denotative words are those that carry less emotional baggage with them, those that tend to be more objective and less susceptible to a wide variety of interpretative responses. Connotative words, on the other hand, are those that are more highly charged for the listener, those that suggest a range of subjective and emotional interpretations. It is pointed out that the same word can be essentially denotative for one person and connotative for another. The word "cat" for many people might simply denote a four-footed, furry feline, a small animal to which there is hardly any reaction. To another person, however, one who has been severely scratched and almost lost an eye as a child in an encounter with a cat, the word can

Style and the Listener's Response

be much more emotionally charged. So denotative or connotative meanings are infused into language by the context in which they appear and by the perceptions of the listener. Nonetheless, in our society, some words do seem to be more highly charged than others: mother, honor, free enterprise, Maoists, reactionary, and so forth, are all words that are liable to conjure up a wide variety of more or less intense personal responses.

The important point to the listener is that charged language not only supports and furthers argument, but it can be substituted for argument. Instead, for example, of pointing out the shortcomings of a particular plan or program, a speaker might simply say, "We should totally reject all such Marxist thinking." In this case, by labeling, by using language that is meant to connote much that the speaker sees as evil or opposed to our American value system, the speaker rejects categorically a proposal which he or she does not like. What the listener must do in this kind of situation is to ask him or herself for the basis upon which he or she will respond. In this example, is there *evidence* that this is a "Marxist," idea? and, even if so, evidence that the *idea* is truly a bad one? If the listener finds him or herself saying without questioning the support for the assertion, "well if this is Marxist then I don't want to have anything to do with it," then the listener may be falling prey to a stylistic substitution for argument.

There are other ways than in simple word choice in which such stylistic substitutions can occur. Consider, for example, some of the devices discussed in the preceding section, when a speaker condemns a particular proposal by saying, "This would make as much sense as playing tennis without a net." The listener must ask him or herself whether or not this comparison is really a good one. Of course, tennis would be a much different game without a net, but how does that really relate to the plan or to the proposal being made? And because a speaker has two ideas as antithetical, "democracy is based on participation, this plan is based on exclusion," does that really *prove* that the plan is undemocratic? In a preceding chapter we considered the need for supporting ideas with evidence. The same principle should be kept in mind when one is faced with persuasive language use. Here, too, the listener will be wary of accepting the speaker's word alone, even if the word is most aptly and interestingly chosen.

Delivery and Predictability

After all the preparation and all the thought and all the work, ultimately the speaker must present him or herself to an audience. Delivery is, after all, only a small part of this total process of speech preparation and reaction. The speaker who stands before an audience for 10 minutes or so has spent hours getting ready to do that. The listeners who hear 10 minutes or so of speaking bring to the situation an evaluative screen made up from years of experience and, hopefully, from careful training. Yet even so, the actual delivery of a message is the climax and culmination of the public communication experience.

Certainly delivery is one of the most obvious aspects of public communication, and one on which both speaker and listener tend to focus automatically at first. If, for example, one were to ask an audience as soon as they had finished listening to a student give a speech in class, what they thought of that speech, the most likely kinds of answers would be something like this: "I think he had a very nice voice." "I think she should have moved around more." "I couldn't always hear him." Delivery may be a small part of the entire process, but it is a very noticeable part. And it can be a very influential part.

Most potential speakers recognize the importance of delivery, and quite often it terrifies them. The phenomenon known as "stage fright" is practically universal. No doubt there are different degrees of apprehension, but practically every speaker does feel a certain amount of discomfort and anxiety before he or she speaks. Part of these feelings come from physiological activities: there is more energy as more blood sugar becomes available to us; we experience the increases in blood pressure and respiration. But these and other physiological influences don't usually make it impossible for the speaker to speak. On the contrary, they can often provide an extra kind of stimulation that will make the speaker think faster and act in a more lively and energetic fashion. But the worst problems that the speaker faces are the psychological ones. The speaker is entering a situation that he or she cannot confidently predict and so a certain amount of anxiety is bound to result. The less familiar a person is with the kind of situation the greater will be his or her anxiety. Part of the solution in dealing with this problem, then, lies in the area of *predictability,* that is, of making the situation one in which the speaker understands and feels better because he or she has some good idea of what will happen.

Unquestionably, it is important for the speaker to remember that it is quite all right to be fearful or uncomfortable; such feelings are normal. Too often speakers assume that they are so "nervous" that they will not be able to speak, as if this nervousness were somehow abnormal or unusual. Everybody feels some distress, so at least the speaker should not be anxious about the fact that he or she does, too. Given the universality of distress, how does the speaker go about reducing the problem by making the situation more predictable?

1. The speaker can make the situation more predictable by being well prepared. It is quite natural to worry about whether or not one will forget specific bits of information, or get mixed up in one's notes, or sound foolish, or seem not to know what one is talking about. The best way to reduce these fears *is* to know what one is talking about as well as possible. All that has gone before in these

chapters has been designed to help the speaker to prepare him or herself as fully and as completely as possible. It does take time and effort to do this, but the result can be some reduction in the fear produced by not knowing what's going to happen in the speaking situation.

2. The situation will be more predictable as it has been more often experienced. That is simply to say that speakers will find it easier to continue speaking the more they do it. The situation will become familiar so that the uncertainties will be reduced. Even the most experienced speaker, like the most experienced actor, is apt to feel some degree of stage fright. Nevertheless, the intensity and feelings of alarm should decrease over time.

3. The situation will be more predictable if the speaker has practiced extensively and appropriately. You may have had the experience of deciding that you might say something to another person that is not entirely pleasant or in some other way difficult. And you may well have run through in your mind beforehand what you thought you would say. And then, as you actually said it, you might have discovered to your chagrin that it was much harder to say than you thought it was. Very often we first play something through in our heads and then experience difficulty when we actually talk out loud about the same thing. This is because we managed to deceive ourselves by filling in little words and transitions, by completing half-formed thoughts. The speaker who decides to run through his or her speech while lying in bed at night before going to sleep, is going to be shocked and distressed when he or she tries to articulate that speech in front of an audience. So one way of making the situation more predictable is by simulating the situation itself, by pretending that one is in the situation. Now, of course, getting up in front of an empty room or in front of your roommate is not the same thing as getting up in front of a larger group of people. But getting up and talking is a similar kind of process in both the real and simulated situation. In both cases you can force yourself to put your ideas into clear, straightforward language, and in both situations you can assess how well you are doing for yourself. Certainly in the audience situation you will be getting some kind of feedback or response as you speak that you won't get when you're all by yourself or when you have a very limited kind of audience. Nevertheless, you can tell whether or not it is possible for you to explain an idea; you can tell whether the notes you have prepared are adequate; you can tell whether that 10-minute speech you planned to give takes 35 minutes. Also, there are times when your practice can be helped if you can use some kind of recording device. By playing back your speech you can make some judgment about whether or not you said what you had wanted to say as clearly and forcefully as you wanted to say it. One note of caution is important here. It is possible for a practicing speaker to be much too hard on him or herself. It is possible to assume that every manifestation of nervousness or anxiety that you

feel will be perceived and responded to negatively by the audience. That's just not the case. While the audience may be aware of a certain amount of nervousness on your part it will not be as concerned nor will the nervous behaviors you exhibit be perceived as importantly as you perceive them yourself.

4. The situation will become more predictable if the speaker has prepared adequate notes. Some speakers try to control the situation absolutely by writing out every word he or she will say. There may be certain situations in which the preparation and delivery of a manuscript speech is the right kind of situation. But these are highly formal, highly structured and very rare situations in the normal course of most public communication. Most of the speaking that most of us will do is the kind that involves careful and extensive preparation but *not* memorization or reading a manuscript. Most classroom speeches will be what is normally referred to as *extemporaneous* speeches. These speeches are those of a kind that we have just been describing: carefully prepared and thought out but not memorized. Some classroom speeches may also be *impromptu*, which is to say speeches that are given on the spur of the moment.

The extemporaneous speech usually calls for some kind of notes to be used. It is important that the speaker prepare these notes and use them during the practice sessions. A very normal temptation when one has things on paper is to read everything that is there, so the speaker will be freer to interact with his or her audience if his or her notes are not too extensive. The important thing to remember is that notes serve as an aid to memory. They do not serve as a complete outline of the speech nor as a major source of the speaker's material as he or she speaks. They help the speaker to keep on the track, but the speaker must know the subject very well (Figure 17).

Figure 17

There are, of course, occasions when it is more appropriate to give a speech from a prepared manuscript. Basically, the same principles of delivery apply: being well prepared, having experience, practicing, and working from a good copy are important. A written speech, however, will cause special problems. *First, the more that has to be read, the less eye contact that can be maintained with the audience.* In order to overcome this problem practice must be extensive so that the speaker knows the material well enough to allow him or herself to look at the audience and to get back to the manuscript without losing the place. A good, readable copy of the manuscript itself is, naturally, essential. It is not uncommon for speakers to discover that their own handwriting is indecipherable, and that what seemed like a good addition, made hastily in ink, becomes an embarassing stumbling block during presentation of the speech. A clean, well-typed, adequately spaced copy of the speech is absolutely necessary. *Second, the manucript speech gives the speaker less opportunity to move around.* The speaker will be reading from a manuscript that he or she is holding or has placed on a lectern. (It is important that the speaker know, if possible, which of these two possibilities will occur and practice accordingly.) Such restriction means that the speaker will not be able to move as freely as he or she might during an extemporaneous speech. The speaker, therefore, will need to think carefully about what movement is possible and take advantage of it. It is still possible to move from side to side or toward or away from an audience. Appropriate gestures are also possible. What is surely to be avoided is the tendency that many speakers have to grasp tightly the podium or the manuscript itself, and hold on as if to anchor themselves in a strong wind. Again, the key to being able to develop some physical rapport with the audience through bodily flexibility is to be well prepared and to have practiced extensively. Preparation should particularly include, in the case of the manuscript speech, attention to ways in which the voice may be used to add the variety, color, and emphasis that lack of movement tends to make more difficult to achieve.

These suggestions should help to make the unpredictable situation somewhat more predictable by pointing to ways that a speaker can prepare to meet this potentially threatening public communication situation. What happens during the actual presentation or delivery of the speech itself and how is delivery to be judged?

Using the Voice Effectively

One of the most obvious aspects of delivery is, of course, the speaker's voice. Now there are those who have significant speech problems of varying degrees of seriousness: the person who is so hoarse that he or she cannot be understood, the person who substitutes or distorts sounds so that "rabbit," for example, comes out "wabbit," the person who stutters. These speech problems are of a kind that require special attention by professionals trained to deal with the pathologies of speech. Furthermore, there are those persons whose difficulties are not severe but who should benefit from work designed to improve their voices. Most beginning speakers, however, will not need such intensive, individualized therapy. All speakers, nevertheless, should consider seriously how best to use their voices to aid them in communicating as effectively as possible. Since the voice itself plays such a prominent role in shaping the listener's perception of the speaker and his or her message, it cannot fail to have some impact on the ultimate successfulness of public communication.

There are certain features of the voice that the speaker can modify by recognizing their importance, by monitoring their operation in his or her own speaking, and by paying special attention to them in oral practice. These features are *volume, rate, clarity,* and *variety.*

Volume

It should be apparent that no idea, no matter how clearly developed, will be understood, and no idea, no matter how persuasively constructed, will be motivating, if the idea cannot be heard. Nor will an audience be able to concentrate on the speaker's message if the speaker is so loud that the listeners are uncomfortable.

The speaker's volume may directly influence the audience's perception of the speaker and the audience's attentiveness to the speaker. One speaker, who later reported that he wanted to be "emphatic" and "forceful," virtually shouted his speech to an audience of about 20 persons in a small classroom. In discussing the speech the listeners concentrated almost exclusively on the excessive volume, describing the speaker as "obviously very nervous," "too aggressive," "too emotional," and, even, "insulting." Members of the audience could hardly reconstruct the speaker's major theme or remember the major points he made, so unnerved were they by the loud delivery. At the other extreme, speakers whose voices come out in soft whispers usually cause an audience first to strain to hear and then to lapse into bored inattention.

The degree of loudness or softness should be determined by the setting in which the communication takes place. Naturally, a small room calls for a quieter voice than does a large lecture hall or an outdoor setting. The speaker, as he or she gains experience, will learn to consider the listeners' needs and increase or decrease volume as the situation demands. Practice is an essential element, of course, in helping the speaker to meet the situation. Standing up and giving the speech, with a volume that seems realistic for the actual presentation, will help the speaker monitor his or her own voice and begin to get the feel of speaking loudly or softly enough for the listeners to understand and be comfortable.

Rate

It is not uncommon for a beginning speaker to sit down after giving a speech, look at the clock, and be amazed to find that the planned 10-minute speech only took 5 minutes to give. Several miscalculations in planning could account for such a result, but frequently the problem is that the speaker has rushed through the speech far too quickly. In his or her anxiety to "get it over with" the speaker can forget that an audience needs time to follow, to absorb, and to react.

The needs of the listeners are paramount. Just as they can't keep up with the too-fast speaker, so they lose interest in and patience with the too-slow one. Often speakers who have not practiced enough, or have not prepared adequately, or have underestimated the audience's powers of comprehension, drag through a speech—stumbling along with "umm"'s and "ahh"'s, pausing too frequently or too long, filling in gaps with the ubiquitous and irritating, "you know." In such situations the listeners may easily give up efforts to grapple with the speaker's intent and meaning.

As with every other factor in speech preparation, the rate is determined in large measure by the speaker's estimate of the nature of the listeners' responses. As was pointed out earlier, listening to a speech can be contrasted with reading a book. The reader can slow down or speed up as his or her needs dictate. The speaker, on the other hand, cannot be stopped and replayed, as it were, by the listener just as the listener cannot skip ahead to the speaker's next point. The speaker must anticipate the listeners' reactions and must be prepared to adjust to the actual feedback that he or she observes. This, of course, means that the speaker's focus is on the audience and on its *response* to the material and not exclusively on the material being presented.

Reacting to and planning for listeners' responses, therefore, forces the speaker to modify rate as the situation demands. Furthermore, the material itself will also influence the speaker's rate. A speaker describing the last few laps of the Indianapolis 500, for example, will undoubtedly speak at a faster rate than will the speaker who is describing the feelings of someone who is going into an hypnotic trance. This is to say that, in order to increase the potential for achieving his or her desired response, the speaker will use a rate that is appropriate to the mood of the speech and will thus enhance the meaning.

Clarity

To be an effective informer or persuader, the way that the communicator speaks must be understood. One speaker, for example, baffled an audience for some time until they finally understood that he was not making frequent reference to a friend, his "buddy," but, rather, to his "body." Another speaker who was generally well prepared and well informed discovered in a discussion following the speech that many listeners interpreted his mispronunciation of key words as a sign that he didn't really know what he was talking about. To achieve clarity—and thus to further his or her communicative purpose—the speaker should aim to achieve primarily three important qualities.

First, the speaker should achieve distinctness of articulation. Dropping the endings of words, slurring sounds, running words together, can interfere with the meaning of a message and cause listeners to work harder to understand what a speaker is saying. *Second, the speaker should achieve accuracy of pronunciation.* Every speaker should feel confident that words he or she uses are pronounced correctly. This means going to the dictionary whenever there is the slightest doubt about the pronunciation of the word the speaker will use. Especially, the speaker should take care that he or she has practiced aloud and checked the pronunciation of words used in quoted material. Mispronunciation can lead to audience misunderstanding and to negative assessment of the speaker's ability. *Third, the speaker should achieve freedom from mannerisms.* It is pointless and distracting, for example, to keep saying "you know." One speaker, to cite another example, obscured the clarity of his message by concluding almost every statement with the unnecessary question, "Right?" Also, there are regional mannerisms that clutter speech and thus reduce clarity, such as the questioning "hear?" at the end of a sentence, or the unnecessary and ungrammatical "at" tacked on to such statements as, "He didn't know where I was *at*." Such mannerisms are distracting to listeners, and listeners who are distracted are less likely to receive the message clearly.

Variety

It should be apparent that certain of the features of a good speaking voice do not always operate in the same fashion. The preceeding discussion points to a general rule consistent with the basic principle of good public communication: in its support of the ideas being communicated, the speaker's voice is adapted to the needs of the audience, setting, and content of the speech itself. One unvaried volume and one unvaried rate will not only effect the listeners' attention negatively, but may distort the basic meaning of the ideas being discussed.

To develop variety, as to develop all aspects of a good speaking voice, the speaker needs to cultivate an *awareness* of his or her own voice. The speaker must learn to listen to him or herself and begin to appreciate what listeners will hear as he or she speaks. Through practice through careful attention to one's own behavior the speaker can produce a voice that listeners are pleased to listen to.

A good speaking voice is an important part, but only a part, of the total process of delivery. Keeping in mind the effective use of the voice, consider now the basic principles that govern good delivery.

If you have ever left a public communication situation or turned off a speech on television and observed to someone, "Gee, that person really has a nice voice;" or "That person sounded pretty good," you would have been responding, in part at least, to the *delivery* of the speech. Sometimes we find ourselves in the uncomfortable situation of thinking someone sounded good but not being quite sure what he or she *said*. Sometimes delivery is so striking that it takes us away from the content of the communication itself. This may be a pur-

The Basis of Good Delivery

poseful act on the part of the communicator or it may be an accident. But in either case it is not *good* delivery. What does characterize good delivery?

First, good delivery grows out of an audience-centered approach to public communication. The speaker whose constant and consistent attention is on him or herself is liable to be far more concerned with what he or she sounds or looks like, or how he or she moves, than with how the *audience is reacting* to what is being said. The speaker, is, after all, not really putting on an "act," the speaker is trying to get a *response* from a particular audience. Good delivery, therefore, reflects such a mental set. The speaker who is delivering his or her speech well, for example, physically focuses on the audience. He or she watches them, talks with them, looks for responses from them. Such a speaker speaks loud enough to be heard by them and does not embarrass them by extravagant gesture or excessive movement. This first characteristic, the audience-centered quality of delivery, naturally leads to the second characteristic of a good delivery.

Second, good delivery does not call attention to itself. The best delivery is that which one doesn't notice at all. It is the kind that the audience will not respond to by obliterating content or meaning because of some physical action on the part of the speaker. This means that what the speaker hopes to do is to exhibit behaviors that are appropriate to the situation, such as the use of a conversational kind of voice when speaking to an audience of fifteen or twenty people sitting close to him or her. It means avoiding distracting kinds of mannerisms as one speaks. One instructor, for example, was notorious for his unique ability to balance a piece of chalk on the end of his finger. This fascinating skill always drew the attention of the students in his class; most of the time the attention was so complete as to distract students entirely from the content of the lecture. Speakers sometimes exhibit verbal mannerisms as well, and these can also distract from the message. The speaker who says, "You know" with great frequency or punctuates his sentences with great numbers of "um," "ah," will divert the audience's attention from the message itself.

Third, good delivery is that which best promotes the listener's belief and understanding. Delivery must be consistent with the rest of the speech. The speaker's body, voice, and gesture must be in tune with the mood and nature of the message. It is not always easy for a speaker to judge in advance the best way to integrate his or her delivery into the speech situation. Probably delivery is best improved through practice and through the critical response of a trained observer. But, the speaker should not allow him or herself to forget that what is happening in front of that audience is all that the audience really knows about the speaker and the topic at that particular moment. The speaker may have some very good and compelling reasons for urging an audience to take a particular action, but, if that speaker, through a dull and lifeless delivery, doesn't seem to care at all, the content of the message may be canceled out.

On Sounding Good and Being Sound

The fact that what the audience sees is for them the total communication experience sometimes puts an undue emphasis on and gives unwarranted influence to delivery. Quite often beginning students of the public communication process will sit in a classroom and listen to a speaker who is poised, who has a good voice, who seems not be at any loss for words, who is confident, and who is friendly. Often, because most people feel so insecure themselves, or are so sure they would be much more nervous and much less articulate, they greatly admire the ability of such a speaker. They tend, in fact, to judge the speaker almost solely on this demonstrated ability to be at ease with a group of listeners. Sometimes, however, such a speaker is merely facile. He or she can speak easily but might not be saying very much. One thing that this book has been designed to do is to prepare you to distinguish between a speaker who is sound and a speaker who just sounds good. A speaker who is sound will be the one whose ideas pass the rigorous tests that grow out of the theory embodied in the preceding chapters. As much as we might admire the ease and grace with which someone can address an audience, we need to be on our guard constantly against the slick, superficial person who is out to sell him or herself and not to grapple with important ideas. One of the chief distinctions between the academic or school approach to public communication and the popular kind that promises you some kind of instant success is this: the former is designed to help you expand your intellectual and communicative powers in order to deal rationally and sensibly with listeners and to prepare listeners to be discriminating critics of what they hear; the latter is designed to help you give merely a good impression of yourself and your personality. The educated person, then, is one who looks beyond the outward facade and hopes to test the firmness of the foundation.

Summary

Delivery, the culmination of the public communication process for the speaker and for the listener, is also the culmination of our consideration of the public communication process. All that has gone before this chapter has been designed to give the participants in the process perspectives and methods that would help them design and evaluate a meaningful message. This chapter has attempted to clarify the role that style and delivery play in the final presentation of a message by considering the way language is used to clarify and interest the listener, and the way it reflects the communicative situation. It has been argued that style can influence the listener's response and, accordingly, should be studied with care to improve effectiveness as well as to sharpen skepticism.

The unpredictability of the speaking situation can be reduced by the speaker's extensive preparation, by the growth of the speaker's experience, by the speaker's careful practice, and by the speaker's adequate preparation and use of notes.

Good delivery, something that the speaker strives for and that the listener expects, is that which is audience centered, does not call attention to itself, and best promotes the listeners' belief and understanding. Delivery that is meant to appeal only to the ear, that covers over flaws in the speaker's thinking is not "good" at all, and must always be regarded warily by the critical listener.

The next, and final, chapter will attempt to highlight the major ideas that have been presented in this book concerning the interactions between the speaker and listener in the public communication process. It also summarizes the principal suggestions for active participation in the process through checklists for speakers and listeners.

Select Bibliography

The following citations, and those listed in all the bibliographies, offer further practical and theoretical information related to the chapter topics, and they provide a starting point for the student who wishes to undertake more intensive study and research into the topic.

Edwin Black, "The Second Personna," *Quarterly Journal of Speech,* **56**(1970), 109-119.

Jane Blankenship, *A Sense of Style: An Introduction to Style for the Public Speaker*. Encino, Calif.: Dickenson, 1968.

Jane Blakenship, "The Influence of Mode, Sub-Mode, and Speaker Predilection on Style," *Speech Monographs,* **41**(1974), 85-118.

John Bowers, "Language Intensity, Social Introversion, and Attitude Change," *Speech Monographs,* **30**(1963), 345-352.

John Bowers and Michael M. Osborn, "Attitudinal Effects of Selected Types of Concluding Metaphors in Persuasive Speeches," *Speech Monographs,* **33**(1966), 147-155.

Ronald H. Carpenter, "A Stylistic Basis of Burkeian Identification," *Today's Speech,* **20**(1972), 19-24.

Theodore Clevenger, Jr., "A Synthesis of Experimental Research in Stage Fright," *Quarterly Journal of Speech,* **45**(1959), 134-145.

Martin Cobin, "Response to Eye Contact," *Quarterly Journal of Speech,* **48**(1962), 415-418.

Richard L. Corliss, "A Theory of Contextual Implication," *Philosophy and Rhetoric,* **5**(1972), 215-230.

Douglas Ehninger and Michael Osborn, "The Metaphor in Public Address," *Speech Monographs,* **29**(1962), 223-234.

William Hamilton, "A Review of Experimental Studies of Stage Fright," *Pennsylvania Speech Annual,* **17**(1960).

Paul Heinberg, "Relationships of Content and Delivery to General Effectiveness," *Speech Monographs,* **30**(1963), 105-107.

Herbert W. Hildebrandt and Walter W. Stevens, "Manuscript and Extemporaneous Delivery in Communicating Information," *Speech Monographs,* **30**(1963), 369-372.

Wendell Johnson and Dorothy Moeller, *Living with Change: The Semantics of Coping.* New York: Harper & Row, 1972.

William J. Jordan, "Toward a Psychological Theory of Metaphor," **35**(1971), 169-175.

Irving J. Lee, *Language Habits in Human Affairs.* New York: Harper and Brothers, 1941.

Idolene Mazza, William Jordan, and Ronald Carpenter, "The Comparative Effectiveness of Stylistic Sources of Redundancy," *Central States Speech Journal,* **23**(1972), 241-245.

Michael Osborn, "Archtypal Metaphors in Rhetoric: The Light-Dark Family," *Quarterly Journal of Speech,* **53**(1967), 115-126.

Anthony M. Paul, "Metaphor and the Bounds of Expression," *Philosophy and Rhetoric,* **5**(1972), 143-158.

J. Donald Ragsdale, "Problems of Some Contemporary Notions of Style," *Southern Speech Communication Journal,* **35**(1970), 332-341.

N. Lamar Reinsch, "An Investigation of the Effects of the Metaphor and Simile in Persuasive Discourse," *Speech Monographs,* (1971), 142-145.

G. Wayne Shammo and John R. Bittner, "Recall as a Function of Language Style," *Southern Speech Communication Journal,* **38**(1972), 181-187.

Jeffrey G. Shapiro, "Responsivity to Facial and Linguistic Cues," *Journal of Communication,* **18**(1968), 11-17.

John R. Stewart, "Concepts of Language and Meaning: A Comparative Study," *Quarterly Journal of Speech,* **58**(1972), 123-133.

Gordon L. Thomas, "Oral Style and Intelligibility," *Speech Monographs,* **23**(1956), 46-54.

Otis M. Walter, "Developing Confidence," *Today's Speech,* **2**(1954), 2-7.

W. Ross Winterowd, "Style: A Matter of Manner," *Quarterly Journal of Speech,* **56**(1970), 161-167.

Peter Wolff and Joyce Gutstein, "Effects of Induced Motor Gestures on Vocal Output," *Journal of Communication,* **22**(1972), 277-288.

Sol Worth and Larry Gross, "Symbolic Strategies," *Journal of Communication,* **24**(1974), 27-39.

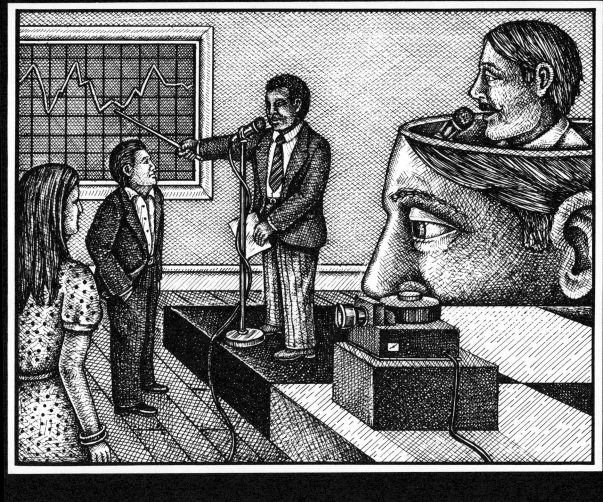

PART FIVE
effective public communication

CHAPTER 10 *effective public communication: a summary*

Students often get together to study for tests. In these study sessions there may be one particular point that one student understands better than his or her friend. In such a case, the knowledgeable student will explain the idea or provide additional information or interpretation for the friend. Both the communicator and the listener want communication to be successful. Much communication is like that; both the source of the message and the receiver of the message hope that the goals will be accomplished. If someone wanted to sell you a motorcycle and hoped to persuade you that it was a good one, and you wanted to buy a good motorcycle, you would want to be persuaded of its quality. If you saw a good movie and wanted to convince someone you liked to go to that movie and your friend wanted and enjoyed the pleasurable experience of going to an entertaining film, successful persuasion would then be a mutual goal.

In many situations, then, communication is a cooperative effort. Public communication often demands that all parties concerned in the process work actively to bring about the kind of response that will benefit all. Speakers and listeners both will be searching for the meaning of their relationship: speakers to understand audience motivations and relate messages to listeners' needs and values, listeners to understand and make applicable the ways in which the speaker's message has the potential for influencing or enhancing their lives.

When an idea is a difficult or complicated one, the best speaker makes every effort to develop to the full the strategies, tactics, and techniques discussed in this book in order to promote the listener's understanding and belief; for his or her part, the best listener aids the speaker by seeking actively to understand relationships between ideas and by concentrating on the evidence presented and its relation to the purpose the speaker seems to hope to accomplish. The speaker who says, "I'm going to say what I want to and it's up to them whether or not they get it," or the listener who says, "O.K., I'm here; see if you can do anything to me," are both failing to meet their obligation to further the public communication process and will probably both be the losers for it.

Speaker and Listener as Confederates

Of course, if you have been reading this book carefully, you know that the speaker and listener do not and should not accept each other's ideas, assertions, and prejudices without question. There are times when the speaker and the listener must assume an adversary relationship.

Speaker and Listener as Adversaries

The speaker cannot always say what the audience wants to hear any more than the listener can always accept what the speaker says without question. While public communication is essentially a cooperative venture, it is not always without conflict between the participants. A speaker may know very well the values of an audience, but he or she may wish to reject those values. A speaker who truly hopes to communicate will adapt to his or her listeners, but that speaker is not expected to adopt wholesale ideas that are repugnant to him or her. The listener should try to fill in gaps and seek structure and unity in a speech, but the listener can't be expected to imagine evidence or relationships that just aren't there. And, as we all know and have experienced, there are times when purposes just are not compatible; we listeners may want to spend as little money as possible, the message may be urging us to spend as much as we have.

The fact that speaker and listener are often in conflict, however, does not mean that their relations should be hostile or antagonistic. In a world of message sending and receiving, we must recognize that we depend on public communication for much of our information, instruction, and inspiration. And we switch roles from speaker to listener as the occasion and situation demands. What is needed is a healthy critical stance on both sides; an awareness that all the participants in public communication will not always be hoping for the same outcomes, and an attitude of friendly, but hardheaded skepticism that demands to be allowed to examine the communication process very carefully and dispassionately before reaching judgment.

All that has been said in this book has been directed toward helping you develop for yourself just such a critical stance, and toward helping you devise ways of improving your participation in the process of public communication. In summary, there follows two Checklists that might help you to review the major points made in this book as well as serving as a practical guide as you get ready to speak or to listen.

A Speaker's Checklist

Consider the following statements. Each time you prepare yourself to speak, check those that you believe adequately represent your planning.

□ I Have Carefully Considered My Audience

□ I know the special characteristics of my audience and how they might relate to my topic.
□ I know the circumstances under which my listeners will be attending to my message.
□ I have tried to determine as accurately as possible how much listeners know about my topic.
□ I have tried to determine as accurately as possible how my listeners stand on the issue that I am discussing with them.
□ I have tried to assess how my audience feels about me and my relationship to my topic.
□ I have as clear a conception as possible of the needs and values of my listeners and how they relate to my topic.

□ I have a Clearly Stated Specific Purpose

□ My purpose reflects what I take to be the overall response called for: informative, persuasive, entertaining.
□ My purpose is a statement of the response that I want from the listeners.
□ My purpose is one that can be realistically achieved in the communicative setting.
□ My purpose is clear and unambiguous.

□ I Have Developed Ideas Designed to Further My Purpose

□ I can state my ideas in clear, complete, and precise sentences.
□ My ideas are simple enough to be understood and followed by my listeners.
□ My ideas are appropriate to the listeners and the context in which they are listening.
□ The ideas are ones that I believe will make sense to the audience.

□ I Have Organized My Ideas Clearly and Appropriately

□ The ideas are arranged in sequence that helps to make them more understandable or believable as chronological, spatial, topical, direct or indirect, problem solution, contrastive, or causal.
□ The total structure of the speech seems to be one that will promote clarity of ideas.
□ The form of the speech suggests the persuasive ends of the speech.

□ I Have Gathered and Arranged Enough Supporting Material to Make the Ideas Understandable and Believable to an Audience.

□ I have carefully and systematically searched through printed material for information relevant to my topic and directly related to my purpose.

☐ I have searched for and interviewed or written to individuals who can provide significant information on the topic.

☐ I have searched for the statements and opinions of experts on the topic and have planned to use their testimony to support appropriate ideas.

☐ I have sought for and used as support adequate statistical information.

☐ I have found specific examples that I have used to make ideas more understandable or believable.

☐ I have sought to bring unusual or new ideas or objects within the experience of the audience through comparison with the more familiar.

☐ I Have Planned Communicative Methods Appropriate to the Ideas in the Speech.

☐ I have planned clear transitions from one idea to another.

☐ I have planned to repeat and restate difficult and important ideas to help an audience follow and remember them.

☐ I have developed visual or audio aids that will clarify and heighten the impact of my ideas.

☐ I Have Tested the Soundness of My Argument.

☐ The relationship between the evidence I present and the conclusion I reach is a clear one.

☐ The amount of evidence I use is sufficient to support generalizations I reach.

☐ I have tried to distinguish, both for myself and for my audience, between those reasons that may be given publicly for the support of an idea and those reasons that may lie beneath the rationalizations.

☐ I Have Considered and Employed Appropriate Ways to Involve Listeners in the Speech.

☐ I have planned to demonstrate for the audience the ways in which my speech bears directly on their lives and experiences.

☐ I have devised ways to arouse listeners' curiosity about my speech.

☐ I have recognized the needs of listeners and associated my ideas with those needs where appropriate.

☐ I have recognized the values of listeners and associated my ideas with those values where appropriate.

☐ I have planned carefully to introduce my speech by stimulating audience interest in what is to come.

☐ I have planned to conclude my speech with a final statement that reinforces the mood and message of my speech and points the audience to appropriate action.

- ☐ I Have, as a Result of My Process of Preparation, Devised a Fully Developed Outline.

- ☐ The outline clearly shows the relationship of the ideas to the purpose.
- ☐ The ideas themselves are stated as complete sentences.
- ☐ The material included does truly support the ideas it is supposed to support.
- ☐ The introduction and conclusion fit into the total scheme of the outline and are carefully prepared.

- ☐ I Have, as Much as Can Be in an Extemporaneous Speech, Planned to Use Language Carefully and Appropriately.

- ☐ I have thought about language that I can use that will be clear and persuasive for listeners.
- ☐ I have considered ways that I can use language interestingly.
- ☐ I have considered the kind of language that will be appropiate to the total situation.

- ☐ I Have Planned My Delivery of the Speech Carefully.

- ☐ I truly believe myself to be as well prepared as I can be.
- ☐ I have practiced my speech out loud, with some audiences if possible.
- ☐ I have prepared and practiced with adequate notes.
- ☐ I intend, as I deliver my speech, to focus on the listeners and their responses to the ideas I present.

A Listener's Checklist

The listener, unlike the speaker, has less conscious preparation for the public communication situation although the listener can and should do some preplanning and thinking. Most of what the listener must do in order to participate effectively in the process, however, he or she must do while receiving the message. Consider the following statements as directions for critical listening in the public communication setting.

- ☐ I Have Prepared Beforehand for the Communication Event.

- ☐ If possible, I have determined the topic and tried to consider the ways it relates to me.
- ☐ I have thought about what I bring to the event in relation to opinions already formed, conceptions already developed, or biases held.
- ☐ I have come to the event prepared to concentrate and to try to further successful communication.

- ☐ I Have Tried to Formulate a Purpose for Myself.

☐ I will ask myself as the speech unfolds, what should *I* be getting out of this?

☐ I will ask, can what the speaker says effect in any way what I do in my daily life?

☐ **I Will Try to Consider the Setting of the Communication and Its Impact on the Speaker and on Me.**

☐ I will try to understand the limitations that time imposes on the message being presented.

☐ I will try to understand how the environment in which the message is produced helps or hinders the successful completion of communication.

☐ I will try to assess the impact of the surroundings on me and my reactions to the message.

☐ **I Will Understand Who the Speaker Is Talking To.**

☐ I will look for evidence that the speaker has analyzed his or her audience.

☐ I will try to understand the ways in which the speaker tries to reach listeners who might be different from me.

☐ I will try to discover whether or not the speaker seems to be talking to an audience beyond the immediate one.

☐ **I Will Uncover the Basis of My Assessment of the Speaker.**

☐ I will identify any preconceptions I might have about the speaker.

☐ I will be aware of the ways in which my perception of the speaker seems to be influencing the way I listen to the message.

☐ I will constantly check my preconception with what I am hearing.

☐ I will be aware of the extent to which I am relying on my own image of the speaker in responding positively or negatively to the message.

☐ **I Will Determine the Speaker's Specific Purpose.**

☐ I will aim to understand what the speaker is trying to get me to do.

☐ I will compare the response that I think the speaker hopes to get with my own goals for the communication interaction.

As I Listen to the Message, I Will Try to Determine the Quality of that Message By Searching for the Answers to a Series of Questions About the Ideas and Their Development:

☐ **I Will Assess the Quality of the Ideas Presented in the Message.**

☐ Are the ideas distinct and readily identified as separate ideas?
☐ Are the ideas clearly stated?
☐ Are the ideas simple enough for me to follow without getting confused?
☐ Do the ideas seem to fit into the message and the setting for the message?
☐ Do the ideas make sense to me as I think about them?

☐ I Will Assess the Organizational Pattern of the Speech

☐ Can I determine a clear sequencing of ideas?
☐ Does the sequence of ideas seem a good one for the topic?
☐ Does the way the ideas are put together help to understand better what the speaker wants me to understand?
☐ Does the way the ideas are patterned suggest that the speaker is trying to get some particular response from me?

☐ I Will Judge the Adequacy of the Communicative Evidence Presented.

☐ Does the speaker support ideas with concrete evidence that makes the ideas more believable or understandable?
☐ Does it seem that the speaker has enough evidence to support ideas?
☐ Does the speaker seem to have taken the trouble to gather as much information as possible?
☐ Does the quantity and quality of the communicative evidence lead me to believe that the speaker knows what he or she is talking about?
☐ Are the examples used typical, accurate, and important?
☐ Are the sources and methods of gathering statistics used uncovered, and do they allow for the possibility of bias or inaccuracy?
☐ Is the testimony by relevant authority, timely, and consistent with the context?
☐ If ideas, events, and persons are compared, are the two items being compared alike in the essential ways to make the comparison valid?

☐ I Will Judge the Quality of the Overall Argument.

☐ Is the relationship between the evidence and the conclusion on which the evidence is based a clear and direct one?
☐ Are the generalizations offered in the message warranted by what the speaker has told the audience and/or my own knowledge and experience?
☐ Does the argument get to the real issues involved in the topic?
☐ Do I really believe the argument as it is presented, or am I willing to accept it as a convenient rationalization?

☐ I Will Assess the Ways in Which the Speaker Tries to Involve Me in the Topic.

☐ Does the speaker realistically relate the topic to my life?
☐ Does the speaker arouse my curiosity?
☐ How does the speaker relate his or her ideas to my needs and my values?
☐ Do the relationships made by the speaker fit my real needs and values?
☐ Does the speaker make an effort to gain my attention and interest?
☐ Does what interests me distract me from what the speaker is really trying to do?

☐ I Will Be Aware of the Way the Speaker Uses Language.

☐ Is the speaker using language that I can understand and follow?
☐ Does the speaker's choice of language help to make the ideas more understandable or believable?
☐ Does the language chosen seem to be appropriate to the setting in which the speech occurs?
☐ Does the language suggest conclusions, generalizations, attitudes, or values that the speaker hopes to further?
☐ Does the language ever function, reinforce, or even substitute for argument?
☐ To what extent am I reacting to people or ideas because of the labels used to describe them?

☐ I Will Put the Delivery of the Speech in the Proper Perspective.

☐ Is what the speaker has to say made clearer or more convincing by the way he or she says it?
☐ Am I doing my best to avoid being distracted by what I see and hear, and am I trying to concentrate on *ideas?*
☐ Do I know *what* the speaker is saying as well as how he or she is saying it?
☐ Do I find myself dismissing the speaker's ideas because I don't like the way he or she sounds or looks?
☐ Do I find myself agreeing with a speaker because I like the way he or she sounds and looks?

The Last Word

Speakers and listeners who can conscientiously cover all the points in the checklists, should feel quite confident that they are ready for whatever public communication situation in which they find themselves. Of course, it will take time and experience in applying principles to develop a well-grounded appreciation for and skill in public communication. This book has laid out for the student the *essentials,* what you must be able to understand and put to use to make communication work. Over time, you will learn much more about the complicated human process of relating to each other in the special way that we call communication. This book, and, more importantly, the personal instruction you have received and the experience you have gained in your study of public communication, should point you clearly in the right direction. This book may also continue to be helpful to you as a reference as you go on developing your expertness as a communicator and as a consumer of communication. In the end, of course, your success depends on you. If you *want* to communicate in an effective way, and if you have the understanding and skills to do it, you will, indeed *be* a more effective communicator, and, consequently, a more effective person in all you do.

INDEX

DATE DUE

GAYLORD | | | PRINTED IN U.S.A.